MW00397259

DIASPORA IS JEWRY'S GRAVEYARD

BY RABBI DR. YEHOSHUA KEMELMAN
M.A., PH.D., D.LITT.

FORMER HEAD OF BETH DIN OF AUSTRALIA AND NEW ZEALAND
RABBI OF THE SYDNEY CENTRAL SYNAGOGUE

URIM PUBLICATIONS
Jerusalem • New York

Diaspora is Jewry's Graveyard
By Rabbi Dr. Yehoshua Kemelman
Copyright © 2009 by Rabbi Dr. Y. Kemelman

This book is an expanded version of the work by the same author first published in Hebrew as *Hit'abdut Ruchanit veLe'umit* in 2003 by the Zionist Library – The Publication House of the World Zionist Organization, Jerusalem.

Printed in Israel. First Edition.
ISBN 13: 978-965-524-024-5
Urim Publications
P.O. Box 52287, Jerusalem 91521 Israel

Lambda Publishers Inc.
527 Empire Blvd., Brooklyn, New York 11225 U.S.A.
Tel: 718-972-5449 Fax: 718-972-6307, mh@ejudaica.com

www.UrimPublications.com

CONTENTS

FOREWORD

NEVER AGAIN?!

AT THE END of World War II, the entire scope of the gruesome horrors, in all their ghastliness and their cruelty, were revealed to our eyes. Thousands of grand and glorious Jewish communities had been laid to waste, completely erased from the magnificent edifices dedicated to Torah, culture, charity, and justice had been destroyed. Among the victims, we saw parents, siblings, children, and disciples of the House of Rabban. Genocide according to a plan executed in deceit, and methodical precision unparalleled since humanity trod on earth. Stunned and aggrieved, we stood opposite the gas chambers and the ovens. We peered into the gloomy depths of mounds of horrifying ashes at Auschwitz, Majdanek, and Treblinka. There, an entire people went up in smoke.

By the grisly light of the bonfire of our millions, we did swear: "never again!" Never shall we forget the lessons of the Holocaust, in order that such shall never recur! We shall do all to prevent the recurrence of the situation in which we are weak and helpless. We shall rush to aid and defend any Jewish community in a state of threatened existence; we will raise a clamor, and provide all the support for shoring up its vitality.

To our dismay and our disgrace, we have all too quickly forgotten this oath. Although a physical Holocaust is no longer in vogue – one cannot know for how long – a spiritual and national Holocaust nevertheless rampages and destroys Diaspora Jewish communities. The similarity is great between our situation today and that of Jews of circa 60 years ago. We were then in a Holocaust of physical annihilation; today, it is silent, but no less destructive in its results. Destruction of a people is not mere physical ruination, but also, spiritual destruction that stems from loss of identity and assimilation.

The epidemic of spiritual loss of identity and biological assimilation strikes us mercilessly, wreaking havoc among the tribes of Israel in the Diaspora. The bond with Judaism continually dwindles; hundreds of thousands of Jews are rendered empty, then drop out, and quietly disappear. This furtive desertion from the ranks of the Jewish people is of catastrophic dimensions. Jews are rapidly slipping through our fingers, and we have neither the strength nor the desire to pursue them…

It is widely known from credible surveys and researches that the number of Jews in America and other Diaspora countries continually dwindle rapidly.

Everyone hears and reads about the phenomenon of many youths abandoning Jewish identity, most intermarrying with Gentiles, in an accelerated process of losing identity and attrition in all Jewish centers in the Diaspora countries. We emit a sigh and shake our heads; however, we close our eyes and do naught to recruit all national resources of various sorts to combat the perils that gnaw at the communal foundations of the House of Jacob.

You stand stunned and appalled: where is the spiritual distress, where is the severe shock at these events for most of our people? Where are the alarm bells to galvanize the heart and awaken us from our slumber in view of the spiritual and national disaster rampant among us? Indeed, we should shake heaven and earth by our deeds and our cry – that of a people adrift.

We are awash in helplessness and spiritual quandary, doing nothing, without any plan in the struggle for the life of the nation. It is as if we have decided to do away with ourselves. Indeed, the existential crisis lurking for our people is fatal, while we are concomitantly plagued with a crisis of leadership that neglects to initiate practical steps to chart a course of rescue for the perplexed of our generation.

The Diaspora Jews are dancing upon the Titanic, while the Jews of Israel who take care not to offend the pride of Uncle Sam, appear as if applauding them.

The Jewish People must mobilize with all its might and fight, given the issue of survival, which faces us in all its fury. The chapters of this book were designated for this purpose.

CHAPTER ONE

THE DEAFENING SILENCE OF THE JEWISH LEADERSHIP

DEMOGRAPHS HAVE ASSERTED that Diaspora Jewry has lost a million of its sons and daughters in intermarriage and assimilation during the last two decades. They predict that in fifty years time only one and a half million of the present seven and a half million Jews will remain in the Diaspora as a result of intermarriage and assimilation. Presently we are loosing sixty thousand young men and women every year.

In addition, 70 percent of the Jewish children in the Diaspora do not get any Jewish education; 20 percent of the American Jewish students do not call themselves Jews anymore. We have sunk to the lowest birthrate of all nationalities, far beyond replacement level; while at the same time we have risen to the heights of intermarriage. In the United States 50 percent of our young men and women intermarry; 60 percent in France and in the other countries of Europe. In Russia it is about 70 percent of intermarriage; while in Australia it is about 40 percent. We are but one generation ahead of the degeneration of American Jewry, in spite of the unique network of Jewish day schools we have created. The statistical data as they have been published suffice to shock any Jew that is concerned about Jewish existence.

Today, wherever we turn, signs of national disintegration are apparent everywhere – the estrangement of young Jews, the alienation from Jewish sources and Jewish thought, the abyss of the Jewish ignorance and the growth of assimilation.

Yet the Jewish leadership is silent, calm and content. No lesson seems to have been learnt from the Holocaust, whose main characteristics appear to be similar to those that afflict us in the present crisis.

First, the Jews of Europe did not know what was awaiting them. They did not believe it was possible. "This is Europe, not the jungle; these people are enlightened Germans, not beasts. What can they do to us? We are better off where we are," they said. The German murderers cunningly hid the truth from their victims. They knew very well that the less they knew about their tragic end, the faster and easier the machinery of extermination would run.

Similarly, today in the midst of the raging plague of intermarriage and assimilation, many of our people are committing the same fatal blunder by believing that it would not happen to their children.

The father is as non-observant as his son. But there is a big difference between them. The father has a good memory, his nostalgia is unimpaired. He had drawn liberally from a religious home a vast reservoir of Jewish attitudes and feelings. He feels perfectly Jewish without religious observance, as he often puts it: "I am a good Jew at heart." Hence, he is sure that his son, like himself, would never betray his people.

The father forgets that his son never saw the real Jewish home, which he had experienced, and that unlike himself, this son has no nostalgia and no memories. Hence he drops it all. He does not particularly care about being Jewish and sees no calamity in assimilation.

The number of Jews who have lost their children in this manner is staggering. And yet there is a deadly silence. The Jewish leadership does not sound the alarm, does not enlighten the Jewish masses of the inevitable plague of intermarriage and assimilation awaiting their children in the Diaspora.

The Jewish house is burning while its inhabitants are asleep, and there are no alarm bells, nor fire brigades. Every visitor to New York, Paris, London, or Moscow, who open-mindedly regards what transpires among Jews, senses that the uprooted are drowning in the depths of disintegration and loss of identity. The great disaster is that those inhabiting these cities and others refute reality and ignore it as if nonexistent. As is known, when the patient yet feels pain, he has chances to recover and to recuperate from its ailments, as the symptoms constitute a form of alert as to the presence of illness in the body. Hence, the patient seeks medical aid and struggles to recover. However, when the patient lies abed without sensing the malady in his limbs, he is in grave danger, for paralysis has set in.

Woe is us that most Diaspora Jews suffer spiritual paralysis, loss of sensitivity about the malignant disease of assimilation, which stealthily labors at gradual elimination, weakening the spirit and strength to resist, dismantling the fabric of tradition, and unraveling the Jewish soul until its extinction. These Jews tumble into assimilation, not due to any certain ideological decision nor because they are convinced that this is the way for them, but rather, they are simply swept up, devoured by gentile society, Jews denuded of their religion, unknowingly led inexorably to assimilation , although devoid of initial intent.

This brings us to the second main characteristic of the Holocaust: The Judenrats, even those who knew about the final solution, followed a policy of silence and non-revelation, which contributed to the illusionary hope of survival and assisted the German scheme of extermination.

We seem to be repeating the same fatal mistake of the Judenrat by not revealing to the people the truth about the severe crisis of Diaspora Jewry and that aliyah is an inevitable step.

Among other peoples, in time of national peril, during crisis and emergency, leadership rises, speaking truth to the people to strengthen the spirit for struggle. It was thus in Britain also during its time of destiny, when Churchill was elected prime minister. In his historic speech, he revealed the awful truth: that he can promise the people only sweat and blood. These words were engraved on British hearts and they carried them on their lips into battle. The leadership of Diaspora Jewry does not understand that it is impossible to fortify a people to withstand grave crisis without analyzing its situation and without presenting effective methods required to ensure its future.

Today, Jewish knowledge and observance are no pre-requisites for Jewish leadership. The lay leaders are part and parcel of the community and are objects of the same weaknesses. Hence they speak and behave as if we live in normal times and circumstances.

But what about the spiritual leaders, why are they silent? Why do they not sound the alarm, while our people are living in the realm of illusion, both in the danger zone and in the countries of freedom and prosperity? The rabbis are described in the Torah as "the eyes of the community." Hence they are in duty bound to see, detect and reveal to the community the real situation.

In the mid-1980's, in the name of the rabbis of Australia and New Zealand, the writer of these lines approached rabbinical organizations everywhere in order to summon a world conference of rabbis to devise a strategy regarding the current crisis that ails Diaspora communities, or at least to raise a loud alarm of lament; to arouse the Jewish world in its entirety, and to dramatically shock the dormant victims. To great surprise, only the "Young Israel" rabbinical organization in the United States fully supported this idea. All the rest replied by cool responses and apathy.

The Jewish people in exile loses circa 5000 young every month, due to intermarriage and assimilation – a loss of circa 60,000 young souls annually. This dread critical state should rightly seize our attention, appall us, and allow us scant rest. How could we remain tacit and tranquil as so many Jewish souls are lost? The Torah admonishes us: "Stand not by your brother's blood!" Moreover, saving Jewish souls in the spiritual and national sense is also a commandment outweighing all others in the Torah. The deafening silence of Diaspora rabbis is terrifying!

The obligation of saving souls applies to every individual of the children of Israel and rabbis. However, public servants are voluntary watchdogs, whereas rabbis are hired guards. Hired guards are held liable for the theft and perdition of souls, just as for the loss of material goods.

There is but one ray of light – Israel, which has the distinction of having the highest fertility rate of any western country; where intermarriage is non-existent; and where Judaism is addressed to the eye. There, children absorb their religion and national spirit unconsciously. It is the only county in which the Jew can live a full Jewish life.

Israel has become the most immense centre of yeshivot and Torah study the Jewish people has ever seen; where young Jews are free, proud and brave, imbued with high ideals and principles. Truly, Israel has developed into the spiritual and national health resort of the Jewish People; while the Diaspora has degenerated into the Jewish Chernobyl, whose poisonous radiation consumes the souls of our children.

The conspiracy of silence is devastating. Our people are entitled to know the truth. Only if they know can they help themselves. And what they should know is that Israel can survive without their children, but their children cannot survive without Israel.

The present process of Jewish disintegration clearly demonstrates the fact that the Jew cannot survive in a Diaspora, where he enjoys freedom, equality and prosperity. Assimilation is the law of existence of the Diaspora. It is fatal to deceive ourselves by assuming that Jewish day schools can preserve us. They can only postpone assimilation but not cancel it; they can only delay it, but not prevent it.

We may now draw a third parallel between the characteristics of the Holocaust and those of the present crisis. The church as well as the Allies stand condemned for their silence and inaction, indifference and callousness to the fearful screaming of European Jews. While they died, the world looked on with folded arms.

Actually, in the present silent holocaust of intermarriage and assimilation, the Jewish leadership is duplicating the dumbness and paralysis of the church and the Allies during the Nazi Holocaust. We see a paralyzed Diaspora Jewry in the face of overwhelming powers of assimilation; without a hint of remedy from its leaders. Thus we have adopted some methods used in the Holocaust in the present process of our self-extermination.

The clarion call: "Liquidate the Galut or the Galut will liquidate you," is as realistic and life-saving today, as when it was originally sounded on the eve of the Holocaust. For the plague of intermarriage and assimilation is sapping us of our people in a way as deadly as gas chambers.

One day we shall be called to account for having remained silent while Israel was calling. Tragically, some positive Jews, certain Chasidic sects, even affirm and justify the Galut. For them, evidently, the messianic idea – which is the idea of redemption – has served as an ideology of wandering – ultimately assimilation; rather than as a stimulus to return home.

What should we do: should we cry, should we laugh? Perhaps both…

While the ship of Diaspora Jewry is sinking, we, the spiritual leaders, are going around with our ordinary rabbinic ministration and ceremonialism, like the stewards on the Titanic – while she was sinking they were serving the passengers drinks and were shining the mirrors.

Should the captain go down with the ship? Moses did, Joshua didn't. In this instance, I would venture to say, that the captain must not go down with the ship. The Rabbi is entitled to leave his flock and go on aliyah for his personal fulfillment and for the salvation of his descendants. But he must not depart on the first life-boat. He should first strive to send off a few life-boats packed with Jews before embarking on his own. The rabbi should preach aliyah not only just in his farewell sermon.

Look and see if a homeland is so precious and vital to national existence, that every nation is prepared and willing to sacrifice its best young sons and daughters for the sake of their country, how much more so should the State of Israel mean to the Jew. Could there be any sacrifice too big for the Jew to be personally attached to his homeland and be involved in its daily life, to maintain it and be maintained by it?

Unfortunately, the Jew in the Diaspora is living and behaving in such a manner as if there had never been a 2000 year bitter exile of persecution and suffering, inquisitions and massacres, blood libels and expulsions; As if there had never been an unprecedented Holocaust, in which half of the nations of the world collaborated with the German murderers in the extermination, while the other half remained silent and indifferent. The Jew continues to live in the Galut, as if there is no more anti-Semitism and Jew hatred in the world; as if no Jewish State exists; and as if no Holocaust could happen again. All the world thinkers claim that it could, only the Jew once more deludes himself saying: "Never again".

Actually, the Galut Jew acknowledges the charge of the anti-Semites, who claim that Jews do not know the meaning of homeland, that they are a nation of chronic wanderers, and that their only ideal is materialistic gain.

Obviously, such an ideal-less generation could not survive for long. Similarly, the generation of the wilderness that preferred Egyptian fish, cucumbers and onions to the Promised Land had to fall in the wilderness. That is the law of the Torah as well as the law of nature.

No wonder that the Talmud ruled that the precept of living in the land of Israel is equivalent to the observance of all the Biblical precepts. For the observance of the former would preserve the Jew and enable and inspire him to observe all the other commandments of the Torah.

CHAPTER TWO

A LOST PEOPLE

AFTER WORLD WAR II, in the Fifties and the first half of the Sixties of the last century, a spirit of optimism ruled among American Jews, a self-confidence that their community would resemble that of Babylon in the Talmudic era, or that of Spain in the Golden Age. During the same years, a theory of the "the Land of Israel and Babylon" began forming in a novel version: American Jewry stands juxtaposed to the State of Israel as a spiritual and cultural centrum, as the original Babylon was vis-à-vis Jerusalem.

The Vision of Israel and Babylon – Second Cycle

Babylon symbolizes a colossal autonomous Jewish center adorned with an exile leader, large, renowned yeshivas, and Torah-education institutions. This wondrous Jewish center existed in its splendor for centuries, and influenced world Jewry by its spiritual loftiness. The Babylonian Talmud was created there as well.

The ambition of American Jewry presuming to aspire to Babylon's pedestal, i.e., as a counterpart to the State of Israel in the spiritual and cultural sense, essentially expresses blatant Diaspora mindset – that the Diaspora is not merely an existing fact or reality born of duress and eventually voluntarily, but rather, a positive phenomenon that occasions bounty and blessing for the Jewish People.

On the other hand, one can somewhat positively judge those holding the opinion that American Jewry stood to replace the original Babylon. Indeed, during the same years, religious awakening and return to roots occurred among American Jewry. Following the Holocaust horrors of European Jewry's destruction, which brought many to consider repentance, people began feeling enormous responsibility resting upon their shoulders. An impetus of synagogue construction flourished among all religious denominations. Imposing new public and educational buildings rose in all American centers, and intermarriages were very few. In addition, rabbis, yeshiva heads, and dynastic Rebbes – remnants of Holocaust survivors – had arrived then in the United States, breathing life in local communities. Parents began to demand comprehensive Jewish education for their children. Torah and educational institutions multiplied, small and large yeshivas were founded nationwide. The number of small yeshivas reached three hundred, from which, Torah and mitzvah observant youth graduated. Many therefore believed that a second Babylon has arisen in the United States.

The author then studied for several years in New York universities, and experienced these optimistic feelings among Torah giants who then stood at the head of the 'Torah uMesorah' organization. Coreligionist scientists and lecturers in universities declared that American Jewry was becoming strong, its spiritual future assured. Indeed, intermarriages were rare then – only 6% as late as 1965.

Pipe Dreams

To our distress, the optimistic estimates have all evaporated. Directly and indirectly, gentile environment and material and cultural conditions influence the Jew and his children's education. They entice him to imitate and blur the Jewish image. Among foreign peoples, the Jew suffers spiritual tension and national suppression, and is forced to adopt their characteristic and another way of life, dividing his mind and deforming the Jewish icon. Hence, the ideology of the 'the Land of Israel and Babylon' was shattered into splinters in view of the curse of the Diaspora. There is no symmetry between these two parts of the people.

The Jew who dwells in the State of Israel, benefits from full Jewish existence: the Sabbath and Jewish holidays are days of national rest, and kashrut observance is customary in the vast majority of hotels. Matters of matrimony are handled by the rabbinate – the vouchsafe of Halacha. Jews dwell in the land of the fathers and circulate among brethren, all of the house of Israel benefits from an atmosphere of freedom and independence; they speak the holy tongue, and Judaism is apparent to the naked eye. At Passover, unleavened bread is neither seen nor found, and only matzoth are found in shops, in restaurants, and in hotels. At Sukkoth, booths crop up adjacent to each building and residential home. During the Feast of the Hasmoneans, Hanukah lights sparkle behind the curtains in homes; at Purim, the festivity is great in city streets, and on Yom Kippur, no automobiles circulate, and 90% of Israelis fast, as it is a holy day nationwide. Indeed, Judaism in Israel lives and thrives – the tradition of ancestors flourishes in the life of its children.

American Jewry

The Jewish community in America is the largest and most stable, wielding the greatest influence internally and externally. Their economic statues are vaunted; they occupy a position of respect in all economic, cultural, and administrative sectors beyond their percentile in the general population. While such a lofty toehold is convenient for them as citizens of the country, it is a negative factor that contributes to their loss of identity. This is a general rule; per the dimensions of equal rights and economic development in the Diaspora, thus also, the threat of spiritual corruption and damaged national stature.

We find corroboration of this horrifying assumption in the fact that the process of loss of identity among American Jewry is heightened every year. Per statistical data, 52 percent of American Jewish marriages are mixed. This percentage refers to large cities, in which Jewish community framework is yet maintained. In small cities, intermarriage rates reach 80–85 percent. Currently, more children under 12 come from a home in which only one parent is Jewish than those raised in a household in which both parents are Jewish. The 1990 survey revealed that, already then, 1,350,000 families were comprised of mixed marriages. That is still not all! In the last survey, over 300,000 American Jews reported converting to another religion – apostasy. Over twenty percent of Jewish students there do not see themselves as Jews at all. Circa half of American Jews who yet identify as Jews have a marginal interest in their Jewish ancestry. There is no connection between them and the Jewish community, they belong to no Jewish organization, and they maintain no atmosphere of Jewish life. Only thirty percent of youth receives Jewish education, one third of who learn in Talmud Torahs and day schools, and the rest only in Talmud Torahs in afternoon hours and Sunday study classes. As said, seventy percent of American Jewish youth has no tie to Judaism.

The Loyal Tribe

Haredi Jewry – the ultra-Orthodox that remains within its own 'four cubits' – numbers about four percent of the American Jewish population. It manages to hold the plague of assimilation at bay; mixed marriages among its members account for just three percent. Even Orthodox Jewry, which constitutes eight percent of the Jewish population in the United States, although it neither limits itself to the traditional 'four cubits', nor abstains from general national culture, largely manages to preserve its uniqueness. Even within its midst, mixed marriages account for about ten percent, according to surveys.

The parents of both of these groups provide their children a comprehensive Jewish education; in Talmud Torahs, day schools, and yeshivas.

Reform and Conservative – Transition to Assimilation

The Reform and Conservative movements constitute a corridor via which a great many are lost to the Jewish people. Together, they both number approximately 40% of American Jews. Disassociation with institutions of Jewish law, dismantling all boundaries in traditional Judaism, transforming it into raw material for revising – indeed 'reforming' – as if the product of humans and their machinations – mixed marriage ceremonies with Christian clergy and reform 'rabbis' all encourage and accelerate mixed marriages.

The Reform and Conservative movements have lost their younger generation. Once the strap was undone, all of Judaism is subject to makeover according to the time and the location. If there exists no observance of Sabbath and Jewish holidays, kashrut, or authentic Jewish matrimony and divorce, and Reform 'rabbis' marry mixed couples, the younger generation concludes that all can be adapted by a human hand, and every individual shall act as he sees fit. Hence, all of Judaism is superfluous at this point! It is merely a burdensome deadweight to be abandoned, and such is transpiring on a wholesale scale. As a result, mixed marriages among Reform is at 53% – a silent holocaust!

We are convinced that massive assimilation in the United States has been occasioned and received great encouragement from the fact that over many years Reform 'rabbis' have officiated at marriage ceremonies for mixed couples of Jews and Gentiles in the Untied States. In fact, those 'rabbis' provide permission and paperwork for legitimacy of assimilation and loss of identity that gnaw voraciously at Jewish communities. Hence, according to the surveys, not only youth, but even most Jewish parents in the United States accept marriage of mixed couples as a natural phenomenon. Fifty-six percent of Jewish parents surveyed reported apathy concerning their children marrying gentiles.

There is also a horrific phenomenon: while American Jews are less than 2% of the general population, 50% of the members of new occult sects are young Jews. Indeed, there is no vacuum; whoever disbelieves in the God of Israel believes in idol worship and various perverse improprieties.

Self-Destruction of Millions

Nearly 70 years have passed since the 1940's when it was known that American Jewry numbers 6 million. If we estimate natural growth at only half that of Israel, which is at 25,000 per each million Jews annually, the significance is that American Jewry should number today close to 11 million souls. In addition to natural growth, 1,735,000 Jews immigrated to the United States in the last 66 years: 135,000 Holocaust survivors, 650,000 Israelis, 700,000 Jews from the Former Soviet Union, 250,000 Jews from Latin America, Cuba, Iran, Syria and South Africa, et cetera. According to all this, American Jewry should now be close to 11 million strong.

According to latest surveys, American Jewry now numbers only 5,200,000. Where did approximately 6 million American Jews disappear? The answer is that they assimilated and lost their identity – self-destruction of circa 6 million Jews; a voluntary holocaust! Indeed, the same surveys revealed 6.3 million non-Jews of Jewish origin. We shout to Heaven and bitterly lament over 6 million victims of the physical Holocaust, and rightly so. However, we are silent and ignore the 6 million victims of the current national spiritual holocaust.

American Jews who did not do enough to rescue their brothers from the physical Holocaust are now doing precious little to save themselves from the grip of the spiritual holocaust rampaging in their midst. Our calamity is that the question of American Jewish existence has already been decided. We must admit that among the great majority of its children, there will be no Jewish continuity of any form whatsoever. As half its Jews have no association to community and institutions, this data is significant; those same millions have lost all connection to Judaism and are in an advanced process of assimilation. The other half of this population, which belongs to Jewish communities and organizations, is circa 75% Reform, which constitutes a point of transition into assimilation. Moreover, intermarriage there has exceeded 50%. The bitter fact is that almost half of the American Jewish community already consists of non-Jewish spouses and children of mixed marriages. The American Jewish community now includes 2.2 million non-Jewish spouses and mixed marriage children. Of the 3.2 million Jewish households, only 1.7 million, namely only close to half are the Jewish families in which both – husband and wife – are Jewish.

According to American World Jewish Congress figures, tens of thousands of youth opt out of the Jewish People in the United States annually. Demographers predict that in another fifty years, only about a million Jews will survive in the United States, and only about one and a half million Jews will exist in all Diaspora lands, primarily of the Ultra-Orthodox and moderate Orthodox. The bitterest words of reproach have come to pass: "Thy sons and thy daughters shall be given unto another people, and your eyes shall look, and fail with longing for them all the day; and there shall be naught in the power of thy hand." (Deuteronomy chapter 28:32)

Influencing the Status of the State of Israel

The spiritual and national holocaust in the United States, that is taking shape before our eyes, greatly influences the State of Israel's existence and future. Israel's standing in the Untied States is based primarily on Jewish influence vis-à-vis the president and members of Congress, due to their importance in elections for the presidency and Congress, both in millions of voters and financial support campaign candidates for the presidency and Congress. While Jews progressively disappear, American Muslims continue to increase because of both births and blacks that accept Islam. Between 1989 and 1998, the Arab American population grew by 25 % to three million. As a result, in anther 15 to 20 years, the influence of Jews will dwindle to negligible insofar as government and presidential and congressional elections, due to their decline. Israel will then be isolated, without benefit of loyal, friendly relations with the Untied States concerning security matters and in the international arena in the UN and the Security Council.

As Diaspora Jewry Disintegrates

A destructive process buffets Diaspora communities the degeneration of spiritual and cultural wellsprings is obvious in most Jewish concentrations.

Jews are being denuded of their Judaism, and are in advanced stage of 'marrying out'. It is discernible everywhere that Eastern European Jewry does not exist as a source in bringing the wellsprings of salvation to the remainder of the Diaspora countries.

In Latin American countries, rapid disintegration of Jewish centers is under way. Argentinean Jewry – the largest Jewish community in South America – suffers from grave assimilation. Approximately 40% of Jewish youth in Buenos Aries intermarries. Outside of Buenos Aires – the capital, the number reaches 60%. The leftist Bundist movement that was prevalent among Argentinean Ashkenazi Jewry contributed to this. The theory not only sided with communism, but also opposed Zionism. The majority of religious Zionist Jews immigrated to Israel, and the conservative movement assumed the place of erstwhile dominant Orthodox Jewry. The Yiddish newspapers that appeared there and the formerly vibrant Jewish theater have disappeared. Argentinean Jews numbered over half a million souls subsequent to World War II and stand at only 230,000 today.

Add to this what is happening among Jews in the rest of the countries, and the picture in its entirety is yet gloomier. According to surveys, a dwindling and aging trend is apparent among the Jewish population in the countries of the Former Soviet Union that now number about 2 million Jews. Nearly 70% of Jewish males married gentile women, while 60% of the women married non-Jewish men.

British Jewry, 450,000 strong in the wake of World War II, lost over one third during the years since then, and now numbers less than 300,000. There also, mixed marriages have reached 45%.

On the other hand, standing at 385,000, Canadian Jewry is maintaining itself, and intermarriages there have reached only 25%.

French Jewry faced disintegration before World War II because of Jewish aspirations to assimilate. However, the community was strengthened in the aftermath, thanks to large numbers of Jews of Algerian, Moroccan, and Tunisian origin that immigrated to France. The majority was Torah and mitzvah observant and inexperienced with intermarriages during its sojourn in North African lands. Currently, even they are largely infected with this scourge. As native-born, the younger generations among the immigrants quickly absorbed French culture. The melting pot in the Diaspora lands strides with gigantic steps toward assimilation and loss of identity to other ethnicities, the summary of which can be expressed in two words: emancipation and assimilation. Just as the Jewish homeland is a melting pot of sects and tribes of Israel into one people…

French Jewry today numbers five hundred and twenty thousand, afflicted with intermarriage at about fifty percent. Intermarriage in other European countries is at the same rate or higher. The rate in Scandinavia is at seventy percent.

The Lesson of Australian Jewry

The majority of Australian Jews live in the two largest cities of Sydney and Melbourne. Australian Jewry, numbering 130,000 was actually in relatively good standing compared to communities in other Western countries. Intermarriages reached less than 20%. This is attributable to the fact that most Jews there are organized in the community and its institutions, and belong to Orthodox synagogues, headed by renowned rabbis, Talmud scholars and Hassidic leaders. It is also thanks to the widespread chain of Jewish day schools.

A change for the worse has occurred in recent years, however, particularly in Sydney. A reform 'rabbi' has been conducting mixed marriage ceremonies between Jews and Gentiles there also. Once among Jews, in Eastern European Jewry, on such rare instance that Jews wandered astray and married gentiles, parents and siblings regarded it as abandonment of family and betrayal of Judaism. They would assume the stance of mourners, even observing Shiva rites of mourning. Such occurrences would shock and revolt Jewish opinion; all were perturbed to hear of the terrible effrontery that had been committed. These dolorous and pained impressions were profoundly etched on Jewish hearts, and distanced them from mixed marriages out of distaste. Today, also, observant families sever all bounds with outlaws such as these.

With the Reform 'rabbi' who conducted mixed marriage ceremonies in Sydney, we saw the exact opposite of what we knew heretofore: an absurd and uncanny instance, a self-proclaimed Jewish 'rabbi' began conducting mixed marriages to sabotage Jews and their Torah. In other words, a 'rabbi' showcasing and publicly presenting practical Halacha: mixed marriage is kosher and pleasant. Such grave injury only weakens the profound revulsion in Judaism concerning mixed marriages, and encourages youth to assimilate and lose identity.

Indeed, to our great dismay, the disastrous results became evident in short order: in one decade, as mixed marriages in Melbourne increased from only 18 to 25 percent, they grew in Sydney during the same period from 20 to 40 percent – a dreadful jump for the worse. This is largely due to the marriages performed by the Reform 'rabbi', at least part of the grave laceration visited upon the renowned Jewish community of Sydney. Hence, one can understand the tremendous scope of the spiritual destruction that these Reform 'rabbis' wreak on the breadth and width of American Jewry by means of such havoc over generations.

A Diaspora – Good as Bad – Consumes its Jews

Two events of great significance to Jewish life occurred in 1848. The Russian Czar Nicolas I then issued the abominable decree to snatch Jewish children from their parents and raise them by priests, with the objective of recruiting them to the Russian army upon their reaching maturity. Prussian emperor Franz Josef then bestowed the rank of aristocracy on several of his Jewish citizens. It is recounted that when the two emperors met, the Russian Czar expressed criticism of the Austrian Emperor, stating: "I am making efforts to destroy the Jews and you grant them freedom and equality, and yet exalt them with aristocratic titles?" Franz Josef retorted: "Know that I also aspire to destroy the Jews, however, you will yet see that my way is more effective than yours."

To our dismay, Franz Josef's malicious scheme has come to pass: under conditions of prosperity and full rights, Diaspora Jewry loses its generations and is stripped of its spiritual and cultural assets, more that it lost and was impoverished in pogroms, inquisitions, and forced conversion. A horrific tragedy for Diaspora Jewry! Not the severity of the situation, but the opposite – improvement of Jewish status in Diaspora lands and their equal rights threaten to corrupt spiritual life and detract from Jewish stature. The dimension of equal rights and economic prosperity is as great as the threat to Jewish existence.

"But Jeshurun waxed fat, and kicked." They once said that it is difficult to be a Jew. It was difficult, but the Jews remained Jews – complete and proud Jews. It is a known fact that it is easy to be a Jew today, although the excess ease tempts Jews to stop being Jewish.

Diaspora Jews Live on Borrowed Time

The peril is that within 20 to 30 years the current generation will also be lost, for most Jewish youth in Diaspora lands receive no Jewish education. Young and old alike are unfamiliar with the letter Aleph. How many Jewish students know something of Judaism or a chapter in Jewish history? Informed individuals reveal that the modern Jew concentrates on only three books, and they are: the phone book, the checkbook, and the cookbook. Indeed, the book has fallen from the hands of the People of the Book, and no one is there to lift it.

Dr. Barry Kosmin, Director of the World Jewish Population Survey, has said that the change in 20th century Jewish demography is not only unprecedented, but catastrophic as well.

Mr. Izzy Liebler, President of the Acting committee of Australian Jewry and joint chair of the Board of Trustees of the World Jewish Congress, cautions about the disappearance of most Jews in the Diaspora – a campaign of assimilation unparalleled at any point. He asserts that Diaspora Jewry faces complete assimilation that will leave isolated clusters of reclusive Jewry behind walls of ultra-Orthodoxy.

Steiner recognized, therefore, that Jews in Diaspora are basically living on a 'borrowed present,' therefore, devoid of traces of a past and without hope for the future.

I do not think that a Jew in Diaspora lands exists who is able to rise and state assuredly that his grandchild, and certainly not his great grandchild, will be Jews. Herein lies the enormous difference between the future of Jews residing in Diaspora lands and those Jews living among their people in Israel, the future of whose offspring is assured of remaining Jews for generations.

You are stunned and shocked in light of the blindness of our brethren that inhabit a paradise of artificial apathy, ignoring a plague of loss of identity and assimilation that rampages around them and threatens to eradicate them from the face of the earth.

Diaspora Jews Resemble Voluntary Suicides

"A country that is destroyed and whose people is yet full of life and strength – shall merit Zerubavel, Ezra, and Nehemiah, in whose wake people shall return to rebuild. But who shall resurrect the people that is annihilated, and whence shall its succor come?"

CHAPTER THREE

FORMER SOVIET UNION JEWRY
ASSIMILATING IN THE USA

Seven Hundred Thousand Jewish Immigrants to America from the Former Soviet Union are in an Advanced Process of Spiritual and National Eradication

SOVIET RUSSIA'S opening gates to mass immigration of its Jews in the early 70's was one of our generation's wonderful miracles. After over 60 years of disconnect from former soviet Union Jewry behind an impenetrable Iron curtain, devoid of any contact with World Jewry, we merited witnessing the hand of God in the process of ingathering exiles: after constant struggle, huge efforts, and complicated, awkward coordination by world Jewry and the assistance of righteous gentiles worldwide, burdensome millstones that for generations paved channels of Soviet bureaucracy were removed, and the gates opened for Jewish emigration. Departure of Jews from the Soviet Union was conditioned by Moscow on their immigration to Israel only, based on the principle of repatriation – return to the homeland.

Arab World Protest against Immigration

The entire Arab world was affrighted and alarmed at this decisive turning point in favor of Israel, its security, and its development. The Arabs raised a howl of protest and threats against Soviet Jewish immigration to Israel. They summoned an emergency conference of all Arab leaders, requesting that Soviet officials close gates on departing Jews. The King of Jordan tremulously warned that Russian Jews would enlarge settlements in Judea and Samaria and force out Arabs. Iraq and Libya threatened to declare war against Israel. President Mubarak rushed to Washington to convince the American administration to increase the number of Soviet Jewish immigrants to the United States in order to direct them away from Israel. Arab leaders also attempted to influence European countries to accept Jews leaving Russia.

Jewish Organization Execute Arab Schemes

Arab leaders got a response to their requests from parties they had not imagined: they were fortunate enough to have their work done by Jewish organizations; leaders and activists executed their wishes in full.

Arab leaders understood the great blessing in Soviet Jewish emigration to Israel from all standpoints: by increasing Israeli population and security, and contributing to the economy, industry, and culture, by immigration of scientists, engineers, and professionals in technology and music. Nevertheless, it was precisely our brethren's leaders and activists of American Jewry who disregarded this manifold national blessing and labored against it with might and main. It is noteworthy that almost all immigrants from the former Soviet Union were then Jews according to Halacha.

Jewish organizations in the United States; HIAS (Hebrew Immigrant Aid society) and the JOINT (American Committee for Joint Distribution) that receive important allocations from the United Jewish Appeal and the United States government, with all their organizations and activists, needed customers in order to actually exist. They found themselves a place to dig in among Jews departing the Soviet Union during their stay in Viennese and Italian transit camps to Israel. They ensnared them there in their net, enticing them to change direction and immigrate to the United States by special considerations financed for them from the United States government.

They say that during World War II, when Churchill as British Prime Minister visited the front, he asked one of the soldiers in position as to his business there. The soldier, instead of stating that he stood there in order to protect the homeland, responded that he was guarding his position... To our dismay, instead of guarding the souls of brethren – that were emaciated under communist rule – and the strength of the State of Israel, activists and officials of HIAS and JOINT guard the positions and welfare of their organizations.

Burgeoning Attrition
American Jewish leaders succeeded in lobbying the American administration to recognize as 'refugees' those Jews departing countries of the Commonwealth of Independent Nations, holding visas of the State of Israel while en route to it, in order to enable them to emigrate to the United States with greater ease and benefit there from special allowances.

The dropouts made a simple calculation: they could always enter Israel, however the United States, if not now, then when? Especially, when this was all connected to luxury travel, hotel lodging, and financial assistance, and moreover, dreams of America as the land of gold and the generosity of its Jews. What encouragement and motivation for dropping out! Indeed, the number of dropouts among those exiting the former Soviet Union reached a frightening increase of up to 90% of the candidates for immigration to Israel. The American HIAS and JOINT organizations had harvested their human crop as it was headed to Israel!

Instruction for Double Deception
Jews of the former Soviet Union left on Israeli visas, on condition that they immigrate there; they automatically became Israeli citizens. The question then arises: how could the American administration consider them as

'refugees'? Moreover, how did the Jewish lobby dare to demand that of the Americans? An independent State of Israel and its Jews as refuges are a double contradiction. If Israel is a Jewish State, Jews bearing its visas cannot be considered 'refugees'. On the other hand, if such Jews are recognized as 'refugees', indeed this is perforce non-recognition of Israel as a Jewish State possessing the right to a unique country, but rather, one of the Jewish communities in the Diaspora. In addition, this recognition also offended the integrity of the former Soviet Union, in that the term 'refugees' attested that its Jewish citizens left it not as immigrants, but rather, fled as refugees from persecution; not as returnees to their homeland, but rather, in preference of capitalist lifestyle to that of the communist regime.

The dropouts delivered a double slap: to Israel and the Soviet Union, which had made a special gesture to Jews in permitting their departure. The Soviets perceived dropping out as a deceitful act, and expressed their protest aloud: "We are disgusted with Jewish intrigues, which are but deceptions." Under the guise of immigration to Israel, the Jews actually travel to the United States. Defamation of Israel's honor!

The HIAS – and JOINT – made breach in the Russian immigration front attracted additional purveyors of human commodity. The Federation of the Jews Assistance Associations – 'Welfare Societies' of Australia – rushed an official to the Viennese transit camp to influence Russian Jews to immigrate to Australia, thus staking a claim to the human wares. Nine thousand dropped out to this country, joined by 12,000 more in time. Chief activists in the organization of Russian refuseniks assert that various parties interested in their coming to American and Canada misled them, enticing dropouts to immigrate to those countries instead of Israel.

Marketing a Humanitarian Campaign
American Jewish leaders, including members of the Jewish Agency Board of directors, vehemently opposed Israel's decision to fly Soviet Jewry requesting Israeli entry visas directly from Moscow to Ben-Gurion Airport to overcome the dropout epidemic that stood at 90%. Appeal heads, also vocal opponents of direct flights to Tel Aviv, threatened Israel, while the American government was prepared to acquiesce to Israel's proposal.

Unfortunately, in abnormal Diaspora life it is occasionally apparent that community activists do no exist for their agencies and their efficacy, but rather, the agencies exist for the sake of the activists and their benefit. They enable them to be involved in public affairs and collect publicity and honor. They help them to be busy, instead of being creators, public guardians and defenders.

To our great sadness, the American Rabbinical Association supported HIAS and JOINT campaigning to allow free choice to dropouts regarding their country of residence. As if "free choice" exists in committing spiritual and national suicide; as if Jewish tradition commands fair payment for liars and deceivers. Dropping out was both an amoral and anti-patriotic phenomenon. It was one of the largest and most entangled international deceptions.

Under the humanitarian banner of "Free Choice," they corrupted Jews exiting the commonwealth of Independent Nations. As customary in the world, all despotism and murders are committed under camouflage of some imaginary idealistic campaign. These dropouts obtained exit permits from the Soviet Union based on requests from Israeli relatives to reunite families in their homeland, based on Israeli visas, as well. It was explicitly stated on these Russian visas that the bearer must settle in Israel. But behold when they had only reached the first station outside Soviet borders, they showed everyone that they had misled Moscow and Jerusalem, and they turned their backs to them. Can public institutions indeed justify "free Choice" by deceit and falsehood? Lies have no basis on which to stand, and in our iniquities, we have stumbled on our leader feet.

Concerning the dropout dilemma in light of Halacha, ethics, justice, and its grave spiritual and national aftermath, see my book: Dropouts in the Light of Halacha, Otzar HaPosqim Publishing, Jerusalem 5745 (1985).

Another Grave Hazard Hampering Immigration

Since HIAS and JOINT found in dropouts a niche for activity, many clients, and endless opportunity, they relentlessly sought them out. As the former Soviet Union crumbled and national gates opened wide, they could no longer claim that Jews were persecuted refugees detained and restrained against their will and consciousness behind an iron curtain. They announced a novel approach, which like its predecessor was greatly detrimental to the fabric of Israeli immigration. These organizations and their leaders and managers, the Jewish lobby headed by Jewish Agency chiefs, launched a comprehensive and persistent campaign lobbying administrative channels in America that President Reagan might allow Soviet Jewry a generous quota of 45,000 immigrants a year.

The result is a doubly damaging national disaster. Not only are 45,000 Jews absorbed each year in the American melting pot with all perils of assimilation, but rather as a first choice of immigration allowed to America, indeed, talented youth and skilled immigrants are attracted. On the other hand, a high percentage of geriatric, handicapped, and single parent families immigrate to Israel, as former Labor and Welfare Minister Ora Namir has declared (5755/1995). When Soviet gates opened for Jewish immigration, Israel had great hopes for receiving human resources of high education and skills to contribute to the professions in Israel. They anticipated many scientists, physicians, engineers, white-collar and other technical workers. Indeed, so it was at the outset of the wave of immigration. However, when

American Jewish relief organizations began to attract Soviet Jews to their country, changes occurred in the composition of the immigration, mainly a dwindling percentage of scientifically trained professionals, free academics, and particularly engineers and physicians, and the percentage of unprofessional workers increased. All began seeking their future in the United States. The Labor and Welfare Minister of Israel also expressed criticism of young immigrants who abandon their elderly parents, refuse to take responsibility for them, depart for the United States, sending their sick, aged, invalid parents to Israel, so that Israel might expend its resources on them.

Moreover, as young professionals with professions and skills immigrate to America, or await a turn to move there, the human inventory of such Jews for immigration to Israel has continually depleted.

Baseless, Bitter Illusion

Despite all the importance of those above-mentioned details, they are indeed minor vis-à-vis the main concern, namely, that the former Soviet Union Jews remain Jews. The assertion of American Jewish leadership that no one can limit the destinations of those exiting the former Soviet Union, as Jewish exit is an overriding factor for rescuing them from spiritual perdition – even if they elect to settle in the United States – is disproved!

To our great dismay, this was but a bitter, baseless illusion that burst on the wall of reality, for which we now pay a catastrophic price for the dispossession of the huge tribe of the Jewish People. The facts prove that immigration to America and other Western countries is actually release from Judaism and national ethnic identity. Former Soviet Union Jewry underwent circa seventy years of the communist melting pot that denuded them of a bond to their past and belonging. They have no knowledge of Judaism, its tradition, language, or historical background of the Jewish people. They know that they are Jews due to the stamp emblazoned in their passports. Such Jews are so estranged that Judaism has no meaning for them, and they harbor no national sentiment. They therefore stand poised to assimilate among the gentiles amidst whom they settled. Above all, these Jews actually require spiritual absorption after all the years of living in a spiritual desert under communism's yoke.

Former Soviet Union Jewry in Israel

Indeed, most of the over one million former Soviet Union Jews who immigrated to Israel have been absorbed in their Israeli surroundings and speak its language – the Hebrew language – which acts as a spiritual and national reviver. Their children are educated in Israeli schools and serve in the army. The national space is redolent with tradition and a Jewish orientation, and the Sabbath and Jewish holidays are easily evident. In short, Israel's atmosphere sanctifies its inhabitants, educating them as to its values.

Many of these immigrants have resumed being observant, assumed the yoke of Torah and mitzvoth and converted their spouse according to the faith of Moses and Israel. None of them are in danger of intermarriage and assimilation. Assimilation in Israel always works in the positive direction of accepting Judaism. These Jews, who fled the Soviet Diaspora, are assured of remaining Jews, and will raise generations loyal to the State of Israel. Not in vain, Our Sages of Blessed Memory said that inhabitants of the State of Israel inherit the World to come.

Additionally, this enormous immigration endowed Israel with a huge contribution for its support and development. The blessing is double for both of them: for the country and its returning children.

Former Soviet Union Jews in Western Lands

This is not so in Western countries, and particularly America. No hope exists for immigrants there to rise along the ladder of Judaism, but rather a plummeting dip into the chasm. All occasions, conditions, and customs of the gentile environment ensnare and attract toward decline and immersion. Indeed, even native Israelis including kibbutzniks that leave Israel to live in Diaspora countries assimilate, most of them losing their children in mixed marriages, despite the fact that they arrived there with a rich national heritage. The Diaspora simply devours its Jewish inhabitants. It is many times over worse with Jews of the countries of the Commonwealth of Independent States, who yet in their native lands were already in a state of loss of identity intermarriage, and distance from Jewish tradition. Upon their arrival in other countries in which there is no real Jewish formation, the process of assimilation is accelerated and overwhelming.

According to the report by Dr. Barukh Gur, director of the Jewish Agency Department for the Commonwealth of Independent States, most of the Jews of the former Soviet Union decided that their future and that of their children lies not in there, and the question that faces them is: to which country should we immigrate? Were there no option of immigrating to the United States, the choice would be: Israel!

Indeed, we see a twin evil in this; Jewish welfare organizations in the United States, by their self-serving and irresponsible actions, occasioned grave and grievous injury to the people of Israel. On the one hand, they prevented ingathering of exiles – a huge group of 700,000 Jews – waylaying them on their route to their homeland: the land of the living the Patria of Israel's statehood and awareness. On the other hand, they have led them to spiritual perdition and loss of identity among gentiles, where intermarriage is truly epidemic, and from which there is no escape even for offspring of its good and best Jewish families. Although American Jews are swept up in catastrophic process of self-extinction, they undertook all efforts and schemes to direct former Soviet Union Jews there, instead of their moving to Israel, for which they have a crucial need.

One misdeed leads to another; hundreds of thousands Jews who have already immigrated to the United States constitute a bridge for their relatives and friends who are yet in the former Soviet Union states, and whoever has chances of receiving an entry visa to the United States prefers to wait several years than to immigrate to Israel immediately.

Loss of Identity among Gentiles

As is known, Jews from states of the former Soviet Union who dropped out to Australia approached offices of the Jewish community only in the initial period of their arrival, when they sought aid and assistance. Indeed, after they exploited the benefits granted them, they exited the Jewish cycle. They are neither seen nor found in the Jewish environment. They belong to no Jewish community or organization and attend no synagogue even on High Holy Days, nor have they any interest in learning a thing about their religion and culture. Australian and New Zealand rabbis exerted themselves to the full extent of their ability and energy to attract former Soviet Union Jews – 20,000 of whom immigrated to Australia – to bring them into the mainstream of local communities and activities and to instruct them in the ways of Judaism. Nevertheless, following considerable efforts and unending disappointments, they were forced to give up on them completely.

In recent years, the author visited several US cities in which most dropouts and Jewish immigrants from former Soviet Union countries have settled, in order to investigate and query what is happening there. To my great dismay, I discovered that it is the same everywhere; their lives and patterns are no different. There also, they are estranged from Jewish life and organization, and their Jewish status there is yet worse. America's enormous melting pot devours its Jews – who know nothing of their creed and culture – and dissipates them without an iota of knowledge of Judaism. I also learned of the disappointment of many in the new environment. Of course! They meandered from one exile to another, finding themselves on strange turf yet again, once more in an unfamiliar and unsettling environment, yet again living temporarily, once more among anti-Semites.

Airbuses to Spiritual and National Destruction

Where did the American Jewish organizations take 700,000 Jews from former Soviet Union countries? To the American Diaspora, where assimilation has reached veritable epidemic dimensions: above 50% of marriages are with gentiles; 70% of Jewish children receive no Jewish education; the youth stumbles in darkness, without any knowledge of whence they came and whither they are headed: hundreds of thousands of Jews are committing apostasy; a large part of Jewish students does not see itself as Jewish at all; demographers rightly predict that only a million Jews will remain in America by the mid-century!

We might imagine what the situation would be, for instance, were certain organizations to lead 700,000 individuals malnourished, weak and exhausted, to an area plagued by an infectious epidemic that exterminates above 50% of its residents. What a bitter cry and tumultuous storm this would arouse throughout the world! Why should we see spiritual and national perdition as a lesser sin than physical extermination? When did we attribute greater importance to losses of the second kind than the first kind?

Above 90% Assimilation!

As is known by top former Soviet Union leaders, the plague of estrangement from Judaism and assimilation with Gentiles is worse in the West than in Russia, the Ukraine, and other neighboring countries, anti-Semitism was so strong and overt there, and Jew hatred is so entrenched for generations among Russians and Ukrainians, that a similar want Jews found no place among them. Such is not so in Western countries, even those in which anti-Semitism exists; indeed, it is not as open and brutal as in Russia, the Ukraine, and neighboring countries. Assimilation and identity loss in Western countries are easier and more convenient.

In the wake of this, Rabbi Mordechai Hanzin and his colleagues, among leading activists of the former Soviet Union Prisoners of Zion Organization, have declared that it is best for Jews to remain in the former Soviet Union than leaving to assimilate in America, for they yet live in hope there, whereas in the 'Free World' they will be dizzied and immediately forget their Jewishness. For indeed, most former Soviet Union Jews who dropped out or immigrated to the West regard assimilation or loss of identity as a natural and proper phenomenon. They explicitly state their willingness to assimilate among gentiles, as they perceive no difference between Jew and gentile: "Religion and nationality do not determine, but rather, quality and character of the individual alone," they claim.

It is our disaster that over 90% of Jews who dropped out or immigrated to the West, particularly America, are in a most accelerated process of assimilation.

Ignoring Warnings

During 5736–5737 (1976–1977), as the number of dropouts began to reach frightening proportions, the author warned from synagogue pulpits and in Anglo-Jewish press articles in Australia and the United States that the dropping out is at once an immoral and anti-national phenomenon. This phenomenon is liable to defeat the battle for releasing our brethren from the former Soviet Union. Any thinking person could expect dire outcome from this sorry affair. Certainly, when sowing defeat and falsehood, one reaps only disaster and bankruptcy.

Nevertheless, the dropout lobbyists, among them US HIAS vice-President and Australian vice-President of the Federation of Aid Societies verbally attacked the author, festively declaring that all would end well. To our great dismay, it is now obvious and evident to all that all ended very badly. The problem with our brethren exiting the Former Soviet Union is not merely one of immigration to Israel and leaving it, but rather, Jewish life in Israel or the kiss of death in America. It is excruciating that 700,000 who reached the same Diaspora disconnect from the House of Israel, losing their identity among the gentiles amidst whom they came to settle, with the aid of Jewish organizations. This is a net loss from the standpoint of Israel and the Jewish people.

National Suicide

One dare not forget that this is not the first time that American Jewish leaders erred and sinned gravely against our people by neglecting the rescue of brethren from extermination. Researchers of Holocaust secrets increasingly discover that American Jewish leaders shirked political action for rescue efforts in World War II.

Indeed Doctor Nachum Goldman, the World Jewish Congress President, declared in a speech in 5723 (1963) in Jerusalem that American Jewish leaders betrayed European Jews during the Holocaust: they convened no mass sit-in by the White House for the president to order Air Force bombing of death camps and railways supplying them. "We refused to do it," Dr. Goldman then admitted, "because American Jewish leaders claimed that it was forbidden to disturb the war effort by loud protests…"

What folly! What hardheartedness and mercilessness! Tens of thousands of our brethren were annihilated daily. Millions suffered sadistic torture to death. Processions of cattle cars leading swarms of Jews to extermination camps; an entire people led to sacrifice and instant slaughter, millions butchered, turned to hills of ash. Victory by allied forcers sooner or later — what difference is there for us? Which practical ramifications has this for an entire people abducted for slaughter? The vanquished armies of the arched demon celebrated their full victory against Europe's Jews. Stonehearted, American Jewish leaders remained taciturn, silently did nothing to save our brothers from the Valley of the Shadow of Death, fearing lest protests disturb the war effort. Thus, the Holocaust era passed in neglectfulness, apathy, ineffectuality, and devoid of any act of salvation.

It is our disaster that leaders and lobbyists of American Jewry learned no lesson from what they occasioned to the people of Israel during days of physical Holocaust forced upon us. Now, they repeat their mistake also during the current spiritual holocaust that is voluntary: they not only accept their catastrophic fate, but rather, they propel a swollen throng of former Soviet Union Jewry to the American melting pot.

We can only repeat the words of the prophet Jeremiah, the national lamenter: "Woe unto the shepherds that destroy and scatter the sheep of My pasture! – saith the LORD (Jeremiah 23:1).

CHAPTER FOUR

JEWISH LEADERSHIP AS MISGUIDERS OF A PEOPLE

THE LEADERS OF the people determine its destiny, its fate, and its future. If fortunate, a people is blessed with wise and spiritual leadership that possesses skill and initiative to pave the way to glory and fame. If not, it is afflicted with stumbling leadership, which deceives and misleads the people to crises and failures. Our Sages, of blessed memory, thus commented: "The body follows the head." In other words, a people march in its leader's tracks. They also said: "When the shepherd errs, the flock errs after it."

The Diaspora Jewry leadership is in a tremendous unprecedented crisis: Jews are disappearing en masse worldwide. Jewish birth rates in Diaspora countries are the lowest in the world, much less than necessary for preserving the status quo. The World Jewish Congress Institute's annual survey indicates in all Jewish communities – save Israel – a higher death rate than that of births. The survey established that 60% of Diaspora youth are entirely disconnected from Judaism and Israel.

The picture is indeed characterized by the paradox of "good for the Jews and bad for Judaism." In many Jewish communities, as the security and economic situation improved, thus the trend of assimilation and accelerated loss of identity increases. American and other Jews are undergoing intensive process of erosion of their Judaism, and their number rapidly declines. Intermarriage brings about loss of hundreds of thousands of youths from the Jewish people. Assimilation is on the rise and has reached terrifying dimensions. Indeed, a horrifying collapse is but another generation away.

Silent Holocaust

This catastrophic process is often presented as a "silent holocaust," as one may perceive a perilous continuation of the treachery of the physical Holocaust. This holocaust is defined as silent, as its horrific result is accomplished quietly and furtively, without arousing the powers that possess to put an end to this growing cancer. Diaspora Jewry is unaware of the dimensions of the ghastly crisis raging within it, while its leadership demonstrates neither the heightened awareness, nor urgency necessary for combating the silent Holocaust, just as it did nothing during the Nazi regime and its murderous policy toward European Jews.

There is a tale of an aged man pursuing a group with the last of his strength, trying to reach them, sweating profusely and breathing heavily. When asked why he so strove to follow them, he innocently replied, "I am their leader…!" Now, as then, Jewish leadership is sadly weak and bending, lacking conviction and vision, self-preoccupied more than setting the tack for the present needs.

We urgently require resourceful leadership wholly devoted to public welfare and survival, capable of earnest, incisive assessment of our constitution; leadership to speak the truth to the masses about their critical dilemma: to summon it to devote itself to act to resuscitate, leadership strong at imagining and envisioning, to pave the course to be followed.

Sweet Music of Sirens
Instead of this, judicial leadership spurned the order of the day and avoided confronting the public with true facts of Diaspora Jewry in the throes of a fatal crisis. Moreover, Jewish leadership misled its constituents with virtual solutions, fantasies detached from reality, imbuing it with an illusory sensation that was the defense mechanism of self-deception.

Instead, the Jewish leadership has not responded to the call of the hour and has avoided confronting the public with the true situation of World Jewry which is in the throes of a mortal crisis. Moreover, the Jewish leadership misled the public by supplying bogus solutions, fantasies detached from reality and chimeras, providing a defense mechanism for self-delusion.

It is worth mentioning here a Greek legend about sea nymphs called sirens. A siren is a female creature whose top half is human and bottom half fish. A siren would lure and charm sailors at sea by her sweet bewitching song, leading them into dangerous waters where they would be shipwrecked on the rocks and abandoned. Homer presents them in the most vivacious way in the ancient Greek literary work *Odyssey*.

I believe there are such sirenic voices among us, false prophets promising a Jewish future full of happiness in the Diaspora, when in fact we are being dragged towards destruction and annihilation.

The First Sirenic Song
Sirenic music is amazing and somnolent as uttered by President of the World Jewish congress who endorsed the right of Diaspora Jewish leaders to oppose certain policy actions of the State of Israel. He describes Western Jewry as strong in the following words: "First, we must recognize that Jews in the democratic world are not weak… from our new position of strength, we must explore ways in which we can bring peace and inspiration to the world, how we can restore our reputation as the deliverers of other minorities who, like the Jewish People, also suffer the hardships of slavery."

How sweet this music sounds to the public ear and how much of it is misleading. It presents Diaspora Jewry as strong, so strong that we are no longer obliged to give an account to ourselves, to our children and to our future, but that we can occupy ourselves with the problems of other national minorities and deliver them… clearly there is an enormous gap between the real situation and what the Jewish leadership says. The truth is bleak and frightening. Never have we known so much personal suffering, an inability by people to live side by side: divorce and broken homes, social ills which have hardly affected us in the past are now every day. All are signs of an illness affecting anguished souls. Nonetheless, the President of the World Jewish Congress claims, contrary to the policy action, that western Jewry is strong and does not experience any weaknesses.

Today, the framework of the Jewish family, which was once the essence of Jewish life and the envy of the international community, has crumbled. The divorce rate in Jewish families and the number of broken homes has grown to 33 percent of all first marriages in the Jewish community. Jewish youth head the list of alcoholics and drug users, Jewish youth by far constitute a bigger percentage of various mystical sects. Furthermore, the vast majority of our youth lacks all knowledge of Judaism and Jewish culture and the trend towards assimilation and absorption is growing.

In view of all these weaknesses, can we still boastfully say that we are strong? To declare that Diaspora Jewry is strong is an illusion which can lead to catastrophic consequences. This kind of assertion gives the public an unfounded feeling of security. If we do not know our weaknesses and failures, how can we repair them? Given this depressing situation it is not surprising that dark prognoses abound predicting the rapid disappearance of Diaspora Jewry. It would be silly and foolish on our part to ignore these facts and to nurture futile visions. But the leaders avoid telling the people the bare truth about the grave crisis in which Diaspora Jewry is plunged; only aliyah to Israel will strengthen the Jewish People and assure its continuing existence. This ignorance of the truth, together with the futile hope of survival, enabled the Germans to carry out their final solution.

The Second Siren's song

The reform movement sung the second siren's song. Spokesmen for this movement admit that tens of thousands of young Jews are lost to Judaism every year in America due to intermarriage. However, they hasten to comfort us; they have found a treatment for this disease which involves converting the non-Jewish spouse. They explain that, in their opinion, the non-Jews who marry our sons and daughters will join our people and swell our ranks.

What an illusion! The reform movement is grabbing at straws when it expects that conversion – or more correctly – adding gentiles, will increase the number of Jews in the Diaspora. They attempt to quiet the nation's anxiety with fantastic ideas such as accepting the children of mixed marriages as Jewish, even when the non-Jewish parent will not convert. This stems from arrogance that these children of mixed marriages will grow up as Jews, and will constitute a generation of young men and women loyal to the Jewish People. This is none other than the siren's sweet music of imagination and hallucination.

What futility! A community cannot depend on intermarried and assimilated couples to strengthen itself and to ensure its continued existence. These ideas completely oppose the norm of "who is a Jew" and lack common sense. If the mother is unwilling to convert how can she raise and educate her children in the spirit of Judaism? To acknowledge these children as Jewish is self-deception.

Telling, Knowing, and Grieving

According to researchers, intermarried couples usually let the children choose their religion. They say to each other: "Don't try to influence the child's opinion. When he becomes mature, knowledgeable, and experienced, he will choose the religion he wants." In other words, the parents allow the environment and the society to influence and act upon the child's soul: the street, the secular school, the environmental culture and its religion. There is no doubt that Christian surroundings overcome the child and conquer his soul. According to surveys, children almost always adopt the Christian religion and its customs.

In addition, statistical research of intermarriages and conversions in America proves that while the number of intermarriages is skyrocketing, the number of conversions is declining drastically. This is in spite of the reform movements efforts to convert these spouses. Ross Phillips, a professor at the Reform Movement's Union College in Los Angeles, conducted a research study, the results of which showed no optimism for the second generation of intermarriages. The reform researcher's findings established that "only a small minority of 18% of children of mixed marriages are raised as Jews." This means that 82% of children from mixed marriages grow up as gentiles. In addition, only 5% of the non-Jewish spouses in mixed marriages identified themselves as Jewish. As opposed to this, 95% retained the religion and nationality which they held before marrying a Jew.

There are two main reasons why reform communities are no longer sensitive to the prohibition against marrying non-Jews. First, a majority of their friends are intermarried. Second, the reform rabbis perform the intermarriage ceremony. The combination of the "Rabbi", the congregation, and the priest, gives the stamp of legitimacy to the very assimilation which consumes the community. It becomes increasing apparent that there will not be a continuation for the reform community in these countries. I write this with tears in my eyes, because we are about to loose myriads of Jews who are from the Reform and Conservative movements.

All of the reform leader's illusions and hallucinations, in their sweet siren's song, exploded on the wall of bitter reality. The reform innovation of running for converting interfaith marriage partners, and declaring the children of Jewish fathers and non-Jewish mothers as Jews, constitutes an additional symptom of a critically wounded nation. The nation is trying to increase its numbers with a blood transfusion of nothing but water, better yet, a transfusion of empty air bubbles.

The Benefits of the Commandment to Settle in the Land of Israel

Religious Jews who learn Torah and observe the commandments certainly know that living in the land of Israel is a positive Torah commandment. It is written "And you inherit it, and you settle in it" (Ramban: Positive commandment 4). This is a foundation in Jewish law, so much so that the Rabbis ruled that settling the land of Israel is equal in value to all the commandments in the Torah (Sifre Rayeha 12:29). More than this, willingly living in the Diaspora is idol worship. On this matter it is written, "Everyone who lives in Israel is similar to someone who has a God, and everyone who lives outside of Israel is like someone who has no God…as if he worships idols" (Ketuboth 110, Avot DeRabbi Natan chap 26, Tosefta 77–85)

The Divine Presence (Shechinah) dwells in the Holy Land, where Judaism is clearly present everywhere and all the time. "The land which Hashem (God) sees at all times: The Lord, God's eyes are upon the land of Israel from the beginning of the year until the end of the year" (Deuteronomy 11:12). Israel is the Land which every weekly Torah portion relates to in holiness and glory. The Holy One's trio is the Torah, the Jewish People and the Land of Israel. They are integrated into one whole, and whoever damages one of them disassembles the trio and also damages the other two elements. The great masters of Jewish Law have already emphasized that, from the beginning to the end, all of the Torah deals with the State of Israel. The entire Torah is filled with the holiness of inhabiting the land of Israel. Many of God's promises to the Jewish people and its fathers relate to the land of Israel as an eternal inheritance. If so, then settling the land of Israel is God's will, as a Torah commandment, Deoraita. Also, according to the Rambam's opinion, there is a special commandment "And you inherited the land and you will inhabit it" (Numbers 33:53).

In addition, the Rabbis emphasize in the Babylonian and Jerusalem Talmuds, that "everyone who lives in Israel is in a category of not sinning," because the Land atones for him. Also, "He is promised that he will receive the next world." He receives two benefits, one in this world and one in the next.

A Strange Mystery

There is something which is strange and mysterious, difficult to understand and explain. How can religious and those who "tremble at God's word," the Haredim, continue to live in exile, when the gates of the Land of Israel are wide open for them? The question of inhabiting the land of Israel, as a separate commandment, existed in every generation. However, in previous generations, it was appropriate to question this due to the difficult and dangerous journey to go to Israel and the poverty and difficult living conditions. There were periods when tyrants who oppressed the Jews ruled over Israel, and moving to Israel truly involved life-threatening dangers. Such is not the situation today, when Israel is under Jewish rule. Today, Israel provides all of the necessities for the good life, nothing is missing. Its Jews earn well and live comfortably and many of them become wealthy. Israel has a rich and well developed economy. With one comfortable and safe airplane flight one can move to Israel.

It is difficult to understand! There are Jews who observe Torah and its commandments, who make great efforts to observe the Sabbath and the Jewish Holy days, and to obtain kosher food and holy objects. Among them, some are very precise about the less stringent and the more stringent commandments, meticulous about glatt kosher food, shemura matza and nice etrogs.

However, they ignore the commandment to inhabit the land of Israel with all of its unique qualities and blessings. They reconcile themselves to life in exile which constitutes a sin. Everyday, on Sabbaths and Holy days, on days of joy and gladness, on days of morning and grieving, they request and petition to "go up and to see the building of Zion. And bring us into (the land of Israel) and let us rejoice in its rebuilding. We will eat its fruits and be satiated from its goodness and bless on the land in holiness and purity." Similarly, "May it be your will, God…to bring us up to our land and plant us within our borders." How can they deny the very words they utter? "Guard what you say and do it" says the Torah (Deuteronomy 23:24). Every morning, before accepting the yoke of the kingdom of heaven we pray: "Bring us in peace from the four corners of the earth and bring us to sovereignty in our land". They say these words but don't implement them, as if they don't hear what they say. Rabbi Yehuda Halevy, in his book *The Kuzari*, has already commented on this. He wrote that all of our declarations about the love of Zion and our prayers to return to Zion are nothing but the starling's song, words disconnected to our true intentions.

On the evening which sanctifies the holiday of our freedom, in accordance with Jewish law, we conclude the Seder with the exclamation "Next year in Jerusalem!" Even more so, on the holy Yom Kippur, we end the day with the same excited promise to go up to Zion next year. When they say this, it doesn't even occur to them to fulfill this obligation during this year, just as they didn't fulfill it in past years. The author, M. Lipson tells the following story. Once Rebbe Yisrael from Rushin conducted the Pessach Seder and told about the exodus from Egypt. When he reached "Next year in Jerusalem," he paused and said: 'Master of the Universe, every year I say next year in Jerusalem and I am still in exile. Oy, how embarrassing, oy how humiliating before that lowly servant'. Similarly, we will compare our own situation to his: Oy, how embarrassing, oy how humiliating before his soul and the souls of his family who are sitting at the Pessach Seder, and even more so before his master to whom he pours out his prayers. The Gomorra warns us that one of the three things that God hates is when one speaks differently than what he thinks or feels.

The Third Siren's Song

There is a third Siren's song, whose sweet music tempts many of our People to continue being battered in the tempest of the sea of the exile. Myriads of these victims are swallowed into the depths of the sea. This pleasant song convinces its admirers that there is no conflict between living in exile by choice and the mitzvah of inhabiting the Land of Israel. Is it possible to live in the Diaspora and pray that the exiles should be returned to Israel? These songs are sung by the Admorim (Chassidic Rebbis), Rabbis, and certain Rosh yeshivas who encourage Jews to continue living in exile and to wait for the Messiah. Only he will gather our dispersed from the four corners of the earth. In other words, sit patiently (shev ve al ta'aseh) and wait for the exiles to be redeemed through heavenly miracles.

Regarding this group, the Talmudic Rabbis and the Zohar warn not to rely on miracles. The Kuzari also warned that a person should not expose himself to danger, telling himself that God will perform a miracle for him, incase He doesn't. Moreover, we did not find any commandment in the Torah to sit idly and wait for the messiah to redeem the People through "sit and don't do" (shev ve al Taaseh). At the same time, the Torah repeatedly emphasizes the commandments to conquer the Land, to settle it, and to inhabit it, with all of its missions. These are positive commandments to do it (Kum Ve Asseh).

Everything that a person does requires God's help; however, a person must make the effort. We see that," If someone claims that he did not try but succeeded anyway – don't believe him." Once, the Children of Israel stood in mortal danger, with the stormy sea before them and Pharaoh's army of cavalry and chariots chasing after them. Then they had reached a dead end and terrible confusion gripped the camp of Israel. They split into four groups who argued with each other about what to do. Hashem said to Moshe, "Why do you cry out to me?" meaning why pray to me? Now is not the time for prayer, prayer will not be effective. Rather, "Speak to the children of Israel and travel" [i.e., advance] (Exodus 14:15). If you remain where you are and await salvation, it will not come. Only when you initiate and advance will help and rescue come. Actually, the sea did not split until Nachshon Ben Aminadav jumped into the waves of the sea. Even then nothing happened until the water reached to his nostrils. Only then the sea split. Nachshon understood that to say "I believe" and to wait for salvation, is not real belief. The Chashmonaim understood this also. Belief which culminates in empty words is only fruitless belief. The Chashmonaim, like Nachshon Ben Aminadav, were not satisfied with "believing". Rather, they were ready to perform God's commandments with deeds, even when difficult and dangerous.

The Rambam's Active, Messianic Approach

Let us access this matter accurately. The Ramban attempted to concentrate the foundations of Judaism into 13 principles, one of them being the belief in the coming of the messiah. What is the nature of the messianic era according to Rambam? In his *Mishnah Torah*, he interprets the messianic vision as natural and idealistic: "Don't think for a moment that in messianic times anything will be removed from the way the world functions, or that there will be anything new added to the physical creation. Rather the world will continue as it always has been." The Sages said that "There is no difference between this world and the messianic era other than Israel's subservience to the nations" (Laws of Kings chapter 12). The Rambam relies on the Talmud: "Shmuel said: "There is no difference between this world and the messianic era other than Israel's subservience to the nations" (Brachot 34b). Rambam's teachings follow Rabbi Shmuel the Amora, who was the Rosh Yeshiva of the Nahardia Yeshiva in Babylon. They both oppose other Jewish philosophies which perceive the messianic era as a period of: supernatural miracles; miraculous redemption; and alteration of natural historical processes. At the beginning of the messianic period the Jewish People will be freed from its subservience to gentile nations and will merit freedom and national independence. Support for this philosophy is found in the Talmud Yerushalmi (Brachot chapter 1). Rav Chiya, Rava, and Rav Shimon Ben Challafta were walking in Arbel Valley in Kretzta, where they saw the first rays of light dawning. Rav Chiya Rava said to Rav Shimon Ben Challafta, "Rebbe, this is similar to [the process of] Israel's redemption. At the beginning it progresses very slowly, but as the redemption advances the pace quickens." In addition, Koresh, the King of Persia authorized and helped the exiled Jews to return to Zion. *Yishayahu* the prophet called him *Mashiach* (Messiah), according to the simple reading of the text.

Indeed, according to the Talmud Bavli, the Yerushalmi, and the Rambam, the generation which merited to see the founding of the State of Israel and the ingathering of millions of our people, is in the period of "the beginning of the Redemption" (אתחלתא דגאולה). The Ramban, the Radak, the Tosefot Yom Tov, and other great sages believed that the redemption can come naturally. To summarize, the messianic era can come miraculously. However, it can also come in stages and through normal development, depending on our efforts and deeds. Whatever happens, we are responsible to fulfill our obligations, and as the Chatam Sofer wrote without burdening the messiah's shoulders (Yoreh Deah 356).

Hidden Miracles in Establishing the State of Israel

Establishing the State of Israel is one of the greatest miracles that Divine Providence has performed for us in this generation. Several unusual and wonderful unnatural events have occurred. They are difficult to explain logically or as natural phenomenon, unless we acknowledge divine intervention. The U.N. decision to establish a Jewish State was itself unbelievable. The vast majority of the countries voted for Israel: 33 for, 13 against. Voting against were those same nations which always voted and continue to vote for the Arab nations. Among them were the Russian Soviets, who have always fought against Zionism and Judaism. Politically, it was almost an unnatural event that Russia joined the western countries to support the establishment of the state of Israel in the U.N. vote. Generally, the western and Eastern countries were divided on every issue. To our surprise, Russia suddenly did an about face and voted to establish a Jewish State in Israel. Wonder of wonders!

Just a few hours after founding the State of Israel, the "War of Independence" erupted. Arab Armies, with huge numbers of soldiers and massive military equipment, poured into Israel from three directions. On the fourth side of Israel lies the ocean, which was controlled by a huge naval empire that was not on our side. Within Israel, murderous Arab gangs were activated. Fueled by furious wrath and murderous lust, all of these forces staged a united attack on the small, poor, Jewish settlement in Israel. The Jews were isolated by the British mandatory Government's navel blockade along the coast to prevent bringing weapons to Israel. Even so, and in spite of all of this, the small, poor army of the settlement overcame the Arab Armies. Another episode of "On the miracles, and on the redemption, and on the strength, and on the salvation, and on the wars" and on passing the "majority into the hands of the minority" [Hanukkah and Purim prayers]. Everyone who remembered these events had tears in his eyes, tears of joy, gladness and thanks to the Rock and Redeemer of Israel.

The Six Day War lasted only six days, ending in the IDF's complete victory over the mighty Arab armies of Egypt, Syria and Jordan. The Israeli Army came out crowned with victory and praise. They bequeathed freedom and honor to the Jewish nation in its fathers' land. This was a war of David against Goliath. It's swift and complete victory brought a strong burst of national joy and glory. The fulfillment of the vision of a united Jerusalem as the capital of the Jewish People brought a spiritual and national awakening. Young Israeli men of the defense army returned to the Ma'arat HaMachpela, to Rachel's Tomb and on the sixth day stood in wonder at the holiness of the Western Wall. Struck with feelings of thanks for the miracles and the wonders, they blew the shofar and blessed Hashem: "That has kept us alive, and sustained us, and brought us to this time."

In the Yom Kippur war, the Egyptian and Syrian Armies surprised Israel. The nation and the army were unprepared for war. The large and well armed Egyptian and Syrian armies advanced on both fronts while the Israeli public was shocked to find themselves under fire. The situation was terrifying, Israel stood in danger of collapse. One of the commanders, a hero at that time, almost had a breakdown when he announced "The third temple is slipping out of our hands." Yet again, the Israeli army turned around and attacked on all fronts, until they pushed back the enemy who sought their destruction. After about three weeks of difficult and fierce fighting, Israel succeed to push the Syrians from the Golan Heights and to cross the Suez Canal. The Israel forces encircled the much larger Egyptian army, laying siege to them until they were forced to surrender.

It's impossible not to see the finger of God in Israel's wars and its continued existence. These campaigns were wonderful and supernatural. The development of this small nation: in building the strongest army in the Middle East; in settling the land and agriculture; in absorbing new immigrants; in science; in industry and economics; in medicine; in armaments; is considered a supernatural phenomenon by the world's nations. Many world leaders visit Israel to reflect on Israel's list of achievements and to apply Israel's methods in their own countries. Meanwhile, we witness the aloofness and coolness festering in Jewish hearts in the Diaspora towards these wonderful developments in Israel. They react as if these developments were happenstance, natural, and uninteresting in the shameful exile.

They refuse to Sense the Miracles and Wonders
Once there was a pious man who expected a miracle to save him from an impending flood. There was a fierce storm, accompanied by thunder and lightning. Strong winds and torrential rains flooded the streets and the water began to seep into the houses. The city sent special trucks just to evacuate the residents of low-lying regions. When the truck arrived to evacuate the pious man, he refused to leave, explaining that he was awaiting a Divine miracle to save him. The sky opened, the rains increased until the water covered the whole area, reaching up to their necks. This pious man also rejected the rescue boat that was sent to save him because he expected a miracle. When the waters covered his head, the pious man climbed onto the roof. Now a helicopter came to save him, but he held firmly to his resolution not to be saved by human endeavor. In the end, the waters overcame him and drowned him. When he arrived in heaven, he complained to God, "Lord of the universe, I believed in you, I prayed to you for a miracle! Why did you disappoint me? The holy one blessed be He answered him: You pious fool, didn't I send you wonderful salvations. I sent you a truck, a boat and a helicopter, what more did you want?

This is similar to our brothers who remain in exile and espouse passive methods of expecting redemption through Divine miracles. Divine providence consoles them and says, 'Look and see, I have given you examples so that you will recognize miracles and wonders: The U.N. decision to establish a Jewish State; saving Israel in the Independence War, the Six Day War, and the Yom Kippur War. These were examples of redemption. What else do you want? However, they close their ears to avoid hearing the truth. They close their eyes to avoid seeing the examples of redemption. Like the pious fool, they await supernatural miracles, such as the messiah hovering in the air and carrying them to the holy land. All of the miracles and wonders that we have seen are insufficient to convince them that the redemption process is an ongoing natural phenomenon, and accompanied by human struggling and sacrifice.

Ingathering of the Exiles

Among the redemption's objectives is to gather the exiles. The father of the prophets, Moshe Rabbenu said: "The LORD your God will return your captivity, and have compassion upon you, and will return and gather you from all the peoples, where the LORD thy God has scattered you. If any of yours that are dispersed be in the uttermost parts of heaven, from there the LORD your God will gather you, and from there He will fetch you. And the LORD your God will bring you into the land which your fathers possessed, and you will possess it; and He will do you well, and multiply you above your fathers" (Deuteronomy 30:3–5). In the Prophets it is also written: "Therefore say: The Lord GOD this: I will even gather you from the peoples, and assemble you out of the countries where you have been scattered, and I will give you the land of Israel." (Ezekiel 11:17) Zechariah the prophet describes the ingathering of the exiles as a wonder since it requires numerous and wonderful acts. "The LORD of hosts says: If it be marvelous in the eyes of the remnant of this people in those days, should it also be marvelous in My eyes, Says the LORD of hosts. The LORD of hosts says: Behold, I will save my people from the Eastern country, and from the Western Country; And I will bring them, and they will live in the midst of Jerusalem; and they will be My people, and I will be their God, in truth and in righteousness" (Zechariah 8:6–8).Yishayahu portrays the ingathering of the exiles as a happy and joyous national event. "And the ransomed of the LORD will return, and come with singing unto Zion, and everlasting joy shall be upon their heads; they will obtain gladness and joy, and sorrow and sighing will flee away. (Isaiah 51:11).Yechezkiel points out that the gathering of the exiles will bring a sanctification of God's name. "Thus says the Lord GOD: When I will have gathered the house of Israel from the peoples among whom they are scattered, and will be sanctified in them in the sight of the nations, then will they live in their own land which I gave to my servant

Jacob. And they will live there safely, and shall build houses, and plant vineyards; yes, they will live safely; when I have executed judgments on all of those around them that disdain them; and they will know that I am the LORD their God' (Yechezkiel 28:25–26). There are many similar prophecies by everyone who prophesied about the following two crucial phenomenons. First, inheriting our Patriarchs' land and living in it securely. Second, gathering the exiles from the four corners of the earth. These two phenomenons will result in sanctifying God's name.

Therefore, the Rabbis gave importance to this day: "Gathering the exiles is as important as the worlds' creation" (Pessachim 88). This is how chazal understood and defined the value of this supreme phenomenon. It's fascinating that gathering the exiles is so important to the Jewish People that they described it as a wonder of wonders, an event of joy and happiness which sanctifies God's name. Chazal compared it to the day that the earth and sky were created. Why did they bother? Because the Jewish People and Torah cannot exist without the Land of Israel! The exile is temporary, destined for destruction, either physical or spiritual. The destruction could be the type that the Nazis and their partners perpetrated. It could be through the kiss of spiritual death, by emptying them of Judaism and its foundations. This is happening presently in the exile. Again, we have been privileged to see the gathering of the exiles, which the prophets foretold. This is the mighty ingathering of millions of immigrants. The vast majority of them were saved from assimilation and intermarriage. This is a historical process occurring now, with God's help, and in partnership with the Jewish People's efforts.

Efforts from the Lower World together with Heavenly Assistance from the Upper World

At the same time, true Jewish believers in the exile continue to petition God every Monday and Thursday as if nothing had happened. "Our father, merciful father, show us a sign of your goodness and gather our dispersed from the four corners of the earth." Look, he did it! Every day, in the morning prayers we say: "Hashem chose Zion, He wants to dwell in it." Similarly in the psalms in the Shabbat prayers: "Plant us with joy in our land, plant us in our borders." There are many similar examples. Yet Jews remain in the Diaspora. They are unique in that they have truth in their prayer books and falsehood in their lives. Belief, unsupported by action is insufficient: it is sterile. "That the LORD your God may bless you in all the work of your hand which you do" (Deuteronomy 14::29). Can one sit idly and do nothing? The verse teaches "in all the work of your hands which you do" If a person acts, does, performs, he receives blessing. If a person doesn't act he will not be blessed (Tanna Debbey Eliahu 14). "A man should not say: I will eat, drink, live a good life, not trouble myself, and heaven will show me mercy. Rather a man must toil, create, and do his utmost and then God sends His blessing" (Tanchuma Vayetze). With thanks to God, we say on Hanukkah: "On the miracles, on the times he rescued us, on the might deeds, and on the salvations. And on the wars that you made for our fathers." Nevertheless, miracles, salvations and wars all took place after the Chashmonaim joined in partnership with God. They waged tough battles and swift surprise attacks against a well manned enemy. They sacrificed many men until they emerged crowned with victory and praise. Jews must be partners with the creator in creating righteousness, integrity, and in achieving redemption and freedom.

Rav Teichtell Z'L explains in his book *Aim HaBonim Smecha* that Messianic belief without positive action is really a pretext to evade the purpose of the messianic era and its mission. For example, the messianic community does not rely on miracles for health and medical treatment. When ill, they are using the best doctors and treatments. Likewise, Admorim (Hasidic Rebbes) who advocate waiting for the messiah to bring the Jews to Israel, when ill, do not stay home & wait for "The Healer of His People Israel" to perform miracles. They go to the hospital! First and foremost they arrange for expert doctors to treat them and then they say Psalms for a quick recovery. Likewise regarding earning a livelihood, they do not sit patiently waiting for "The One who feeds the world in his goodness" to miraculously send them bread from heaven. Only in the most important issues of the Jewish world, such as saving souls who err through assimilation, is passivity, "sit and do nothing," preferable.

Certainly, Jews who observe Torah & mitzvoth believe in the coming of the messiah, when the Creator sees fit. However, it is forbidden to refrain from activity to gather the exiles and to quicken their complete redemption. To remain in the spiritual holocaust of exile: to delay saving Jewish souls through immigration to Israel, thereby preserving them until the messiah comes; is as insane as the pious fool who drowned due to his foolish stubbornness to wait for a miracle.

A Question of Saving lives

The problem we encounter is more than fulfilling or breaching a particular commandment, or the legal framework of the Torah. It is a question of saving hundreds of thousands of our Peoples lives. This takes priority over all of the Torah's commandments, except for three.

All over the world, a whole generation of our People's young men and women are wandering aimlessly, and being swept away by every random custom and idea. They have abandoned their past and neglected their life source. They have no spiritual home. Like infants who were raised by gentiles, they lack Jewish beliefs and reject Jewish principles and ideals. They are people with no past and no future. They don't know where they came from or where they're going. It's heartbreaking to see the unfortunate souls. They are like fallen leaves, which have been separated from their branches and roots. They are shaken and driven from place to place by the winds of history. Some of them hide their identity, because they are embarrassed by their background. Many of them roam around the chaotic world, searching for something. In the end, they are swallowed up by alien influences. Some are trapped by Christian groups or mystic cults.

What do our messianic Jews who observe Torah and the commandments say about this? It's unbelievable! The exiles should wait patiently for the messiah to bring them from "distress to wellbeing," and bring them to the holy land. This is their attitude, in spite of the very heavy death toll, reaching hundreds of thousands and, millions throughout the years! This Sirens song is so misleading and destructive, to leave Jews in the Jewish Death valley, until they drown in assimilation and intermarriage. This happens when, on the other side of the planet, there is a different Jewish world which is so much better. A world of the new adolescent Israeli nation. A world of revival, prosperity, pioneering training, fulfillment, and an army to defend the People and the country. A world full of hope for a strong and magnificent Jewish future.

A Safe Shelter for Jews and Judaism

The Jewish People, with Heaven's help, succeeded to build this world, in the old-new homeland. The State of Israel raised a proud and brave young generation, and entrusted it with the States' security. This youth has proved itself in the wars. It is able to stand courageously against all enemies and dangers, and to make the ultimate sacrifice for its people and country. Israel is the only Jewish community in the world who is able to sustain itself spiritually and physically. It is the only place where Jews can live a true and full Jewish life. Despite all of the real criticism, it is a Jewish state, in the image of the Torah's People. It is the only country in the world where: Shabbat and Jewish Holidays are national days of rest; the holy tongue, the Torah and prophet's language, is the children's mother tongue; the Hebrew culture is an inseparable part of every man and woman.

In Israel, the level of Torah study and Jewish studies are the highest in the world. There are thousands of Yeshivas, Kollels, yeshiva high schools and women's seminaries. The big yeshivas have tens of thousands of students, and are the largest yeshivas in history. These yeshivas have more students than the prewar, European yeshivas and more than the first and second Temple period, Israeli yeshivas. Israel's air is replete with Judaism. Its children absorb their religion and their nationalism naturally, every day. In Israel a one of a kind phenomenon is achieving results, as increasing numbers of secular Jews embrace Jewish tradition. Also, the large repentance movement is a natural outcome of a nurturing Jewish environment.

In the State of Israel the damage of intermarriage doesn't even gain a foothold. Assimilation works in a positive direction, pulling people to Jewish tradition and holiness, because "the air of Israel makes people wise," uniting and sanctifying its Jewish residents. The State of Israel is the only Jewish community that can influence Jewish youth to want to remain Jewish. The younger generations seeks a mission and meaning for which to fight. In Israel, this generation finds this meaning. More than Israel needs this wonderful youth, this wonderful youth needs Israel.

The Plague of the Loss of Spiritual Identity and Biological Assimilation

During the last few years, we have reached a period of national emergency in which the exile threatens the Jewish soul and its existence. The plague of loss of spiritual identity and biological assimilation strikes us mercilessly and kills the Israeli tribes dispersed in exile. Our People loose hundreds of Jews every day. A silent holocaust is occurring before our very eyes. Every year it swallows tens of thousands of young men and women through intermarriage. Over the years, millions of Jews are disappearing through the kiss of death. The bitter reality is that the bonds to Judaism are diminishing and disappearing, and the Jewish population is shrinking and being destroyed. Exile is in essence a process of assimilation which damages the Jew's spiritual and religious wellsprings. It becomes clearer and clearer that the gentile environment, with its material and cultural presence, does not allow Jews to cope over the long term. In this situation, we cannot reconcile ourselves to the exile, because the chances for continued Jewish life are very slim. The choice is for the Jews to end the exile before the exile ends its Jews. Therefore, it turns out that immigration to Israel is not just a Zionist obligation, not just a Torah commandment, but rather a commandment to save lives. It is equal in value to all of the other Torah commandments.

Surveys conducted in the United States revealed that while the reform Jews had a 53% intermarriage rate, the Charedim had 3%. It is true that 3% is much less than the rate of American Jewry at large. However, this rate is still significant. For every one thousand marriages, 30 are intermarriages. In addition, many of the Charedim and orthodox switch to conservative and reform movements, where eventually their children intermarry.

Religious Jewry, Where are You?

First and foremost, a heavy charge lies on the believing Jews who follow Torah and the commandments. They ignore the mitzvah to return to Israel, even though the Jewish soul depends on it. Even more so, they transgress the law in the *Shulchan Aruch*, that, when a plague breaks out in a city, one should flee from there as soon as the plague begins. It is forbidden to rely on miracles and put oneself at risk (*Shulchan Aruch* Y.D. 116:5). Our tragedy is that the plague of spiritual and physical assimilation is rampant, slaying many in every city and country where our people reside. In this situation, we could expect that Haredi Jews and religious Jews would fulfill the Torah's commandment, per the Shulchan Aruch. Pack their possessions and flee with their souls, since spiritual annihilation is no less grave than physical extermination, according to Torah and Jewish law. Instead, there are Admorim and certain Rabbis who preach to communities to continue peacefully in exile. They should wait for the Messiah, who will gather our far-flung people from the four corners of the earth. What a tempting Siren, which leads so many Jews to their annihilation!!! They also supply the rest of our people with an excuse to reside in the cursed exile. When the non-orthodox Jews see that the Hasidim, who perform the commandments punctiliously, remain serenely in exile, the others find no reason to move to Israel. They are just like those who lived in the ghettos, and waited patiently for the trains to Auschwitz. Today, the Jews continue to cling to their homes in exile until they are devoured by the ravages of the Christian ambience. They are bereft of their children who no longer remain to continue the Jewish chain of generations.

Rambam Versus Messianic Jews

Rambam wrote "Igeret Kiddush Hashem" about the wicked decrees which were issued against North African Jewry. At the end, the Rambam writes that when there are evil decrees against the Jews in a certain country, they are obligated to emigrate from there. He writes "However, for those who seduce themselves, saying, continue living here until the Messianic King comes to the western countries…and brings you to Jerusalem, I don't know how God will revoke their persecution? They transgress and cause others to transgress" (מקורות לתולדות החינוך בישראל), edited by Rabbi Simcha ASAP, fourth volume, page 10).

This is very significant for our subject! Was it not the Rambam who defined the belief in the messiah as one of the thirteen principles? However, where one suspects that either physical or spiritual annihilation is immanent, one is obligated to flee. Rambam mocks those who preach passivity when endangered with annihilation. He mocks those who sit and wait for the messiah to come and save them from their troubles. He also accuses them of sinning and of causing others to sin.

To entice Jews to remain in the "valley of humiliation," and to sacrifice their sons and daughters to the Moloch of assimilation, is truly a grave transgression. It is a tremendous and terrible crime to prevent our brothers, the children of Israel, from moving to the chosen land. Living in Israel is the foundation of the nation's existence and its Torah. It is weighed against all of the commandments of the Torah. These people are teaching Torah that is not according to the Jewish law (halacha). Unfortunately, they are carried away by the klipah (the husk) of the spies' sin. "They were disgusted by the precious land" because of misleading reasoning and false and seductive claims: The Torah obligates every Jew to do everything within his ability to save himself and his countrymen, both physically and spiritually. Judaism emphasizes that it is a crime to rely on miracles when Jewish life is in danger. The Torah demands that we strive to improve our lives and sacrifice for redemption. There is a cult in our people who unknowingly destroy us with spiritual and national suicide under the banner of faith in messianic redemption!

Turning the Redeemer into the Destroyer

Apparently we did not learn the lesson of the holocaust. Even before Hitler rose to power and before the setting of limitations on immigration to Israel, hundreds of thousands of Jews were prevented from immigrating to Israel. They were ordered to remain in exile and to wait for the messiah. They remained and were lost in the fires of Auschwitz. The bitter destiny of those masses that trusted in those leaders who mislead them, must have laid a heavy burden on their leaders' consciences. Instead, they repeat the same mistakes today during the spiritual holocaust. The history of mankind is supposed to teach us a lesson so that we will not repeat the same mistakes again. However, this is not true about our People's leaders. The purpose of the exile is to motivate the Jews to repent and to return to Israel. Those who justify and advocate exile apparently confused the idea of the messianic age with the ideology of exile, whose end is assimilation. They have, de facto, converted the messiah, who is supposed to bring redemption to the Jewish People, into its annihilator, while they remain in exile and wait for him to come!!!

The national poet correctly blames the People's mistakes and sins on the shepherd. "The shepherd who leads the people astray is the root of failure. They spread deceptive instruction and continue the affinity for living with 'good gentiles.'" In his lamentation, the prophet of the destruction foretold: "Your prophets have seen visions for you of vanity and delusion; neither have they uncovered your iniquity, to bring back your captivity; but have prophesied for you burdens of vanity and seduction." (Lamentation 2:14).

CHAPTER FIVE

THE DESTRUCTION OF THE TEMPLE
[I.E., THE JEWISH HOME]

A VOICE FROM HEAVEN roars and says: "Woe to me regarding my house, my children, where are you? ... Woe to the children who were exiled from their Father's table, my children have left and are no longer." (Opening of Eicha Rabba, Yermiyahu 10:20)

Today, Jewish youth who live in exile face anxiety and crisis. As "children who were raised among the gentiles as captives," they know nothing about Judaism or the Jewish People. They don't understand who they are, what they are, or why they are Jews. Youth is the hope of every nation. Youth carry the promise of the future for their People and their land. Youth, in healthy nations, with all of its naiveté and enthusiasm, with the blood pumping full speed through its veins, carry on its nations' language, culture, traditions and practices, and they abhor everything which does not align with their nation and religion. Each man guards his own camp and flag, and according to his deeds, his reward is great. This is not so with our youth in exile. The vast majority distance themselves from everything Jewish, and sink into the 49 gates of secularism. Their souls are empty, so much so that they cannot distinguish between: holy and profane, pure and impure, and the Jewish People and other Peoples. Our youth wonder in the nations' wilderness, confused, embarrassed, and lacking leadership and inspiration. The Torah, which has enabled us to prosper for so long, appears useless to them. They are estranged from their nation's customs and the values which have been sanctified for generations. They leave the synagogue behind and become guests there for a few hours per year on the high holidays. When mourning their relatives, they attend synagogue for a few days to say Kaddish. "A father can bring merit to his son," however the son receives merit while alive, but not when dead. "The nation cries for its families" – for families that have been destroyed, because there are hardly any families that did not loose at least one member to intermarriage. The end for those who remain is – assimilation and a prolonged expiration.

Those who run Jewish institutions in the Diaspora sit on this time bomb and ceremonially confer about how to return the children to the fold. Many people voice their opinions vociferously, while wise men blame modern times which have brought evil influences which "kidnap" their children. They speak as if the times influence society, rather than society influencing the times. They also make the environment a scapegoat, spewing blame on it. It is as if the environment acts on the people, rather than the people acting on the environment.

Parents Have the Greatest Influence

Fathers and mothers, examine your behavior. We all know that education does not begin at school or at kindergarten. It begins at home, in the family's social-framework. The main lessons are learned at home. This education determines the child's soul, nurtures his spirit, and charts the way that the child will lead his life.

During the months of Elul and Nissan, members of the Australian Jewish Court and its leader used to visit Jewish day schools, to size up the students and to converse with them about Jewish issues. One time I inspected – among others – a classroom of school children who had learned the creation story in the book of Genesis. I asked them, who can tell me where God resides? One boy answered that God lives in heaven, because he saw that when his father prayed, he raised his eyes to heaven. The second child, whose father was a doctor, reasoned that God's house was in heaven, however, the office where he met people was at the synagogue. This is like his father the doctor, who lived with them at home, but treated people in his clinic. Later, a six year old jumped to his feet and proclaimed, 'Rabbi, I know where God lives. He lives in our bathroom!' I was shocked to hear this strange answer, and asked the boy, 'Why do you say that?' He answered innocently; "I know because every morning my father knocks on the bathroom door and yells: Dear God, are you still in there?" This illustrates that children naturally absorb and imitate what they see and hear. They learn by seeing examples. Every word and every deed makes an impression on a child.

Parents must serve as role models for their children: in word, deed and good behavior. Deeds are most important and have more impact than words. When does one start to educate children? Rav Yisrael Salanter's answered: twenty years before the child is born. Educate the parents so that they will be excellent role models. Indeed, children and youth are influenced by the personal example of their parents: for better, if the parents are positive; or for worse, if the parents are negative.

The child's parents have the greatest influence on his education. The parents are his friends, teachers and preachers. Home is the child's first school, synagogue, and playground. The parents can perform the teacher's role: but the teachers cannot perform the parents' role. The home can be a school; however the school cannot be a home. Experience teaches us that all good traits, faith, and religion that people possess – and the opposite characteristics – all derive from the parents. There is an English expression which says: "My home is my fortress." For Jews, their homes were not only their fortresses, but also their temple, filled with belief, holiness, love, and brotherhood. Most of the positive and negative commandments are performed in one's home – the edifice of religion and its laws. The prophet says: "This is the law of the house: upon the top of the mountain the whole limit thereof round about shall be most holy" (Yechezkiel 43:12). The gentile prophet also envisioned Israel's greatness and its existence in the land – of which the Hallel says: How goodly are your tents, o Jacob, your dwelling places o Israel." (Bamidbar 24:5).

Breeding Ground for the Nation's Soul

Once, the Jewish home was solid and idealistic: the parents, like the priests in the Temple, served Hashem in love and awe, and observed the Torah's commandments to the last detail. The boys and girls were educated in the tradition of their fathers, to live with integrity, and to find favor in the eyes of God and man. The home was the breeding ground for the nation's soul. The home enthused its children with a burning love for its people and land. It inculcated Torah and proper character traits. It nurtured spiritual beauty and pure hearts; and enriched their essences and their personalities. In the Jewish home the treasure of Mount Sinai was established: "The entire nation saw the voices." – according to Tanchuma: "They saw the soul." The children saw everything that they learned at the Talmud Torah School being implemented at home. They saw: Sabbath and holiday observance, father putting on teffillin, and mother meticulously fulfilling the kosher food laws. The parents showed their children, through their own behavior – the precious strength and splendor of the holy people of Israel. It is no wonder that they influenced their children more than any teachers or experts could. "And ye shall observe this thing for an ordinance [חוק] to thee and to thy sons for ever." (Exodus 12:24) If something was an ordinance for you, then it will also be an ordinance for your children and grandchildren. This system works. However, you should know that if something was not ordinance [חוק] for you, then it will not be for your children either.

The Destruction of the Jewish home in the Diaspora

It is painful to witness the Jewish homes' destruction in the vast majority of the Diaspora's Jewish neighborhoods during recent years. "In the past it was called the house of God and now it is called the house of sin." (Brashit Rabba 39:15) Their parents can say our tithes pronouncement proudly: "I have completely removed all of the holy things from my house" (Deuteronomy 26:13). I have removed all of the holiness, all of the Torah and commandments from my home, and have nullified them as the dust of the earth. There is no memory of the God's kingdom or of prayer and blessings. There is no comprehension of holiness and purity, and no vestige of the Sabbath and the holidays. However, I do have one small consolation: "I have given it to the Levite and to the convert" (ibid) – to the Rabbis and the teachers who came from Israel. Let them attend to holy matters and educate my children. My conscience is quiet, because I have fulfilled my obligations.

No, No! These are dreams and fantasies, desires and chicanery. A child is not a piece of cloth and Jewish schools are not dyeing machines, which change the child's color and soul. That all of the fads and bad influences that are in the child's home and environment will not change his soul. The Jerusalem Talmud propounds a fundamental principle of education; "All Torah study which does not have the parent's home, is not Torah." (Shabbat chapter 19, Halacha 6). In other words, if the Torah that the child learns at the Jewish school does not share a place in his parents' home – it is not Torah; it will not become a permanent part of the child's life. If we carefully examine the concept of "The soul is burnt [and destroyed] but the body continues to exist," we must reach the conclusion that the parents are responsible for the situation of the child's soul. They and only they are responsible for the child's soul.

Jewish Studies teachers try to relay the Torah and commandments to the students, using the Torah's terminology. Examples are: "Observe the Sabbath day to keep it holy", memorizing: "Seven days shall you sit in Sukkoth" and the remaining Jewish festivals and also "And you shall eat and be satisfied and bless the Lord" etc. However, when the child arrives home, he sees the opposite. There is no Sabbath or holiday observance, father and mother don't pray or bless grace after meals, and the "blessings for pleasure" are unknown. When the child innocently objects to the desecration of holiness, his mother counters, listen son, I didn't send you to Jewish school to become a rabbi! That's funny! Do you think it's so easy to become a Rabbi! The parents' actions contradict both his teacher's lessons and the Rabbi's guidance. The child is emotionally confused. He thinks in his heart: either his teacher is a liar and the Torah is just old myths which are incapable of providing a viable lifestyle, or he thinks that his parents are hypocrites and sinners. He will despise either his teacher, who taught him things opposing his family's lifestyle; or he will despise his parents, whom he views as bad; or he will despise both of them. This results in disappointment and bitterness which raises doubts in the child's' mind, and leads him to skepticism and spiritual exhaustion. Eventually, living with this conflict overwhelms the Torah that the child learned in school.

The House's Plagues and their Effects
The story is told of an immigrant to Sydney, Australia who wanted to open a store. Since he didn't have business experience in his new country, he decided to walk around and see how the local businesses operate. During his walk he saw a store with a huge sign on the storefront: "Grand Opening party – Bargains!" The store was packed with customers and there was a long line outside. He continued walking until he saw another store with a

huge sign on the storefront: "Going Out of Business Sale". This store was also overflowing with customers. The immigrant went and opened a store and followed the two business models that he had seen. He hung two huge signs on the front of his store: One sign read: "Grand Opening Party" and the second sign read: "Going Out of Business Sale".

Regretfully, most of the youth behave like that immigrant. They burn the candle at both ends: They have the grand opening bar mitzvah party with myriads of guests to celebrate accepting the yoke of the commandments. The next day they celebrate the: "Going Out of Business sale", alienating themselves from Torah and its commandments. This is not surprising since it results directly from their parents' behavior. When children are being trained to put on teffillin before their bar mitzvah, they sometimes ask their teacher an innocent question: When will my father have his bar mitzvah? The children had never seen their fathers performing commandments or wearing teffillin. The youth, knowingly or unknowingly, follow their parents' example, rather than the teachers' instructions. The home not only does not help the Jewish school, but opposes it. The home ruins what the school aspires to repair.

"The plague is spread in the house." (Leviticus 14:44) The signs of impurity, which are given in the Torah portion of plagues and leprosy, are of "base appearance". The appearance of the house shows baseness of soul, baseness of spirit, baseness of tradition and nationality. "The plague on the house" is surely "spreading." Its infection is spreading in all directions, poisoning the mouths and the hearts. It penetrates deep into the soul and pollutes its very foundation.

Yirmiyahu Ben Chelkiyahu – prophet of Israel and national lamenter, arise from your grave and raise your voice on high again, a voice of wailing and weeping: "Behold, and see our reproach. Our inheritance has been transferred to strangers, our houses to foreigners" (Lamentations 5:1–2). Our homes, which were sanctified with prayer and divine commandments, have become "a house of non-Jews" through their adoption of "foreign" names, languages and customs. They are no longer ours. They are not "The tents of Jacob and the dwellings of Israel," Rather, they are like "strangers and foreigners" to the spirit of traditional Israel and its Torah.

Righteous Women

The fathers are guilty and the mothers even more so, because the homes' management and spirituality is dependent on women. The home is her domain, it is her sphere of influence where she reigns. As Rav Yossi said: "I never called my wife – "my wife," but rather "my home" (Shabbat 118) because "his home is his wife." The commandments to light Shabbat and holiday candles are only given to women. This is her privilege and her responsibility – to light God's candle, giving the light of Torah to the home.

With the light of faith and mitzvoth she influences her children. "In the merit of the righteous women who lived in that generation, Israel was redeemed from Egypt (Sotah 11, b). "The midwives feared God... they saved the lives of the male children" (Exodus 1:17). Those midwife mothers, those righteous women, they themselves believed deeply in Hashem! "The midwives feared God" and this very faith and awe of God that was in their hearts, they implanted in their children's hearts. It is no wonder that they "saved the lives of the children" that they gave the dry bones life and breathed courage and hope into them. Together with the kneading dough troughs that the Jewish women carried on their shoulders, they also brought tambourines to provide the beat to dance in joy at the downfall of Pharaoh and his soldiers. The mothers' trust in Hashem and his redemption of Israel is what spiritually prepared the whole generation for redemption.

We Survived Thanks to our Mothers
It is very interesting that all three of the ancient civilizations which contributed the most to the advancement of civilization, the Jews, the Greeks, and the Romans, had a similar tradition. They all believed that the father of the nation was an endangered child who was miraculously saved. Zeus was the top Greek god, responsible for ruling over the other gods and maintaining law and order. According to Greek mythology, in his childhood a goat saved him from death. According to a Roman legend, Romulus, the founder of Rome, was abandoned as a child and a wolf saved and nursed him. According to the Torah, Moshe Rabbenu, at age 3 months, was left alone and was in danger of drowning in the Nile River. He was saved by his mother who nursed him. "Moshe is considered equal to all Israel" (Mechilta Beshlach 15). Truly, we survived thanks to our mothers.

The Jewish mother in her wisdom, concern, and self-sacrifice for her husband and children, united the family and created a family life. This became the vibrant and fundamental core of our nation and its glory. She strengthened her home as a fortress and sanctified it as a temple. The wise man praised her above all: "Her children gave approval, her husband exalted her." "My Yiddisher Mama" that song of praise and thanks was sung to her: That motherhood became the symbol of loyalty to God and Torah, the symbol of strength and sacrifice for their people and land, the symbol of every good and noble trait which they displayed in leading the precious, mighty, and splendor of holy Israel. Those mothers influenced their children with more goodness and blessings than all the expert teachers. Today, these Jewish mothers are estranged from Jewish values, and fill their homes with foreign ambiances and lifestyles, which penetrate the entire soul, until the souls themselves become foreign.

Jewish Motherhood in Western Countries

The angel who brought Avraham the tidings that he would have a son, first inquired into Sarah's character. Was she worthy to be the ideal mother? Was she a promiscuous woman or a merchant, sitting in coffee houses and frequenting theaters? Therefore, he and his companions asked Avraham: "Where is your wife Sarah? And he said, "She is in the Tent" (*Brashit* 18:9) Due to her holy merit, light and blessing: "A candle remained lit from before Shabbat until the next Shabbat, her dough was blessed, and a cloud hovered over her tent" (*Rashi Brashit* 24:87). Then they understood that she was worthy to educate a boy fitting to be a righteous Hebrew. Today, in answer to the question, where is your wife? We cannot answer that she is in the tent. Sadly, the modern mother in the western world has rejected the principle that "The entire honor of the kings' daughter is internal, in personality and her soul." She behaves like Hagar, the maid servant. "She cast the child away… And she went, and sat her down opposite him, but far away." (ibid 21:15) She has exchanged her kingdom for toys and diversions, for coffee houses and theatres. She also throws parties, organizes social dances and charity events. These activities are good and would be praiseworthy, if she would make not them into ends in themselves, but would realize that these are only means to an end. The trouble is that the Jewish mother lives under an illusion that through these activities she fulfills her purpose and her Jewish and maternal obligations. She has sanctified the means and lost focus on her exalted purpose. Therefore, all of her activity is simply for the sake of activity.

There is no association or social society where Jewish women are not found. She has also founded organizations and institutions especially for women. Many mothers attend parties or sit in coffee houses talking with each other and passing the time. However, they are not at home. The best among them know how to spend their time and energy to help funds for "Youth Aliyah", "Jewish Students", "poor children", may Hashem bless these women. However, they have forgotten their own children and don't take care of them properly. They know how to establish kindergartens and charitable institutions. However, they don't concern themselves to provide wholesome Jewish homes for their children. They do not worry about the character and the spirit of their homes. The opposite is true. They act negligently regarding sanctified Jewish values. They nullify the commandments which depend on the Jewish home. They have neglected their positions; the role of the mother is to educate her children. They have cast off the responsibility to guide their children towards a fulfilling Jewish life. These mothers have ignored their homes and have abandoned their children to whatever influences the environment provides.

The Collapse of the Jewish Home on its Very Foundations

How can one hope that children from these homes will be loyal to their Torah and People? If the mothers are as described, what can we expect from their offspring? This follows the principle of "The derivative law can't receive more of a punishment than the source law." Indeed, King Shaul also knew this in spite of the evil spirit that possessed him. When it seemed to him that his son Yehonatan had corrupted his life, King Shaul placed the responsibility on the boys' mother, when he chastened his son saying; "distorted son of a rebellious wife." Is it any wonder that the holy foundations of the Jewish home in Diaspora have crumbled? The love and loyalty between husband and wife withered. The unity and togetherness of the family was weakened. Hasn't the parents' influence over the children declined lower than ever? This is what God told Ezekiel Ben Buzi, who prophesied about the dry bones: "You, son of man, tell the house of Israel, that they should be ashamed of their iniquities!" (Ezekiel 43:10)

We are accustomed to hear women demanding "equal rights." I think that they have already taken more than equal rights. And the time has come for men to demand for themselves "equal rights." What would happen if men disregard their responsibilities to work and making a living outside the house, just as women disregard their responsibilities to maintain a traditional home and to provide Jewish education for their children in the house? The children would wither away from lack of necessities and physical starvation, just as they currently withering away from spiritual starvation, due to women's negligence.

There is No Substitute for Home and No Replacement for Mother

Jewish mother, don't even consider fleeing from your responsibilities, because if you will be silent now, comfort and salvation will not come to the Jews from somewhere else. Neither teachers, nor councilors, nor youth clubs nor Hillel houses will save our youth from assimilation. They will not raise sons and daughters faithful to their people and dedicated to our fathers' tradition. It will never happen! There is no substitute for home and there is no replacement for mother. Only a home can serve as a fortress against assimilation. Only a home determines the child's soul, charts the way that he should proceed in life and develops his spiritual capabilities which will help him throughout his life. Both the home and the children are under the mother's influence, and she has the key to help her teenagers observe Judaism.

Our father in Heaven, the Rock and Redeemer of Israel, save your People and enthuse Jewish mothers with one burning desire: to be homemakers; the children's happy guides. May she have one and only one goal: to run her house according to Jewish tradition and to establish her family life on its proper foundations.

CHAPTER SIX

VISITING INIQUITY OF THE PARENTS
UPON THE CHILDREN

MAN IS DEPENDENT on various resources to cope with the demands of life and its challenges. Just as the body needs to be healthy and vital, and receive its nourishment from essential vitamins to enable it to develop and grow, so too, the soul is dependent on certain resources in order to be able to respond to the constant demands of the moment and ones surrounding environment, attain self-fulfillment, self respect and rejoice in life. When these resources are lacking, the expectations and demands of life become larger than the inner means available to a person to help him confront them. As a result, this creates pressure on one's soul and spirit, which can bring about unwanted responses and a distressed spirit.

Nourishment for a Child's Soul
A man needs these resources from the beginning of his life and till its end. A child is hungry for love, warmth and hugs, which are the life and sustenance of his being.

However, this is not enough. Together with the physical development of the child one must care for the development of its being. This can be achieved through showing respect and admiration by those who care and come into contact with him, whether it is his parents, family, teachers, or friends. On the other hand, showing disrespect and contempt can force a child to become secluded within himself. He creates a world, different and separated, from the one surrounding him. There he lives separately and cynically. The child or youth becomes uncompromisingly bitter. He suffers a lack of self-confidence and hates everyone, and, sometimes even himself.

Social factors influence how one's personality is formed, in particular, during the early years of one's life. A child is dependent on the environment around him and the people close to him. It is from them that he absorbs his primary impressions and awareness about the cycles of life. Love, admiration, and understanding the emotions of the child, determine the development of his personality, well-being, and self-confidence. Nevertheless, if the worlds of expectations of a young person clash with the worlds of reality. His instincts become confused and he enters a state of inner confusion. As a result, he becomes aggressive and daring, which can lead him to becoming violent.

Psychological Complexes from Infancy to Adulthood

Psychology is aware of inner complexes that develop and are suppressed during childhood and adolescence. These problems can disturb a person's inner development during adolescence. Paterson, an experimental psychologist, found that parents, who ascribe importance to their children, relate to them with admiration. This is a very meaningful act that increases a child's self-worth and esteem. They feel respected and see themselves as people whose opinions are considered. Their ego strengthens and grows. Their being respected obligates them to behave with reason, since their self-esteem has been aroused. The opposite occurs in a negative surrounding or society. Youth whose surroundings humiliated them are hostile and full of grudges. They have no self-confidence and will most likely become part of the fringe elements of society. Some will chose to isolate themselves from society. In other words, a life of alienation and isolation. This explanation comes to tell us how severe the emotional state of a Jewish youth can be in the Diaspora.

The Difficulties of Attaining a Meaningful Identity in the Diaspora

A child needs a role model that he can identify with and internalize. This process begins at home and continues through school. If the child has strong models who strongly believe in what they do or represent, he will imitate them and identify with them. Professor Moshe Adar correctly asserted that the essential challenge facing an adolescent is the search for meaningful identity which they cannot attain in the Diaspora. Today, parents are not prepared to serve as a fitting model to imitate and learn from. Parents have no direction and are perplexed, and have not yet achieved a meaningful identity. The farce of family life, the collapse of family and social traditions and values, create for the adolescent a detrimental, confusing and depressing view of the world. Teachers are not considered examples to amplify Jewish identity. Most Jewish children learn in non-Jewish schools where the teachers are not Jewish. A small minority of children receive a bit of Jewish education at Sunday Schools. Most of the teachers only know a little Hebrew and their knowledge of Judaism is limited. They are perplexed and do not have a strong Jewish identity.

The Jewish Child in an Anti-Semitic World

The world is full of different kinds of anti-Semitism. To the wonderment of the Jewish child, he will discover that his people are attacked and humiliated everywhere. It is difficult for him to accept this degrading and shameful reality. For indeed, the Jewish adolescent seeks to experience self-esteem and admiration. Surely all of us seek to be related to positively. The bitter reality of anti-Semitism is expressed by the American Jewish author and educator, Solomon Schechter: "I remember, when I would come home from heder, full of blood and screaming from the pain of the wounds inflicted upon me by non-Jewish youth, my father would say to me: 'My son, we live in the exile, and it is upon us to receive this as the will of the Holy One, Blessed be He.' He explained to me that this is just a temporary period in our history, since we, the Jewish people, belong to the-end-of-days, when God will console His people. So, therefore, my pain was only physical. However, my real pain occurred later on. When I left Romania and went to countries considered cultured and sophisticated (United States of America) I found the supreme anti-Semitism, one that burns the soul even though the body is alive.'"

School is the first place where a Jewish child encounters anti-Semitism. He innocently expects that he will be treated the same as any other person; however, he hears his classmates calling out, "filthy Jew," and other hateful remarks and curses. To his amazement and anguish, a Jewish child becomes aware that he is not like other children, but different. When he goes through the streets and sees graffiti in large letters, with the curse, such as, "death to the Jews," he sees there is something offensive in what he has been called and that separates him from other youth. He hears about synagogues that were burnt in his city, cemeteries and tombstones that were desecrated – even the dead cannot rest. In his aguish, he feels he is different from everyone, because every one hates him. The Jewish youth loses his self-esteem and suffers from a conflict of opposing desires and expectations, which is a source of stress. He tries to suppress his true identity and hide through another one, so that he will be accepted by every one.

As a result of this, his true identify as a Jew becomes debased and embarrassing, falsely identifying as a non-Jew he respects and admires. There is no greater inferior complex or lower level than this. Inner wounds and a distorted view of things occur in young and sensitive souls. Inner destruction is caused from long oppression. The children – infant creatures, innocent and pure, fragile and sensitive – their confusion is great, causing them to play hide-and-seek with themselves. They become partners with insulters and oppressors, to the point that they succumb to self-denial. This is essentially a spiritual and inner destruction that is decreed upon them.

The Loyal Jew to the Heritage of his Fathers
In the past, the Jew was faithful to the purpose of his creation, and whole heartedly believed in his distinctiveness, as it is stated: "Who chose us from all the peoples, and exalted us above all languages." The Jewish people saw itself as chosen by the creator of the world and proud that the Jewish people enriched the world with religion and culture. He adhered devoutly to the observance of Torah and Mitzvot, and it never entered his mind to resemble a non-Jew. On the contrary, for the Jew had the ideal: "It is a people that shall dwell alone, and shall not be reckoned among the nations." A Jew

established this principle as an ideal, and lived according to it. The ideals of Judaism were highly valued by ones parents, who made great efforts to bequeath them, in deed and thought, to their children. Then, one did not need to worry about Jewish identity since it was deeply rooted in family tradition. One knew from where he came and to where he was going. He was completely aware in his thoughts and deeds of these essential ideals. This made him a sincere and complete Jew when at home and away from it.

The Jew has Become a Spiritual Refugee

This ideal situation has changed for the worse and there has begun negative transformations in Jewish life in the Diaspora. As an immigrant he has now become a spiritual immigrant. He has become someone empty of Judaism and its ideals, a stranger to our authentic culture. He has become snared by the ways of life and culture of the peoples with whom he lives. Fleeing the traditions of his ancestors the Jew has become a spiritual refugee. This is no longer a Jew in exile, but the exile in the Jew. It has invaded his spirit and soul and has transformed him into someone without a spiritual address and nationality. Nevertheless, the mezuzah is still ready to receive our presence at the entranceway. But the Jew of the interior side of the entrance is lacking any Jewish knowledge, as his bookcase is bereft of any Jewish book.

The problem of youth in the Diaspora is essentially the problem of parents that was passed on to their children. The dropout justifiably accuses the parents: "The fathers have eaten sour grapes and the children's teeth are blunted." (Ezekiel 18:2)

A Parents Cruelty to the Souls of their Children

In the years when I served as a Rav in the central synagogue in Sydney, Australia, I was personally in touch with the mainstream of youth and student groups, with whom I had many conversations and gave lectures. Frequently the youth, in particular the younger ones, would converse about matters bothering them, such as, when their fellow non-Jewish students would sometimes burst out against them, yelling, "filthy Jew," or "Jews, go back to the gas chambers." These bursts of anti-Semitism made a terrible impression and troubled these youth. From one aspect, the Jewish youngsters wanted to be considered like all other youth. But they rejected them often with curses and insults. Understandably, these embarrassing incidents cause difficult and painful conflicts in the lives of the victims, and can cause constant inner tensions for longs periods of time. These insulting incidents shocked the Israeli children, who grew up and learned in Israel, where all their classmates were Jewish. These sudden outbursts of anti-Semitic incidents weakened their senses. Frequently they would cry bitterly, because they were fed up with these attacks and life in Australia. They yearned to return to Israel and study there with their own people.

All of this, which came out of their innocent and pure hearts, touched me. I saw them as young chicks uprooted from their natural surroundings and put into a hostile one, which left them with inner complexes that will trouble them for years and rob them of peace of mind. When I raised my concerns to their parents, their apathetic answers usually were: "They will get used to it," or, "there is nothing one can do." I was shocked to hear from the parents such cold and indifferent responses. What does this mean: "They will get used to it"! Why do the parents dismiss these serious incidents with the apathetic response of, "there is nothing to do"? These troubling incidents and outbursts can cause deep stress and leave a scar for life! However, it is possible to transfer the children to a Jewish school to save them these oppressive and depressing incidents! They yearn to be in a sympathetic and supportive environment with their own people. Deep in their hearts they are fed up with the atmosphere of the exile. These parents, and their like, are treating their children cruelly. They are damaging their self-confidence and their peace of mind.

During the course of Jewish history, never has the sense of responsibility of parents towards their children been so defective and inadequate. In light of this, it is stated in *Sifri* (*Ki Tetze*): "Men die because of their iniquities; children die because of the iniquities of their fathers."

Devoted Parents in the Animal Kingdom

Our Sages have taught us (*Eruvin* 100): "If the Torah was not given to us we could have learnt from the righteous ways of animals." Indeed when we observe the animal kingdom; birds, animals, and wild creatures, one can see how a mother raises and teaches her offspring the basics of survival: How to fly, run, seek food, and survive predators. Even animals, wild creatures and winged animals will feed their offspring before they eat from the food they found for them. They will defend their young with all their might from predators. This is the natural fatherly and motherly instinct of parents toward their children.

Therefore, we would expect that human beings, who are higher creatures and who have the ability to speak, would display a form of behavior that would lead to stability and faith – the path of Judaism. Meaning to say, that parents guide their children to remain faithful to their people and religion. However this is not the case. In contradiction to the rules of nature, these parents abandon their children to foreign influences that will prey on them. They have been abandoned without any means of defense. They have no way of life, values or ideals, Jewish identity, faith or self-esteem. Without any of these it is impossible to survive.

The Exchange of Packages

A horrifying story came to us from the abyss of blood and tears of the holocaust. A young woman, from a respected and wealthy family in

Bialystok, saw from her hideout the Germans drag her parents from their home and shoot them to death, and the Poles club her husband to death. She decided to escape at night to the Russian border, which was far away. The young woman took with her two packages. She put her one-year-old son in one package, money, jewelry and a few precious items, in the second, in order to buy food. In the darkness of the night she began her long journey, dragging her tired feet under the weight of the two packages that she carried with her gentle hands. Tired, and about to collapse, she arrived totally exhausted. She fell to the ground and rested for an hour. When she woke up she felt she could no longer carry the packages. She decided to take the package that contained her baby son, and leave behind the package with the valuable items. When she just passed the Russian border she checked the package she was carrying, she suddenly screamed: Oh my God!! Where is my baby son?! I left him in the field! Weak and exhausted, distressed and confused, she lifted the package with the gold and silver coins, instead of the one with her infant son.

In this tragedy, the changing of packages happened due to events beyond the mother's control. However, many of our brethren do this willingly. They place the package of material goods above everything. Whereas their children, with a sigh, they leave abandoned in foreign fields. They act like ants: They always go on collecting and gathering, but do not continuously and devoutly care and give.

The Inferiority Complex and Jewish Intellects

Inferiority complex claims many victims among the intellectual professionals of our people, such as, doctors, engineers and lawyers. The modern assimilated Jew knows nothing about Judaism and is barely aware that he is Jewish. He has lost his self-esteem. He sees his non-Jewish friend as superior to him, and all he aims for is to be like him. But the non-Jew does not accept him as one of his peer group.

I merited to head the Rabbinical Court of Australia. A number of non-Jewish women married to Jewish men asked the court to convert them. When the court asked them, "Why do you want to take upon yourselves Torah and Mitzvot?" they explained that their husbands suffer from an inferior complex because they are Jewish. When they meet non-Jews they are nervous and perplexed about their being Jewish, and they try to hide it. The stress from this badly influences the daily routine of their lives; therefore, these women explained that through converting to Judaism they wish to strengthen their husbands' spirit by showing them that they are proud of their being Jewish.

Inner wounds should not be taken lightly since they are more difficult and severe than bodily wounds. Psychiatrists claim that when an inner complex affects the fabric of one's personality and wounds deep inner emotions, it is difficult to reverse the process or heal the person. A Jew that conceals his identity and pretends to be non-Jew is hiding from himself. He is always wearing a mask and trembling from fear that someone might reveal his true identity. This is a game of hide-and-seek between himself and others. He cooperates with his pursuers and those who insult him and uproots himself from his being. This is one of the most degrading and offensive things that a person can do, because there is no greater self-destruction than this. No person in his right mind would destroy his soul, or being, then rise, and go his way in peace. Such a person is wounded and broken, and as he matures he will increasingly suffer pangs of conscience. Many Jews of the Diaspora are plagued by these complexes and suffer difficult pain. It is just cruelty to human beings.

Steven Spielberg, the well-known movie producer, publicly acknowledged that throughout his childhood and adolescence he suffered from an inferior complex about his being Jewish. Only when he produced the film Schindler's List, did he learn the Jewish people's history, its values and ideals, in contrast to that of evil Gentiles and their deeds of murder. Only then did he become free of his inferior complex, and became convinced to be proud of his being a Jew. Kirk Douglas and other well-known America Jews, after reaching renowned celebrity and financial fame, complained about their having suffered from anti-Semitism.

A community in exile is one that lives outside it true home, and since it has been denied its homeland, it has lost value and respect in the eyes of the world and itself. No community, or individual, can exist for a long time without faith, ideals, and self-esteem.

Anti-Semitism in the Diaspora

Jews were always convenient scapegoats to be used as the reason for diseases and epidemics. Anti-Semitism is different from other forms of racism and discrimination, because it is more traditional, and has deeper roots. Furthermore, Jews have integrated more successfully into Western society than other minorities. Hate for Jews is an illness that cannot be healed. It is like cancer, which spreads to other parts of the body, and there is no cure for it.

The Jewish people are hated more than any other nation of people, since anti-Semitism is deeply rooted in ancient Christian sources and the New Testament. They are considered as collectively guilty for the death of Christianity's messiah and his suffering, and responsible for delaying his return. Jews appear as demonic and satanic, as a people always to be hated. As long the New Testament exists Jew will be hated. When Christians, whether they are young, or adults, read the New Testament, they become filled with wrath and hatred against the Jews. Jews are also despised because of their unnatural nomadic way of life. Another reason for hating Jews is that they are successful financially. Everywhere the amount of wealthy Jews is more than the rest of the population. Twenty-five percent of the multimillionaires in America are Jews, even though they comprise less than two percent of the population. Fifty percent of the billionaires in Australia are Jews, even though they make up less than one percent of the population. Similar situations also exist in Russia and in other countries. The richest man in England is a Jew. This reality arouses jealously and anti-Semitism, even though many Jews do not have substantial financial resources, and are even poor. But they want only to know about the rich and their villas. They are contemptuous of all Jews, especially anti-Semites, who do not need any real reason to hate Jews.

Anti-Semitism on the University Campus
The data about anti-Semitism in the world shows an increase in the amount and level of anti-Semitic incidents. This is very troubling and should worry Jews worldwide. Particularly, regarding the fact that anti-Semitic activity increased greatly on university campuses throughout America, and in other places. This is a cause for great worry, since the virus of anti-Semitism is increasingly spreading to the younger generation and to intellectuals. Today anti-Semitism is thriving.

Global Tsunami of Anti-Semitism
The Chief Rabbi of Great Britain, Jonathan Sacks, expressed his deep fears about the growing global anti-Jewish sentiment. He warned of a global tidal wave of anti-Semitism. One sees how *The Protocols of the Elders of Zion* is promoted as a best seller in book shops and on prime time television in many parts of the world. Anti-Semitic incidents have increased in many countries and are now at record levels. All of this is a kind of a tsunami of anti-Semitism of which the Chief Rabbi is very scared. He pointed out that throughout Europe, Rabbis have been assaulted and synagogues desecrated. The U.S. anti Defamation League shows that 35 million Americans are blatantly anti-Semitic.

How then could Jews, possessing any self-respect, dwell in such a hateful and damaging environment? How cruel it is to raise children in this kind of atmosphere.

Further, the recent appearance of wealthy Israeli investors worldwide will bring about a mightier tidal wave of anti-Semitism. The Hebrew press recently proclaimed that Israeli billionaires are conquering every corner of the globe, what will the Gentiles eventually say and how will they react?

Surveys and Jewish Students
In America surveys are conducted, mainly among Jewish youth, in order to find out to what extent anti-Semitic tensions influence their lives. In a survey carried out in New York and Los Angeles it became evident that they are

sensitive to anti-Semitism, especially young adults. They describe the non-Jewish world as enemy territory. Nevertheless, they do wish to be part of the general non-Jewish society, even though it is clear to them that this is very difficult to achieve unless they hide their Jewish identity, which many are willing to do.

The surveys revealed qualities typical of Jewish youth and should be reason for concern. For example, Jewish students accept the negative ways non-Jews view them without doubting or objecting to them. The students were asked to choose among many characteristics which characterize Jews. They chose the following: He is intelligent, a seeker of knowledge, clever, shrewd, arrogant, greedy, seeks to be wealthy, a kike, and uncivilized, etc. The students did not understand that the characteristics attributed to the Jewish people were negative qualities that anti-Semites attribute to Jews. As to the question, what is the reason for anti-Semitism, various answers have been suggested which are basically a repetition of the characteristics attributed to Jews by anti-Semites. Many responded that Jews are responsible for how non-Jews view them. Jews arouse anti-Semitism because of their uncivilized behavior and manners. The answers of these students prove that American Jewish youth suffer from a complex of inferiority and self-hatred, which is a direct result of anti-Semitism that youth encounter in schools, universities, clubs and the street. Above and beyond this, most of the students showed they have no knowledge of Jewish religion, heritage and culture.

Alcohol and Drugs

Dr. N. Sargeant, an expert sociologist at the University of Sydney, Australia, did comprehensive research on students with a tendency to drink alcohol and students that take drugs. His research revealed that Australian students led the list of drinkers with 32 percent. After them were the Jewish students with 19 percent, Japanese students with 7 percent, and Chinese students with only 3 percent. On the other hand, of those that took drugs, the Jewish male students achieved first place with 20 percent and Jewish female students led with even a higher percentage, 29.7 percent. The Australian male students comprised 12.4 percent, female students 16.3 percent, Japanese students 4 percent, and Chinese only 3.7 percent.

These students, and similarly, with the rest of our youth, escaped to drugs and alcohol. In the past, a Jew was innocent and knowledgeable, and knew how to sing: "A drunkard is a goy!" Even on Purim, when Jews are commanded to become intoxicated to the point that they cannot distinguish between the cursed one Haman and the blessed one Mordechai, they were not found drunk on the streets. A Jew was prepared and invited to fulfill the commandments of the Torah according to Jewish law in the most meticulous way. However this particular commandment to drink till when one is not able to distinguish, a Jew was not able to fulfill completely, because of his pure and upright nature. The bottle was foreign to him. Today, to our shame and anguish, our Jewish youth have become experts on the use of alcohol and drugs. We have many who are alcoholics and drug addicts.

Dr. Victor Frankel, the world-renowned psychiatrist, wrote that today we have found new neuroses: Severe inner complexes that derive from boredom and a lack of self-confidence, and which lead to alcoholism and drug addiction. Indeed this is true, since our youth are ignorant of their culture, aliens to their rich heritage, void of Torah and Mitzvot, without traditional religious homes, suffer from boredom and an inferior complex, and lack self-esteem.

Jewish Youth in the Diaspora are in State of Crisis

Jewish students and youth are going through a major crisis in the Diaspora. Most of them avoid their Jewish identity. They are embarrassed of their Jewish identity. They cannot accept the fact that they look like Jews, and that their destiny and how they live is that of a Jew. Judaism makes them perplexed. They relate with mockery cynicism to Jewish nationality. The vast majority of young Jews in the Diaspora are seeking one aim, and that is to be like the non-Jewish population. Such is the desire of Jewish youth in the Diaspora, which leads only to one direction – spiritual destruction.

These are the words of a Harvard University graduate: "The majority of Jewish youth in universities view the fact that they were born Jewish as the greatest tragedy of their lives. They always want to be seen as non-Jews by others, and they make great efforts to assimilate as quickly as possible… as much as their facial features allow them.

The Torture of Jewish Youth in the Diaspora

The author David Harden of Uruguay explains the existentially feelings and hardships of Jewish youth in the Diaspora regarding their Jewish identity. "A young Jew who was born or immigrated to a Western country, is educated in that country's language and assimilates it's culture, identifies with its history and ideals, does not feel any loyalty toward another culture, nor towards a religion that he does not believe in, and nor towards one that he is intimidated by it. He is not a being of his own will, but merely born biologically a Jew. He views this as an arbitrary incident of nature, like someone born with a defect, or flaw in his character. The presence of this defect eventually reveals itself with intensity, and when it does, it can leave one with a scar. The youth becomes aware that the concept of a Jew has a certain place in peoples' awareness, whereas, he has always considered himself equal to others. He eventually learns that the status of being Jewish is not necessarily an honorable one, since it is linked to preconceived judgments and prejudices. He becomes aware that the Western secular culture that he chose is linked to Christian culture where the concept "Jew" does not have a respectable place. Something that one considers being a defect exists in him, which makes one hesitant to deal with it and not willing to tolerate it. The defect, no matter how small or large it is, influences a person's actions and how he interacts with people and situations, for better or for worse. It can cloud his experience of reality and make it difficult for him to relate to his handicap with a calm state of mind. It always stands in his way and troubles him. It prevents him from fully assimilating. Sometimes he despairs because he is not able to free himself from the handicap. There are times when he even hates himself. He also hates the various causes of his defect, such as, his Jewish past, tradition, religion, and essentially, anyone or anything Jewish."

Self Denial

The French author, Albert Memmi, in his book "Liberation of the Jew," describes the tendency of assimilated Jews to conceal their Jewish identity as a form of self-denial. It is a pitiable and cunning way to be accepted in non-Jewish society. They are always playing hide-and-seek with their contemporaries. All their lives they make great efforts to instill belief in a personality facade that does not exist. They become accustomed to living like chameleons, shrewd and frightened lizards that change their colors to the colors of their surroundings, so that they will not be noticed. Jews, likewise, through fear and deceit, hide behind a camouflaged identity, so that no one will discover their true identity.

To deny one's identity is one of the most dreadful acts that one does discreetly and secretly. Negating one's being and surrendering to the oppressor, can only be viewed with irony and with anger.

Destructive Self-Hatred

Albert Memmi goes on to explain that when one negates his being he does not solve anything. This matter is even more critical: Self-denial, which was intended to save the oppressed, eventually destroys him. As much as he succeeds in negating himself, he destroys himself more. A person cannot remove himself from his inner being without continual inner injury. Usually, the oppressed experiences a feeling of humiliation about his previous identity, because it reminds him too much of his downfall. Incidentally, he is to some extent the same person he was before, but he is still different from others in various ways... the past is a proof of this, even in spite of his running away... he has little patience, he becomes angry about anything that interferes with his commitment to appear like everyone else to the point that no one will notice him. Oh! If he was only given the chance, he would tear mercilessly the old layer of skin that separates him from others, even if he wounded himself seriously! The negation of oneself ends in bitterness and self-hatred.

A mixed marriage will not change his situation and bitter destiny. On the contrary, it will only open another hostile front against him, and further embitter his life! His children will despise him because he defamed their Christian mother's honor by imposing on them to be seemingly half-Jewish. We know of cases where children severely accused their father, or mother, for having had married a Jew, or Jewess.

Young Souls Lost in a Wilderness

These youth, who are ignorant of Hebrew culture, aliens to our rich heritage, void of Torah and Mitzvoth, and without traditional homes, suffer from emptiness, boredom, a lack of self-esteem, and self-hatred. These souls, wandering in a world of nothingness, arouse contempt and compassion. "The well has no water, therefore it has snakes and scorpions." Where there are no Jewish ideals and values, one becomes vulnerable to the evil forces of the world. People without roots and no vision of the future do not know where they come from, or to where they are headed. They are swept away and thrown from one place to another. They are thrown and dumped by every passing trend. They change their ways according to what is fashionable at the time, or change their values according to some insignificant movement void of any ethic or ideals. Like falling leaves, they land wherever the wind blows them. They threw away their rich past, lost their sense of direction, and the ability to see a future. The problem is princes have become paupers. They gather the crumbs under the table of any damaging plant.

Religious Youth Live with Faith and Pride

Contrary to lost youth, religious youth that grew up in traditional homes and received a Torah education, derive inner-confidence and patriotic pride and joy from his being Jewish. He knows his peoples' history and how he is connected to it. He is familiar with his rich heritage. He has a sense of, "and He has chosen us." He feels close to God and sees himself as one the select of the Creation. On the other hand, he views the Gentiles as partially idolaters. He is proud of the fact that the Jewish people have enriched the world with religious and cultural treasures, and given the world access to a living God and the Prophets. Judaism has endowed it with a sense of justice and righteousness. It has taught the humanity about the kingdom of heaven and the brotherhood of humanity in the days of the Messiah. The pure faith of the Jew has always given him a spiritual advantage over his surroundings. It was decisive in his being able to exist as a Jew: "It is a people that shall dwell alone, and shall not be reckoned among the nations."

Visiting the Iniquities of the Parents on the Children

To one's great regret and sorrow, most of the Jewish youth in the Diaspora do not believe in the spiritual superiority of their heritage. They know nothing about their heritage. Their parents prevented them from having any encounter with it. On the contrary, they see non-Jews as superior to them, and their goal is to be the same and equal to them. Therefore, they consider mixed marriages as an achievement and a means to further their social status and relations with non-Jewish world.

Sigmund Freud, the father of psychoanalysis, studied the unconscious mind. He treated people with complexes and neuroses through his analysis of the world of the subconscious. He viewed Jewish education as a source for empowering the Jewish soul. Freud rebuked and warned irresponsible parents who were not giving their children a Jewish education: "If you do not raise your child as a Jew you are depriving him of a vital source of energy which cannot be replaced by anything else. You should know that your son will have to fight as a Jew, and he needs every bit of energy to persevere this struggle. Do not deprive him of this asset." Thus, Freud advocates Jewish education and urged parents to provide it. He did so, not because of patriotic or religious reasons, with which he did not associate, but rather in order to strengthen the spirit of Jewish youth and their ability to exist as Jews.

The vast majority of parents refuse to provide their children a Jewish education, and do not teach them Jewish values or love for Jewish tradition. They alienate their children from their glorious Jewish history, and from their chance to participate in the lofty and heroic struggle for the Jewish People's spiritual and national existence. One must make parents aware of the need to worry about their children's inner spiritual strength and happiness, no less than being concerned about their children's health and physical welfare.

The Jewish Home has no Judaism

The foremost educators are one's parents and to a lesser degree, one's teachers. The problems of Jewish youth in the Diaspora begin at home. Parents design their children's characters and influence their patterns of behavior. Children are instantly influenced by their parent's words, actions, and way of life. It causes us great anguish that most homes are not prepared to bequeath the Jewish heritage to their children. The opposite is true. The home serves as a negative force in everyday life. There are no signs of Jewish life. There is no Shabbat and Holidays. A foreign language is the only one spoken and no Jewish book can be found anywhere. As is well known, the most prominent books that people study diligently at home are: the phone book, cook book and check book.

Children that grow up in such a disfunctional Jewish home are prone to the forces of assimilation. They have not seen, heard, or known a Jewish lifestyle. How can we expect them to become fed up with and abandon the Gentile lifestyle? Parents absolutely do not understand the need to maintain the Jewish people's special lifestyle. They do not know that a Jewish lifestyle and worldview exists, and that it is treason to transfer loyalty to a foreign camp. "If parents have transgressed and eaten sour grapes (*boser*) how can we expect children's teeth not to become blunted?" Our children are not corrupt – their parents corrupt them. Where is the love and devotion of a father toward his son? They left their sons to sigh, like lost souls wandering in a world of emptiness.

Neglecting the Soul is a Criminal Act

Many times we read in the news about harsh court decisions against parents who neglect their children's physical well-being by not providing them with proper nourishment or other material needs. If all of the parents who ignored the mental health and happiness of their children and who prevented them from receiving spiritual nourishment and enthusiastic patriotism were ordered to appear in court, who could imagine how long the line would be? Parents cause their children severe psychological damage by depriving them of self-confidence, a sense of security, and national pride.

Abuse is not only physical but can also be psychological. Parents are responsible to provide their children their material needs and spiritual nourishment. Children are more than merely sacks of flesh that have to be filled with food and drink. Parents ignore the fact their children have souls which need spirituality, morality, and patriotic ideals. The home cannot fulfill its role as long as parents see the home merely as an inn for providing food and shelter. There is no greater injustice than relating to a child as a body without a soul. Every possible gift one can give a child cannot fix this terrible injustice. Because if the parents relate to their children as if they have no soul, then the children soulless they become. This is mainly because of the cruel way that parents relate to their children.

Worshipping the Golden Calf

In Greek literature there is an ancient moral tale. It tells of a nobleman named Midas, who had a loving and devoted wife, handsome and talented children, a good livelihood, and a spacious home. Nevertheless he was very unhappy. He desired abundance and longed for great wealth. Eventually Dionysus, the Greek god, fulfilled his wish. He informed him, "Everything that you will touch will turn into gold!" Midas became overwhelmed with great joy about this generous promise. He quickly ran home to tell his family about the wonderful tiding. He burst into his home, embraced and kissed his wife, and told her, "I am about to become the richest man in the world, because everything I will touch will turn into gold!" But suddenly, he looked, and noticed something strange. His wife's lips turned cold and became frozen like a piece of metal. He became terrified and yelled for his children. His children came, and began to cry out, "Mommy, Mommy!" But their mother remained deaf and motionless, like a golden statue. She glanced at them with a sharp and piercing look, with cold and terrifying eyes that lacked the light of life. They approached and lovingly caressed their father, trying to console him. He, too, embraced them, and, suddenly they turned into lifeless pillars of gold. Midas insanely lamented, "Oh, My loving wife!" A deceitful voice then called out, "Gold! Gold! Gold!" Midas cried back, mourning, "Where are my precious children?" The deceitful voice again called out, "Gold! Gold! Gold!"

This terrifying legend describes the tragedy of materialism and how it dominates most of Jewish Diaspora life. They run after the Golden Calf and worship it. In their homes one finds people that live without a Jewish soul or vision, they live merely for the moment. The father is totally stuck trying to figure out ways to accumulate wealth, instead of enriching himself and his home with spiritual content and patriotic ideals. The mother is swept away by pleasures and idleness. Shabbat and the Festivals do not exit. There is no tranquility or anything sacred. There is only a race after materialism. In this race everything important is ignored, and the most precious thing is lost, one's children. These abandoned children either forsake the Jewish religion, or despise and loathe their ancestry. If someone were to describe this kind of living to a reasonable and intelligent person, he would certainly respond: This is nothing but spiritual suicide!

Children Criticize Their Parents

Occasionally the author of this volume heard Jewish students expressing themselves with quite sarcastic language and with sharp criticism of their parents. One of the common critical remarks was: "How can I respect my father if he is merely a machine for making money? He is always busy running after money. I can tell you that he is like an automatic robot that never stops, even on Shabbat and the Holidays." Some of these students strongly criticized their parents for abandoning religion and patriotic values, and burying themselves in a world without meaning and ideals. They condemned their parents with sharp words, because their homes lack Jewish content and meaning.

Of course, these are strong accusations voiced by children about their parents. If we were to ask parents: Why do you work so hard, without stopping or resting? Everyone would answer: "I work for my children's sake." In fact, their children not only do they not appreciate their hard working parents, they even ridicule and criticize them. We are not exaggerating, that in the criticism of some of these children there is a hint of indignation towards their parents.

You should know that you can give your children special treats and presents, provide entertainment and trips, and even buy them a car. However you will not succeed to gain their love and admiration. One cannot win over the hearts of others through money. An adolescent, in spite of his parent's intentions, thinks that he is owed these privileges. Give them not only a life of luxuries, which our ancestors were not able to provide us. But our ancestors did succeed to abundantly provide us with a life of spirit, faith, sense of holiness, tradition, and love for other Jews. One would receive their admiration and respect if he would succeed to be a good and responsible person, a Jew loyal to his God, People and country, through commitment and self-sacrifice. Through these ideals which penetrate into the heart, one would truly earn their sincere admiration.

Inferior to Animals

Every cat finds a place to guard its young. Crocodiles swim miles to reach dry land and dig a pit in a hidden place, in order to lay its eggs. She then covers them so that no predator can discover them. When the young emerge from the eggs, the crocodile moves them with its mouth to the safe haven of the waters of the river. Chickens cover their chicks. The chicken is known as someone who guards the chicken coop, to prevent anything bad from happening to the other chickens and their young. He does not allow any birds to prey on its young. Other birds and animals behave in a similar fashion. However, the Diaspora Jew is like a Cuckoo. It lays its eggs in the nests of other birds and abandons them to forces of nature, until they are devoured, or nurtured by the host mother.

These are the iniquities which parents visit on their children.

CHAPTER SEVEN

CAN THE DIASPORA SURVIVE?

THE CENTRAL ISSUES in this chapter are: Are the Jewish people in the Diaspora able to survive and ensure future generations of Jews? What was the backbone that anchored and united the scattered Jewish nation? They were a people without a country, without a land, and a people dispersed among Gentiles. In every generation enemies rose to annihilate them through evil and cruel decrees. In spite of all of this, beyond the graves of oppressors and tyrants, the Jewish people continued to march forward on the world stage, with their eyes raised towards the Holy Land. What was it that prevented the Jewish people from vanishing from the world scene? The answer is clear. Even the Jewish historian, Tzvi Graetz, stressed that when the Jews traveled through the desert of life during their two thousand years of exile, they carried the Holy Ark with them – the Ark also carried them. The spiritual mission planted high aspirations in the Jewish people's hearts, and shone through the stigma that they bore.

A Midrash, which clarifies this point, says: "When the Israelites stood at Mount Sinai and received the Torah, the Holy One Blessed be He said to the angel of death: You rule over all the nations of the world, but you have no rule over this nation (*Midrash Rabbah Shemot*, 32:7).

Judaism as a Life Preserver

During the Jew's journey through the turbulent sea of life, Judaism served as a life preserver. National unity was created through the observance of the Torah and the celebration of the Jewish holidays and festivals. The Jew viewed the ideal spiritual and moral character of Judaism with strong feelings and as a source of inspiration in his struggle for the Jewish people. It has been fittingly said that, "more than a Jew guards the Shabbat, the Shabbat guards him." In other words, the Jewish religion is what preserved our identity against those that rose to annihilate us. During the thousands of years of exile the mitzvoth (commandments) shielded the Jewish people. Without the mitzvoth, the Jewish people would have been destined to assimilate, which is what happened to most of the ancient peoples. They became extinct, and a memory of them is found only in history books.

In the exile, for many generations the Jewish religion was the cement that bound our people together. It enabled them to exist without having their own country. Moreover, the Torah succeeded to fulfill the task of being a replacement to a homeland. It created an artificial environment which enabled a Jew to fulfill his religious, cultural and social needs. "Wherever the

Jews were in exile, the Torah went into exile with them." With the Torah the Jewish people created wherever they were a Torah state. Torah observance prevented assimilation. It aroused in the hearts of Jews a spirit of might and national pride. His personality radiated the difference between Yaakov and Esau, the holy and the secular, and light and darkness. His table was greater than theirs and his crown was superior.

The Negative Impact of Decrees and Oppression

The negative impact of decrees and oppression was a major force for unifying the Jewish people. A shared hatred for non-Jews, and the difficulties of everyday life in the ghettos brought people together. The Jewish people are, "a people that shall dwell alone, and shall not be reckoned among the nations." The Jew's hatred for the cruelty shown towards his people, separated him from Gentiles, and prevented him from assimilating. Gentiles refused to accept Jews. Even Jews that converted to other religions were eventually rejected by the Gentile society. This created strong barriers between Gentiles and Jews. However, thanks to Jewish tradition, Jews preserved these barriers.

Actually, the Jews themselves, because of their tendency to remain distant from Gentile society, created the ghetto. Only afterwards did the Gentiles build walls around it. The Jews of the ghetto succeeded to persevere due to their ability to create religious and well-organized frameworks. These enabled them to successfully confront hostile surroundings and threats of assimilation. The Jews had their own independent and well-organized institutions. These enabled them to maintain a thriving and autonomous way of life. Even though crises and oppression often struck Jewish communities, Jews succeeded in achieving an amazing amount of independence, regarding their way and style of life. They lived according to the Halacha, and Jewish courts adjudicated court cases according to Torah law.

In short, the ghetto was a paradigm of a Jewish state in the midst of a non-Jewish one, in which Jews lived a pure religious and national life. The Jews in the Diaspora suffered insults, oppression, evil decrees and pogroms. All of these imposed on Jews physical suffering, and in spite of this, they were not injured spiritually. They viewed their Gentile oppressors as predators and barbaric idolaters. The Jew felt himself pursued in this world, but, as a servant of God, he was chosen to merit the world-to-come. The ghetto Jew had deep personal faith and Jewish pride!

Brutal anti-Semitism prevailed ceaselessly in the hearts of Gentiles. Frequent persecution, which was part of the life of Jews, enlarged their spirits and strengthened a sense of social responsibility towards other Jews and the community.

The Revival of Zionism

During the last century, the struggle to establish a national homeland was a tremendous source of national hopes and ideals. The Zionist movement is a century old phenomena of our times. Its struggle for a state united the Jewish people and served as a decisive force against assimilation. The Zionist idea is an ancient one, and is as old as Judaism. It began at the dawn of the history of the Jewish people, when God spoke to Abraham, the first Hebrew. "The Lord said to Avram: Go forth from your native land and from your father's house to the land I will show you" (Genesis 12:1). The dream of the redemption, the gathering of the exiled, and the deep, inner connection to the Land of Israel, were deep wellsprings from which Jews in the Diaspora drew moral and spiritual strength to able to overcome the oppression and suffering of the exile, until the coming of the redemption.

The hope of returning to Zion never ceased throughout the exile. A renewed national revolution took place. This was an orderly and prepared plan to carry out the aspiration of every generation: The revival of the State of Israel. This aspiration strengthened the feeling of unity among Jews and raised the awareness of their joint destiny with all Jews in the world. Jews from all over the world began to immigrate to Israel. The gates of Israel were partially open. In spite of this, thousands of illegal immigrants, traveling in dilapidated boats and ships, burst into the ancient, but new land, with patriotic passion. Jews, who for generations had no secure and reliable source of income or profession, returned to working the land. They established settlements and farmed the land. They planted vineyards, fruit trees, and harvested the fruits of the field. There arose a proud national awakening. World Jewry gathered, with their soul and money, to help Israel. They were so positively influenced that they turned their backs to assimilation.

The Zionist movement was an important instrument for creating the State of Israel. She proved her strength in her diplomatic and political struggles, and in her ability to build urban and rural settlements. She was able to draft into this project Jews from Israel and from the Diaspora who were far from Judaism.

The Threesome Becomes Weak

Today, the threesome that we described above has become severed. The three foundations served as decisive factors: One, they helped prevent assimilation. Two, they supported the traditional religious way of life: these three factors have almost vanished. Jews in the Western world enjoy equal social status and economic comfort. However their ties to Judaism are weakening. This reality will lead to the disappearance of Diaspora Jewry.

The negative factor, which helped unite all of our people throughout the generations, no longer exits. These are the walls of the ghetto. Thank God, there are no more pogroms. However, it is known that Esau hates Yaakov, and anti-Semitism does erupt in various places in the Diaspora. It is not violent, or like a storm, as it was in the past. The emancipation served as a turning point in the life of the Jew. When the Jew left the ghetto, he began to be part of the general society and culture. Jewish tradition was no longer a source of joy and happiness, but a burden and obstacle. Heinrich Heine summarized this by saying: "Judaism is a tragedy for Jews."

Today, in most parts of the world Jews dwell in improved economic and political conditions. Economies are open to all. Discrimination against Jews is less than it was in the past. Don't forget, that in times of prosperity, when most Gentiles accept and are tolerant of Jews, the Jewish people lose their children, more than in times of decrees and pogroms. The more the surrounding society becomes open to Jews, the more their independence becomes limited. The dynamics of our inner strength lessen. Not the poor conditions of the exile, but the improved material conditions and equal opportunities in the Diaspora threaten our existence.

Jewish Philanthropy

Zionism has lost its character as a political movement, a movement fighting for the liberation of its people and its homeland. It no longer embraces the whole people, unified in a shared aspiration. Today Zionism is an ideologically weak movement. The activities of the Zionist movement do not represent the urgent problems in Jewish life in the Diaspora and outside of it. The shallowness of Zionism is apparent, since it has no real commitments. Zionism ceased to be an ideal. It is no longer capable of breathing life into the Diaspora.

This point brings to mind the American Jew that entered a coffee shop in Tel Aviv and ordered a cup of coffee. The waiter explained to him that a cup of coffee with sugar costs six shekels, and without sugar, five. He chose coffee without sugar. But when the waiter gave him the coffee, he stirred it with a spoon. The waiter was surprised, because he served him coffee without sugar. He asked him: "Excuse me, Sir. Are you a Zionist worker? You are stirring and mixing, but you put in nothing in it." Indeed, Zionism rejects the Diaspora. Zionism obligates Jews to immigrate and settle in Israel. If he does not do this, he uses the name Zionist in vain. However, today there are many communities in the Diaspora that have representatives of the Zionist movement. They do not invest their time and energy in actualizing Zionist aspirations. They have many conferences and meetings, and the only things they accomplish are the empty words they speak at these gatherings.

Fundraising Campaigns Instead of the Realization of Judaism

The Zionism of these activists is merely philanthropic. It demands of them shallow commitment. Fundraising campaigns in the Diaspora, donating money and asking for donations, has taken the place of the Zionist movement. Who remembers the true function and meaning of Zionism? Today Zionism is willing to be satisfied with so little. Zionists erroneously attempt to make the Zionist movement as large as Judaism. But the opposite is the case. They merely succeed in putting Zionism into a charity box, with the words, "Fundraising Campaign," stamped on its face. According to Zionism the world is based of three foundations: Money, money, and money! The fundraising campaign silences the Jewish and Zionist conscience. It is as though he is saying to himself: I have fulfilled my obligation and done my part for the Jewish people and the State of Israel. Basically what he is saying is: "This donation is in place of me. (I am not going to Israel, but the money is.) Because of this donation I can now live a good, long, and peaceful life in the Diaspora.

To realize Zionism means to immigrate to Israel and to leave the Diaspora behind. For this kind of Zionism, the Jews that reside in the Diaspora are not ready, and the processes of assimilation grow every day. Before the establishment of State of Israel, the anticipation of the redemption united and excited Jewry. These shared yearnings with even those who left the world of Torah observance. Now that the yearnings of generations have become fulfilled, and there is the State of Israel, emptiness is tearing the nation apart.

Judaism of the Past and Present

The same is also true about Judaism. Tragically, traditional Judaism occupies little space and time in the lives of most Diaspora Jews. Long ago, Jews received their education according to the Torah and heritage of their ancestors. They experienced learning the discussions between Abaye and Rava, which formed the way they thought and reasoned. They had one criterion for judging things: Is it forbidden, or permitted? Is it kosher or non-kosher? Is it bad, or good? They reasoned according to the Torah and lived their lives according Torah traditions. In the past, the roots of Jews in the Diaspora were rooted in Judaism. It formed the character of the Jewish people, and it enriched their national ideals and values.

Faithful and sincere Jews struggled and persevered with great difficulties. Six days of the week were filled with very hard work and worries just to provide the bare necessities of food, even bread. But when Shabbat arrived, they returned to themselves. On Shabbat there was no work, toil and effort. This was a day of rest, sanctity, tranquility and peace of mind. The unity of the Jewish family manifested itself around the Shabbat table through songs, prayers, and words of Torah recited at the meal. Shabbat and the Festivals were dedicated to family life and education of the children. Jewish life was something you could clearly see. Each member of the household had an active part in it. In the Jewish home, Shabbat enabled the "special additional soul" to be felt and perceived. The family enjoyed the "radiance of the Divine presence." For many generations, the Jewish family, it laws and ways of life were an example of respect and honor between parents and children, and husband and wife.

The Jewish Holidays and Festivals
The Jewish calendar is sown with Holidays, Festivals, and monthly and annual celebrations, which are rich with content and meaning. There are *Yamim Tovim*, and *Yamim Nora'im*, which are known for their beauty and sanctity. Some of these days are celebrated with great joy and happiness, and others are for soul searching and correcting one's behavior. These days rescue a Jew from boredom and emptiness, and from falling into alcohol, drugs and crime. When Jewish Holidays and Festivals are observed according to the Halacha, they have the power to enable one to educate his children. He can connect them to their forefathers through the threads of the Hebrew soul with which our spiritual and national life were spun and woven.

Shabbat is Not a Holy Day, and a Holiday is not a *Yom Tov*
Shabbat has a major role in family life and educating children. When the family feasts together, singing pleasant and happy melodies, everyone becomes closer. The joyous atmosphere leaves a lasting impression on the children. Most families in the Diaspora have become alienated from any religious ritual and worship, which could have served as a source of Jewish education. The Jewish child is denied the holiness of a religious home. He is denied the inspiration of the Holidays which preserve the memory of the Jewish nation's spiritual and national history. Nature does not like vacuum, and likewise, human society does not like the life without meaning. A young person feels that his home is empty, and is not able to endow him with spiritual nourishment or anything that can satisfy his soul. He finds it filled with materialism. He seeks nourishment in other people's religions and they receive him with open arms. It is therefore only natural that young people in the Diaspora abandon their religion and nation.

In light of this, one remembers a very tragic incident that occurred during the Spanish Inquisition. During the turmoil of the inquisition a mother lost her child. Terrified, she almost lost her mind, from anguish and grief. The voice of her cry shattered hearts. Suddenly, it became known that the child died a natural death, while everyone was trying to flee. The beadle of the community brought the child to burial quickly. This reached the mother's ears. Seemingly, this tragic rumor should have made her lose her mind and become despondent. On the contrary, this horrible rumor calmed her spirit, and she inwardly accepted the tragedy. Innocently, like her ancestors during the Bar Kokhba massacre, she said the blessing, "He is good and He does well," she was comforted that her child was brought to a

Jewish burial and did not fall into the hands of the priests of the inquisition. Otherwise, God forbid, he would have been raised as a non-Jew.

For generations Jews suffered in this cursed exile from oppression, humiliation, slaughter and banishment. But they knew how to live as Jews, and how to die as Jews. They knew how to recover from suffering, and find solace in the midst of mourning. They were able to rejoice when they should have been sad, and hope when in a sea of despair. They preserved their belief in the coming of the Messiah. Even death did not rule over them.

Intermarriage in the Past and the Present
In the old world, in Poland and Lithuania, and similarly in Russia before Communist rule, parents would sit on the ground and mourn for seven days when their child intermarried. This strong reaction against intermarriage by parents, and by the Jewish community, served as a severe warning to youth not to mingle with Gentiles. Today, most parents have reconciled themselves with this plague. A survey held in America revealed that when parents were asked: What would their response be if their child married a Gentile? They answered that they would relate to it with understanding. In other words, they would consent to it.

The Sages taught that assimilation is the fruit of the weak and the oppressed. This was caused by the culture and status of the strong nation that ruled over them. Our ancestors, who adhered to their faith and guarded the Torah, were not wounded in any way by this self-deprecation. On the contrary, they had an inner independent faith and a feeling of superiority of being a Torah nation. They suffered from the Gentiles and were persecuted by them. Even though they suffered physically, they did not suffer spiritually or morally. Indeed, every morning they uttered the blessing, "that You did not make me a Gentile." It is generally accepted that people do not marry someone who is of a lower status than them. Someone from the aristocracy will not enter into marriage with someone who is a common person. A faithful Jew, who observed Torah and mitzvoth with love and self-sacrifice, saw being Jewish as fulfilling a prophetic and historic mission. Sincere faith and messianic hope gave the believing Jew a sense of religious and moral superiority. He looked upon Gentiles with contempt, and even with pity, as though they were creatures sinking in idolatry and sin. The Gentiles' hatred and cruelty influenced Jews not to join them and waste away spiritually and morally by intermarrying. The religious Jew saw assimilation and intermarriage as degenerating spiritually and morally, in addition to being an act of betrayal. A proud man does not like to fall. What! He is marrying a Gentile? That cannot be!

On the other hand, the modern Jew has lost all of his elevated traits. As a result of this, his identity and the foundations of his life have been shaken. He has no national pride and spiritual strength. He sees his Gentile friends as superior to him. He longs to be equal to them, and he does not consider intermarrying with them as a decadent act. Rather, on the contrary, he is fulfilling his dreams.

The Collapse of the Foundations of Jewish Life and Existence

All the strong foundations that were mentioned above constituted a source of strength for Jews to persevere even in the Diaspora. Now these foundations are eroding and collapsing. Moreover, East European Jewry provided world Jewry with its spiritual wealth and traditions. And thanks to her they could maintain a Jewish existence. The holocaust destroyed the source for growth and existence of world Jewry. Jewry in the Diaspora is advancing with giant strides towards further disconnecting itself from Jewish religion and culture. It is tightening its connection to non-Jewish culture and Christian values.

Assimilation is taking place quietly. It is happening without its victims knowing it. Therefore it is difficult to fight it. Everything seems to be fine in the Diaspora community's institutions. There are large synagogues, fancy clubs, nice old age homes, kindergartens, and Hebrew day schools. The Jewish community, in general, is not afraid of unseen dangers. These dangers threaten more today than in any other time in our history. In nature, a group of people, like a lone individual, can only exist for a limited period of time without enough nourishment. On the surface it seems that everything is fine. However, gradually he will collapse and never rise again. Diaspora Jews, the majority of whom are undernourished in terms of Judaism and spirituality, will not be able to exist for long. They also have nothing with which to nourish their children. The children wander far to seek spiritual and cultural nourishment in the fields of strangers.

The Holocaust, the Revival of Israel, and Jewish Identity

In general, either a national victory, or a threatening crisis, awakens and strengthens one's national identity. This is particularly true for youth, who are easily enthused and excited. In the last generation, there were two major national events that brought about important changes. Our people were shocked to their feet when they saw the murder of a third of their people, six million Jews. The Holocaust should have boiled the blood of every Jew. It should have awakened and shocked Jewish youth everywhere, and brought them to a new awareness of Judaism.

On the other hand, there has never been such a nation in world history: A people, wandering in the desert of nations for two thousand years, mercilessly oppressed and persecuted, has now returned to its homeland! It has been a great miracle of God that He has done for the Jewish people! Like in the days of Joshua Ben Nun, and the Chashmonaim War, Jewish youth went to fight a war of "a few against the many". The Six Day War surprised military strategists worldwide. With great decisiveness and alacrity the Jewish people were victorious. They brought freedom to the Jewish people in the land of their ancestors.

The horrible and catastrophic holocaust, and the revival of Israel against the background of its amazing struggles and glorious victories, did not influence the Diaspora Jews to cling to their heritage and people. If these two major historic events were not able to have any influence on its youth, their national future as a people is very slim. It is apparent their vision is blocked and that they are not able to see these major historical events as crucial and decisive moments in the life of the Jewish people. These events should have caused a spiritual revolution and breathed a new spirit of life into the nation.

Education – There is No Magic Wand

The Sages correctly said that, "no one is wise as one who is experienced." The main cause that motivated me in 1968 to accept the invitation to be Rabbi of the Central Synagogue of Sydney, Australia. I discovered that I should devote myself to Jewish education. During a lecture tour in Australia I found a neglected Jewish education system. Except in Melbourne, only five percent of the Jewish children learned in Jewish day schools, and mixed marriages were ten percent. I felt that a network of religious day schools would help prevent assimilation and mixed marriages. These schools would produce students loyal to their ancestor's heritage and to their nation. This is what I honestly hoped for, and devoted my efforts to. By virtue of my being head of the education department of the local Zionist Federation we carried out a comprehensive plan. We held meetings for community leaders, spoke at synagogues, and published articles in local Jewish newspapers. All of this was done in order to influence our brethren to establish religious Jewish day schools in Jewish population centers of Australia. And so it came to be.

With God's help, after a few years, more than sixty percent of Australian Jewish children attended Jewish day schools. Isn't this a big accomplishment? However, to our great sorrow, we still do not see the vast majority of youth in synagogues or participating in cultural and Jewish national events. By 1985, mixed marriages doubled, reaching twenty percent. Today intermarriage is forty percent. Jewish schools are not magic wands. There is a limit to what they can do. It is very doubtful that the school can solve the problems of assimilation.

Three Factors in Educating Youth

Certainly we must advance Jewish education in the Diaspora. However, we cannot view Jewish education as the only answer to the problem of assimilation. School education is not the only source of assimilation of Jewish youth. There are three factors which help form the spiritual, patriotic and moral character of a young person: The home, the school and the street namely the environment. Education is not limited to the walls of the school.

The home and the street are the most responsible for influencing his character, behavior, and loyalty to his people. It is there that he absorbs customs, lifestyle, behavior, and opinions. Schools succeed when they are supported by the rest of the child's experience of the world. Namely the home and the environment.

The Jewish Home

Talmud Torahs and Jewish day schools cannot be the only source for providing Jewish education. The heart of Judaism – the Jewish home – is the secret for transmitting the Jewish tradition from one generation to the next. Throughout the history of civilization the family has always been the main source for educating the young. As we mentioned above, most Jewish homes in the Diaspora do not observe Jewish tradition. They are lacking Torah and Jewish culture, and are not a means for transmitting the Jewish tradition to their children. On the contrary, they are a negative influence. How can a student in a Hebrew school absorb values that have no practical application or relevance in everyday life? How can he not be influenced by the customs and values of his Christian surroundings?

The relationship between Jewish schools and the home is painful and tense. Neither of them acknowledges each other, or, they are always battling each other. The children end up being victims of this conflict. They learn about observing Shabbat and the Festivals, prayer, the laws of kashrus, and other mitzvoth. However, the child, who is sensitive and clever, sees that his parents do not observe what is sacred and pure to his people. The contradiction between the home and the school destroys the faith of the younger generation in their parents and teachers. The Sages stressed this in the following statement (*Brachot* 7): "Evil culture in one's home is more difficult than the war of Gog and Magog."

Jewish Religious Environment

In addition to the Jewish school and the religious home, it is also essential that there be a Jewish atmosphere that has a traditional religious environment. Such an environment does not exist in the Diaspora. The whole atmosphere of life in the Diaspora does not allow the observance of Shabbat and the Festivals to fully reflect the spirit of the Halacha. Even if an individual benefits from human freedom, the surrounding environment depresses the Jewish soul and disturbs the national personality.

It is a natural development that the lifestyle of Jewish youth in the Diaspora is similar to that of their non-Jewish neighbors. They speak the same language. The Jews dresses like them, study in the same universities, and work in the same profession or business. They like the same sports and forms of entertainment, and they participate in the national and civic events. Jewish youth eat their foods and drink their wines, and their thought processes are in a foreign language, not in Hebrew. How can they not assimilate? They have no ability to contend with the power of their surroundings. As Jews they are empty, weak, and meager vessels. The strength of the non-Jewish environment to attract and influence them is so great, that their Jewish identity dissipates and its strength wanes, without any intention or effort. The Diaspora, knowingly or unconsciously, fills them with foreign and alien influences, which disfigure their Jewish presence and crush their souls.

What Can be Learnt from Australian Jewry

The importance of the three basic factors in educating Jewish youth – the home, the school, and the surrounding environment – become stronger in light of the percentage of mixed marriages in different centers of Australian Jewry. Sydney and Melbourne are the two largest cities, where most Australian Jews live. Sydney, like Melbourne, has around fifty-thousand Jews. However, whereas mixed marriages in Sydney have reached forty percent, in Melbourne they are only thirteen percent. The large difference is because the Jewish community in Melbourne is a more religious community that of Sydney. Parts of the community are even ultra-orthodox. The Melbourne community succeeded in establishing yeshivas for younger and older students, and even Kollels. A large number of the Melbourne community observes Torah and mitzvoth. They live in the same neighborhood and comprise the majority of the residents of the neighborhood. Most mixed marriages in Melbourne occur in neighborhoods where Jews comprise a small minority, or where the majority do not observe Torah and mitzvoth.

Although the Jewish communities in Sydney and Melbourne are in the same country, they are distant spiritually. In the Sydney community, as in the larger communities, there is a plague of intermarrying. The loyal Melbourne community, however, is known for guarding its youth against mixed marriages. This is because they benefit from the three basic factors in educating youth: Torah education, a religious home, and a religious environment in the community.

The above delightful illustration about the Melbourne community was done about a decade ago, before the eve of publication of the first edition of this book. But since then, things unfortunately, deteriorated. The intermarriage rate has doubled to 25%. It demonstrates that whatever you may do, Diaspora will continue to consume our young. "Escape for thy life lest thou be consumed" (Genesis 19:17).

The Exile is Temporary

In general, the first generation of immigrants from Eastern Europe had strong religious faith and brought a wealth of Judaism with them. However, with the passage of time, the second generation became accustomed to the surrounding Christian environment and the whole foundation of Jewish life began to crack and fall apart. It is difficult to swim against the current and against the social pressures of the general Christian society that expects you to appear and behave like everyone else. The third generation was prepared to assimilate.

Of the six million Jews that were in America after the Second World War, four million came from Eastern Europe. The majority observed Torah and Mitzvoth, or at least, came from religious homes and received a traditional education. Where are they today? The vast majority of their descendents are in the process of assimilating. This is a natural process that happens to peoples living in exile. The first generations are still somewhat connected to their homeland, but eventually they assimilate. The way of assimilation is that people mix and merge into the surrounding society without intention or effort. Nationalities that live together naturally influence each other. A new social reality is created.

Know Whence You have Come!

When I would visit a Jewish home in Sydney or Melbourne, sometimes I would notice a picture on the wall of "a person from the old world". There was a portrait of a face with elegant characteristics, a grown beard and long peyos on each side of his face. He wore a black kippah, and a silk kapotah as an overcoat. His wide-open eyes, broad forehead, and radiant appearance conveyed the splendor and beauty of a Torah observing Jew. And next to him in the picture was a pious and God-fearing woman, with a scarf covering all of her hair. In her hands she held the book, "*Tze'inah Ur'enah.*" She had the appearance of being a modest and kind woman, and yet she had the presence of being the pillar of the household. She was a *Yiddisher Mama*, in the fullest sense of the word. Afterwards, my host surprised me by telling me that, "these are my parents, my mother and father, of blessed memory." I thought to myself: These were your parents? It's hard to believe! The way I know you and your lifestyle, I would have never guessed they were your parents. There is no resemblance between them, you and your children. If your mother and father were alive, they would not recognize you. They would feel like strangers in your home and would not allow themselves to eat your food. If I would reveal to my host what I was thinking, he would most likely answer me: Today we live in modern society. I would have responded: I know this, yet I also know that it is absurd and self-annihilating to live as though life just began now, without having had parents and a glorious past. Only orphans do not have parents. Only strangers do not have a past. Empty people do not know where they come from and where they are going. Only those deeply rooted in their heritage can continue succeed in the future.

A Self-Made Holocaust

These Jews were certainly not heretics, God forbid. They were not intentional transgressors, but rather mistaken Jews. They don't intentionally allow their Judaism to dissipate, not at all! The exile, the gentile environment, the physical and social conditions all directly and indirectly influence Jewish life and their children's education. These factors, like magnets, draw Jews to imitate their gentile surroundings and to blur their Jewish identity. These factors assimilate them into the gentile population and culture. The result is that assimilation and intermarriage occur in the proportions of a holocaust, but this time it is a self-made holocaust.

The Exile's Curse

With great sorrow I witnessed the stress of my congregants during the years that I served as the Rabbi of the Sydney Central Synagogue. Occasionally a worried member of the community would approach me: "Rabbi, please help with a problem I have. My daughter is dating a non-Jew. Please talk to her. Maybe she will listen to you." Or: "My son is about to get engaged to a non-Jewess. Please explain to him about the pain and humiliation that he is causing his parents." I am sorry, my brother and friend, it's too late! However, we still try to talk to the hearts of these young people, in order to appease the futile hopes of the distressed parents. Experience proves that when the relationship between young people reaches this intimate stage, it is difficult for a third party to separate them. For the Bible says, you reap what you sow, and, this is also a law of nature. The less you observe Judaism, the more you have increased the chances of a Gentile taking your son or daughter away. When Judaism's influence is weak, Jews are willing to imitate Gentile's lifestyle to the point of assimilation.

Truthfully, these tragedies also occur to young men and women from religious homes, however, in fewer numbers. In the Diaspora, no Jew has any real security. When the plague of assimilation spreads, first and foremost, it strikes the sick and the weak. It can also strike the healthy, especially those that lack spiritual immunity.

The People and Its Land

"And the Lord said to Abraham: Go forth from your native land and from your father's house to the land that I will show you. I will make of you a great nation, and I will bless you. I will make your name great, and you shall be a blessing" (Genesis 12:1–2). Seemingly, it is difficult to understand this passage. God reveals himself to Abraham, and the first thing He says to him is: You, leave!

Let's consider the following: When God reveals Himself to the Children of Israel at Mount Sinai, He revealed Himself in the following words: "I am the Lord your God who brought you out of the land of Egypt, the house of bondage" (Exodus 20:2). In similar language, God could have revealed Himself to Abraham, saying: I am the Lord your God who has created heaven and earth and all the hosts. Or, when God reveals Himself to Moses at the burning bush, He declared: "I am the God of your fathers, the God of

Abraham, the God of Isaac, and the God of Jacob" (Exodus 3:6). It would have been more appropriate to reveal Himself to Abraham in similar language: I am the God of your father Adam, the God of Noah and his sons, and not merely, "You, leave!"

According to the intention of God's first command to Abraham, it becomes clear that the purpose was to found the Jewish nation through Abraham. To realize this goal, the first and foremost condition was that the founding father of the nation leaves his native land, and acquires a particular land for his descendents, the Land of Canaan. For a people to exist and develop it needs its own homeland, like a human being needs his own home.

The Nations' Ways of Life

For the benefit of mankind, the Creator established that each people should have its own land. He created the world in such a way that there is connection between the soul of a man and the territory he dwells in. This is a connection of strong emotion, self-sacrifice, and a covenant of life and death. Indeed, humanity has shown throughout history that there is nothing more elevated and holy than defending one's homeland. Millions have sacrificed their lives for this.

Natural Territorial Instinct

Territorial instinct is a natural instinct that both man and animals are born with. All birds build nests to lay their eggs and raise their young. Every animal takes over a certain space of land and marks its boundaries. He will stay within his boundaries and not go out to exile. There he will give birth to his young and raise them. He will defend his territory and fight fiercely to defend it against intruders. An animal that has left its territory and family to wander in a foreign land will not exist for a long time. Sooner, or later, it will fall prey to an animal, or to the forces of nature. How much more so regarding the Jewish people, when they ignore the laws of nature, and dwell among alien peoples. Human beings are not only material beings, but also spiritual ones. Therefore, they are more susceptible to being wounded, not only by their physical surrounding, but also by the spiritual, cultural, and social environment around them. They are surrounded by a world full of contradictions and foreign influences, which wound them.

The Exile is a Deviation From the Natural World Order

The Torah scholar and thinker, Maharal of Prague, wrote in his book, *Netzach Yisrael* (Chapter 1) that nature – made by the Creator – is the powerful superior force, and it can overcome anything that stands in its way. If something is no longer in its natural setting, it is obviously outside of its correct location or place. It cannot exist in a place that is not its natural setting. Nature will not let anything be an obstacle to where something inherently should be. Even if there is interference, it is temporary. Indeed, with the passage of time, nature will overpower the interference, and things will return to their right location or function.

There is no doubt that nations dwell in their lands because of laws of nature. It is natural that a person is proud of his nationality and enjoys how his country's culture and that the economy is flourishing. Contrary to this, the exile is a departure from the natural order of the world, and against the laws of nature. Hence it cannot last for long.

Assimilation is the Nature of Exile

Assimilation is a natural process of the exile. The Diaspora experience, because of its nature and essence, is fundamentally interrelated to assimilation and intermarriage. The Creator of the world determined where each nation belongs, and within this plan dedicated for the Jewish people the Land of Israel as their eternal homeland. In light of this, to be exiled from the place where you are meant to be, is a departure from the laws of nature. The atmosphere and context of life in the Diaspora, in which Shabbat, the Festivals, religious daily life and education take place, is alien and prevents a Jew from having a total Jewish experience. Whoever refuses to live according to the rules of nature, will fall prey to their forces. Sooner or later, nature will overpower him and cast him aside. The laws of nature do not allow someone who ignores them to exist for a long time.

These are the laws of exile, their curses and punishments. If the place of exile is an evil one, it will end like the physical Holocaust in Europe. If it is a pleasant one, it will end through a spiritual and national holocaust of assimilation and intermarriage, as in America and Europe, in Russia and France. There is no way to avoid the forces of nature: A people without its own land ends in Auschwitz.

The Most Critical Sin

We find in the Torah that the Children of Israel were forgiven for all the severe sins they committed. The Golden Calf was a grave sin, and nevertheless, they were forgiven. They sinned when they complained in the desert, craved meat, and joined the Korach's controversy. Nevertheless, they were forgiven. Only regarding the sin of the spies, when they spoke against the Promised Land, they were not forgiven. Their judgment was: "Your carcasses will fall in the wilderness." Since they resented the land of their fathers, they themselves passed their own judgment to be annihilated in the wilderness of nations.

The Land Determines the Destiny of Its People

Therefore, the most decisive and critical test for Avraham and for his offspring was certainly the first of the ten tests: "go forth…to the land." It would have been impossible without it for the Jewish people to fulfill its destiny to develop and exist as a nation. Exile is an unnatural and negative phenomenon, and its end is doomed. Having a land is the foundation that enables a people to develop and grow and provides the basis for an independent nation. *Rashi* certainly stressed this point: "You, go forth, for your pleasure and welfare, and there I will make you a great nation. Here, you will not have any offspring." Outside of the Land of Israel your descendents will not remain yours, but will assimilate into other nations. A People without a homeland has no right to exist. This is a law of nature and a law of the Torah.

What did God demand of Abraham in their first meeting? That he leave the things that he was most dedicated to: birthplace, family, and possessions. Ur Kasdim, the birthplace of Abraham, was a magnificent metropolis, and the capital of the Kingdom of Sumer and Akkad. The city had large and magnificent buildings, with a relaxed and pleasant life. Abraham left for Haran, and from there he went to the Land of Canaan. "And there, was a famine" (Genesis 12:10). The Sages in Midrash Tanhuma, said: "There was never a famine like this in the world." Abraham left the exile, an affluent and tranquil place, and wandered to a land stricken with famine. But it was his land, a present God gave to him and to his descendents: "Go forth…to the land." The mitzvah of settling the Land of Israel is an all encompassing commandment. In God's eyes, it is not only equivalent to all the mitzvoth of the Torah, but was also the first mitzvah that He commanded to the first Jew, Abraham. There is no safe refuge for the Jewish people and Torah of Israel except in the Land of Israel.

It is important to point out that in spite of all the persecutions, pogroms, and the Holocaust, if the Jewish people had not assimilated during the exile, we could have become a population of more than two hundred million souls. Only those Jews who faithfully and zealously observed Torah and mitzvoth, and who maintained complete faith throughout the exile remained among the Jewish people.

Diaspora is Jewry's Graveyard

Historians have estimated that during the Second Jewish commonwealth there were six million Jews in the Land of Israel and in the countries which were under the Roman Empire. All of them descendants of the Kingdom of Judah. Historians have also estimated that during the same period of time, there were twenty four million Chinese. Today the Chinese number well a milliard people.

Two thousand years ago the Jews numbered a quarter of the number of Chinese. Let us assume that tens of millions of Jews were lost in pogroms, inquisitions, and in the holocaust. Today, we should still number over two hundred million souls, while we barely number thirteen million?

Evidently in all the counties of exile and throughout the generations we lost in intermarriage and assimilation those two hundred million Jews. And then where are the descendants of the Ten Tribes of Israel, who numbered five times as many as those of the Kingdom of Judea, consisting only of two tribes? Evidently, they were assimilated and absorbed by the nations in whose countries they were exiled, informed us the Talmud (Shabbat 147).

Indeed, Diaspora is Jewry's Graveyard!

Informative Facts

I cannot end the chapter without citing a number of informative facts about my family. Between 1881–1914, 2,400,000 Jews emigrated from Eastern Europe to Western countries. The vast majority went to America, without any hesitation or doubt from any authority or camp. During the first years of this period, my grandfather's two brothers left Odessa, Ukraine. One went to America, and the other to Brazil. They adapted to the new country, and tried to persuade my grandfather to leave and also come to America. However, my grandfather, who was a scholar and God-fearing, decided to immigrate with his family to Eretz Israel, and establish his future there. His relatives and friends tried to dissuade him not to carry out this critical step. They said to him: "Look, you are a bright and sensible Jew. If you have already made the decision to leave your relatives, friends and community, you should go to America, the land of plenty and prosperity. However, don't go to Eretz Israel, which is barren and poor, a land full of swamps and diseases." Indeed, it turned out that because he was firm about his decision to go to Eretz Israel, he was truly a "wise and sensible Jew," just as his family and friends said about him.

In 1897, Rabbi Shmuel Kemelman z'l, left Odessa with his wife, three sons and two daughters, and immigrated to the Holy Land. Among those he left behind were two married sisters and their families. The trip to Eretz Israel was long, difficult, and exhausting. Living conditions in Eretz Israel were difficult and meager. His work barely provided means to support his family. He labored with one hand, and studied Torah with the other. He was grateful that he merited living in Zion. His lips always expressed gratitude to God that he merited to work the earth of the Holy Land, which he saw as a sacred mission.

More than a century has passed since my grandfather and his family arrived in the Holy Land. His two brothers, like him, came from orthodox homes, studied in yeshiva, and observed Torah and mitzvoth, before leaving Odessa. Yet all the descendants of his brothers, those in America and in Brazil, disappeared and assimilated. His two sisters' descendants who remained in the Ukraine perished either in Babi Yar, or in the concentration camps. My grandfather, who immigrated to the Land of Israel, was viewed by his friends and relatives as a fool. In spite of this, he was blessed to father over two hundred descendents in Israel, grand and great-grand children. Some of them are already the sixth generation, may they continue to multiply. Most of them live in Israel, where they have established homes faithful to Torah and the Jewish people.

The Diaspora Devours its Jewish Inhabitants

Every exile is doomed to annihilation, physically or spiritually. Jews may be annihilated as the Nazis and their helpers did. Alternatively, they may die from the kiss of death, through assimilation and intermarriage, as customary in the Diaspora today. Whoever allows himself to believe that Jews can survive in the Diaspora as well as they can in Israel, is bitterly wrong. His illusion will be at his children's expense. Exile is an unnatural phenomenon. For a nation to thrive and develop it needs a homeland and environment of its own. The Diaspora is a temporary abode which devours its Jewish residents.

The Solution is to Return to Zion

Contrary to this, the State of Israel is a positive phenomenon. It is a natural place to continue the chain of Jewish generations. The land was promised to Abraham and his descendents; it is only there that the Jewish people will find its permanent continuation. Jews and Judaism have no other solution other than returning to Zion. This is the only remedy to the malady of exile. Israel is the only land in the world where people are considered *aliyah*, to "ascend" when they immigrate to it, and *yeridah*, to "descend" when they leave it. This is a special quality about the Holy Land. On one hand, anyone who immigrates to Israel absorbs the unique atmosphere that uplifts and makes one wise. He feels a strong sense of having a national home, a spiritual serenity, and an inner security that a Jew cannot experience anywhere else. On the other hand, anyone who leaves it, even if he observes Torah and mitzvoth, eventually will descend and become distant from his religion and his people.

The Torah was given to the Jewish people to be observed in the Land of Israel. This is a normal, healthy and thriving Judaism. Returning to Israel is not merely a Zionistic duty, but rather a Jewish one, to guarantee the promise and our very right to exit. For it is said (Leviticus 26:5): "And you shall dwell securely in your land." The Sages stressed in *Torat Kohanim*: "In your land you will dwell securely, and you will not dwell securely outside of it." The State of Israel is not only the solution to the redemption of the Jewish body, but also to the Jewish spirit and soul.

The State of Israel is the only country in which a total Jewish experience exists. It is the country where Judaism belongs to the public domain. Israel is the sole place where Judaism is addressed to the eye, where the Shabbat and the Jewish festivals are parts of the calendar and where Hebrew is the language of everyday life.

CHAPTER EIGHT

HAVE WE LEARNED OUR LESSONS
FROM THE HOLOCAUST?

THE JEWISH PEOPLE's history has been overflowed with suffering and tribulations, persecution and expulsions, pogroms and inquisitions. However, we have never known any phenomenon as threatening and terrifying as the German's "final solution." Never in world history, has such a terrifying slaughter and destruction been so cruelly, satanically, and deviously perpetrated to burn an entire nation and send it up in smoke. These were cold blooded murderers: who built gas chambers and ovens to burn millions of people; who slaughtered men, women and children like flies; and transported their ashes to fertilize their fields; or who used their victims flesh to make bath soap. Humanity has never seen these kinds of monsters.

Although sixty years have passed since the concentration camps were liberated our wounds have still not healed. Then the truth was revealed about the German oppressors' terrible and shocking behavior: their annihilating one third of the Jewish People. We see these pictures over and over again, passing before our eyes.

A Terrifying Sight
Sometimes, in the darkness of night, I lay on my bed, rolling from side to side in throes of sleeplessness. I see in my minds eye a terrifying and shocking sight. This gloomy nightmare of tremendously dark fear awakens awful feelings and revulsion. The entire scroll of suffering and torments, all of the physical and emotional suffering caused by the evil perpetrated on European Jewry, the destruction of an entire oppressed and tortured nation, physical starvation, and physical and emotional torture through sickness and plagues, pass before my eyes. I see the humiliations and the nightmares that the Nazi monsters, in their unspeakable evil, inflicted on their victims, day and night, before murdering them. Historians refer to the systematic and methodological murder of our beloved fellow Jews as the "death culture." The German nation, that highly cultured "Aryan race", committed these monstrosities for their own sadistic pleasure.

I see in my minds' eye terrifying parades of thousands upon thousands. They are a mass funeral on their way into the depths of the earth. Men and women, grey headed mature people together with young children, march with bowed heads, as if they were accompanying themselves to the grave. They walk quietly and calmly, a parade of sheep on their way to eternity. I see trains with many boxcars, overflowing with thousands of Jews. They are galloping to the hellish concentration camps which sprouted from the earth. There the Germans quickly unload their Jewish cargo. With whippings and gun butts, they push the Jews towards the "shower" rooms, along the street the Germans call "Himellstrasse." Men and women, old and young, children and sucklings, were brought from every European city. These were terrible parades in which a whole nation was brought to be murdered, millions slaughtered in lightning fast massacres, the nation's sea of blood.

The process was organized and precise, according to the "superior race's" character. The Jews are corralled into gas chambers, which work around the clock, 24/7. They are packed in until there was no room for anyone else. The doors close, the gas suffocates them and the realization of what is happening drives them insane. Their murderers – cold as stone – peer through a small hatch to see what's happening inside. They stand there, enjoying the sight of the suffocating people, twitching in their death throes. These two legged horror machines are thrilled by their own destructive proficiency, while inside their victims scream and climb the walls, trying to escape, until the final twitches of death overcome them. I hear millions of Jewish souls groaning, purified by separating from their physical bodies. A trapped people walk astounded and are burned in the central European ovens, in the "Enlightened nation's" monstrous death industry.

The Prolific European Jewry was Destroyed

Six million people were annihilated, women, children, our people's old and young, spiritual giants, mighty Torah scholars, the righteous, the kind, the philanthropists, the wise men, them, their students, and their children. The populous European Jewry was destroyed, together with its tens of thousands of beautiful synagogues. These mighty and numerous buildings were dedicated to Torah and culture, to kindness and charity. These major centers of Judaism, whose teachings were disseminated throughout the Diaspora, were utterly destroyed.

The Divine Presence rested in each and every city and town that was destroyed. The large cities were roaring and the villages were noisy. Life surged through the holy Jewish People, a People of pure faith. The people bubbled with life, strength, and courage. Synagogues were filled beyond capacity and overflowed, morning and evening. In the *Bate Midrashim* (study halls) they drank the holiness of life from the wellsprings of salvation. This holiness accompanied them when "they went along the way" and when they rested at home, when they went out and when they came in. They did not forget spirituality, the eternal spiritual connection with their master. The holy ones finished their lives with the song of pure life, "Shema Yisroel" [Hear O Israel].

There were thirty thousand Jewish communities, including large, ancient and vigorous communities. These communities served as spiritual wellsprings and sources of inspiration, ensuring the vitality and continuation of the nation. They were destroyed and wiped off the face of the earth. A whole nation went up in smoke and was turned to ashes!

We have not yet found a second Jeremiah who could express the lamentations for European Jewry. Who could write the scroll of hellish sufferings and tribulations which even Satan could not imagine? Where is the poet who could express at least one thousandth of the national tragedy which has smitten us? Who is the lyricist who could capture the anguish and shame which burn in our hearts for Jews who went on those shameful marches to their eternal rest, and for those refined Jewish girls who shrieked in terrible suffering while the Nazi marauders defiled them and then snuffed out their lives? The piercing lamentation has not yet been written that could recount the moaning of this unfortunate mother whose infant was wretched from her breast and thrown into the burning furnace before her very eyes.

The National and Spiritual Last Will and Testament
The special importance of remembering the holocaust, over and above the fact that many people around the world deny it, is to learn lessons from it. The holocaust taught us, first and foremost, that the attempt to be a nation, or even an independent community, without our own country, ends in Auschwitz. It also taught us that "The mercy of the nations is transgression" and therefore not to rely on strangers for our security.

The silent cry of the holocaust is that the existence of the Jewish People as a nation in exile has ended, and the time has arrived to serve the exile with a writ of divorce. Through their deaths, the holy and pure Jewish departed souls have ordered us to rise to the challenge of eternal life.

The Crimes of the Nations Against Us
The Jews were tortured and murdered not only by the German Nazis, but also by their accomplices: the Ukrainians, the Lithuanians, the Latvians, the Pollacks, the Russians, the Hungarians, the Czechs, and others. They all banded together to slaughter, to murder, to steal from, to rob from, to torture and to destroy sucklings. Even the French, an enlightened people in terms of championing the rights of man, a symbol of freedom and equality, handed the Jews under their sovereignty to Nazi executioners. Without the French Police's help and the Vichy Government's cooperation, the Germans could not have succeeded to round up and transport the Jews to concentration camps. The Vichy government, headed by Marshall Pettin, worked with excessive enthusiasm to organize traps to capture Jews. They gathered them to camps to be shipped eastwards to destruction. Seventy six thousand French Jews were sent to the death camps and only two thousand

five hundred returned. The French police gathered thousands of Jewish children without parents and sent them on special trains to their deaths.

The German Asmodeus (the king of demons, according to Jewish sources) was not an isolated phenomenon, but rather the accumulation of the all of the nations' hatred combined. The outburst reflected the loathing that has been stored up over hundreds of years. The Vatican knew everything and was silent. The "holy father" did not raise his voice against the genocide of the Jews. The various Christian sects saw everything and didn't move themselves one iota to help. Their silence and ignoring the horror stemmed both from the weakness of their imperviousness to a whole nation being destroyed, and also from their unspoken consent. They felt joy that the end of the Jewish People had come, and the world would be free from them. The Vatican, as the head of the entire Catholic Church, had preached hatred of the Jews throughout all of its history and prepared the [emotional] climate conducive to destroying Jews. The Vatican saw the holocaust as the punishment for crucifying the Christian God, and as releasing the world from the "sinners," from the Jews.

The Entire World Knew and Stood Aloof

The enlightened nations knew that European Jewry was being led to the gallows. They closed their eyes and ears and played dumb and mute. They did not lift a finger while the smoke from the Nazi Asmodeus's furnaces spewed darkness over Europe. The Jewish world's leaders demanded that the allied superpowers warn the Nazis to refrain from their criminal activities and mass murders of Jews, for after the war they will face punishment. Nevertheless, they ignored it as if they didn't see or hear anything. Even more so, they closed their borders to the pitiful refugees, and did not try to save their lives. These miserable acts proved that the allies ignored the miserable cries of the Jews subjected to tortuous deaths. The allies gave tacit permission to Hitler to murder Jews to his heart's content, to eat Jewish flesh to his stomach's content and to drink Jewish blood to satiation. Jewish Organizations begged the American and British governments to bomb the Auschwitz concentration camp: "Every day 40,000 Jews are transported from Hungary, straight to the gas chambers. Bomb the railroad tracks that bring their human cargo to the gas chambers. Bomb the gas chambers and the crematorium!" The Jewish leaders begged and pleaded before the Americans and the English. It's a world of lies, go talk to a wall. Their planes bombed targets near Auschwitz. They had enough planes to send weapons to the partisan fighters in Poland and other places. However, when it came to saving the lives of hundreds of thousands of Jews, all of the "righteous gentiles" could not find one bomb to blow up the crematorium. The United States refused to send a plane to bomb the German's murder factories, as they later did against Iraq in order to free Kuwait. "For the violence done to thy brother Jacob, shame shall cover thee, and thou shall be cut off forever. In the day that thou didst stand aloof, in the day that strangers carried away his substance, and foreigners entered into his gates…" (Obadiah 1:10–11).

Those same countries that closed their borders to the Jewish refugees opened them wide to Nazi murderers after the war. Let's say it bluntly: The "enlightened" nations are guilty of incinerating a nation, of eternal silence, of refusing to save Jews, of closing the gates before refugees fleeing for their lives, of shirking the humane obligation to bomb the gas showers and crematorium, and of relating to slaughtering Jews like exterminating ants. All of this proves the truth in the most brutal way: The Jews must take the initiative to fight their own battles, for their own land and country, to save themselves, because "If I will not be for myself, then who will be for me!" (Ethics of the Fathers 1:14)

We look into the dismal abyss. We see before our eyes the millions who were, but are no longer. This tragic site is shocking: the remaining emptiness and the silence. The world has been depleted of our brothers, our upright and pure country men – the tortured of this world. This silence terrifies our soul, preventing it from screaming in horror. The alarm and warning before the eruption of the volcano is still ringing in our ears: Dear Brothers, the lava is on its way. Wake up and choose life, run for your lives, flee to the Land of Israel!

Where Should the Remaining Refugees Go?

When the war ended and the gates of the death camps were opened, the immediate question that the survivors faced was, where do we go from here? Dr. Moshe Biasky (Mashua) recounts: "I will never forget the Russian officer who, on the morning of May 9, 1945, was the first to enter our camp. Our camp had about 1200 Jewish prisoners and this officer had come to proclaim our release. Just a few hours ago, groups of SS soldiers had withdrawn. We could still see German soldiers fleeing westward. The Russian officer gave an impassioned speech, praising the liberating Red army and their commander, Stalin. He dramatically threw the gate wide open and declared that whoever was able had permission to leave. When he turned to leave, a few prisoners accompanied him to ask about the situation in the Polish cities that he had been through. When the officer heard that all of the inmates were Jewish, he revealed that he was also Jewish and started talking in Yiddish. He was asked about the various places that he had passed through during the fighting. His singular and inclusive answer was: There are no Jews anywhere; you are the first Jews that I've met. Before he left us, the Russian Jewish officer was asked: What should we do now? Where do we go? His answer summed up the tragic situation of those who were liberated at that time. The officer said: "Don't go to the east and don't go to the west. They don't like us anywhere." He was silent and disappeared.

Anti-Semitism Remains Forever!

That officer expressed the dirty situation as he, as a Jew, saw and felt it. Ancient Jew hatred and modern anti-Semitism are found everywhere and at all times, even where only a handful of Jews survived. Nazism was not uprooted, but continues to plant its poisonous roots in many areas of the world. The neo-Nazi movement continues to grow. We also hear loud and clear the messages of hate for the Jewish People that they disseminate.

Hatred for Jews is different than other forms of racism and discrimination because it is traditional and has deeper roots. It has religious foundations, nationalistic sentiments, and economic motivations. Anti-Semitism is a deadly, infectious disease that is still incurable. The singular medicine for this disease is the return to Zion. The Holocaust's silent cry to its survivors was: go to Zion, to redemption, and to freedom.

The Jewish Partisans Officer's Commands

At the last inspection before the underground partisans disbanded: the partisans' officers commanded their Jewish soldiers in particular and also holocaust survivors in general, "Brothers in arms and destruction! I tell you it's enough! Our suffering and torments are indescribable, and our losses are uncountable. The time has come to go our own separate ways forever, and to leave this cursed exile which eats us alive. We have shouldered the nations' sins. We have sacrificed our blood and bodies in other people's wars, in foreign countries. I command you to leave here as fast as possible, go up to Zion and fight for our freedom, for our land, and for our nation's future."

On parting from his division, the Jewish partisans' officer later told the holocaust survivors. "Never again will there be another Auschwitz! We should make a different type of march, a march where Jews fight valiantly until the last man, rather than surrendering to their cursed enemies and going passively like lambs to the slaughter. We should say to the nations: Jews no longer believe you because you are deceitful liars. We no longer put our trust in your rotten humanity, which has put us through seven levels of Hell. We will no longer be the wondering Jews and the scapegoats sacrificed to *Azzazzel* by every crazy tyrant. We are disgusted with you and refuse to live among you, because of your guile and deceit. You are filled with torture and deadly suffering. Whatever happens, for better or for worse, we are going home – to Zion and to Jerusalem."

These words were spoken to spur people on, however they were also an accurate description of reality. They are true and correct. The time has finally come to leave the cursed exile which consumes us. The main question is: Did the holocaust survivors accept this and carry through with it? Did they pass this fateful and crucial test?

Father, Where is the State?

Some of the holocaust survivors answered the holocaust's silent call by immigrating to the Land of Israel. The holocaust served as yet another negative proof of the Jewish People's problem of lacking a homeland and national independence. The solution was to renew a Jewish state in the Land of Israel. A Midrash relates the following story. A father and his son were walking on a long and exhausting journey. The worn out child turned to his father and asked: Where is the state that we are trying so hard to go to? His father answered him: Son, your landmark will be a cemetery; when you see it, you will know that the longed for state will be after the cemetery and that it is near by... (Midrash Shochar Tov, Psalms 20).

Likewise, those holocaust survivors left behind a huge cemetery with millions of Jews and many of them secretly made their way to the longed for land. They made the statement: We prefer the four cubits of the holy land to the spacious grazing lands of the Diaspora. They joined the freedom fighters in the War of Independence. Together with native Palestinian Jews, they advanced from battle to battle and victory to victory, until the longed for State of Israel was established. They fulfilled the obligation that they had undertaken, that they had dreamed about in the ghettos and death camps.

They settled in Israel and raised generations loyal to their father's traditions and to their nation. Among them were learned and active rabbis, who established large yeshivas and other praiseworthy educational institutions. There were also Admorim who established exemplary neighborhoods in Israel, as living memorials to the holocaust victims.

"I Love my Master... I will Not Go Free"

To our sorrow and embarrassment, approximately half of the holocaust survivors did not pass the test. They preferred to choose other options. Some returned to their birthplaces in Europe, where fathers, mothers, brothers, and children were murdered, where their family members were incinerated. Some settled in countries which had hardheartedly closed their gates to fleeing Jewish refugees, thereby refusing to save their lives. These nations refused to bomb the gas chambers and crematorium; rather they looked on calmly while our nation burned. We would presume that these terrifying experiences and horrible visions caused permanent psychological wounds which would prevent the holocaust survivors from remaining in these cursed countries for even one day. However, this positive result was not achieved. "I will not go free," They are stuck in and cling to the exile's lifestyle and cannot break free. Future generations will certainly be amazed at the survivors' reaction in the darkest period of world history.

I am well acquainted with many holocaust survivors, some of whom settled in the U.S.A. and many who chose to live in Australia. My congregation in Sydney comprised two thousand worshipers, close to fifty percent of whom were holocaust survivors. These survivors brought a good spiritual "baggage' with them, because most of them grew up in Torah observant homes with Jewish culture and tradition. Their main goal, upon arriving in their new homeland, was to quickly settle into their new environment and to succeed financially, even if that entailed compromising Jewish values and lifestyle. They succeeded to settle into their new country and many advanced economically. However, the second and third generations paid the price for acquiring the means and sacrificing the ends. They grew up and were educated in a foreign culture and environment. They, like the majority of the Jewish youth in the Diaspora, are ready to assimilate and intermarry.

A Triple Tragedy

As mentioned above, close to fifty percent of the members of the Central Synagogue of Sydney, in which I served as Rabbi, were holocaust survivors who had wandered from one exile to another. It is very strange that the eternal "wandering Jews" did not learn even from the gas chambers of Auschwitz and Maydanek that the most secure Jewish future for their children is in the land of their Fathers. I will never forget a Shiva visit that I made to consol an elderly holocaust survivor on the loss of his wife. Most of the time tears were streaming down his eyes. From time to time he would let out a gloomy sigh of grief. Calm down, I told him, you must try to find consolation. This is the way of the world. Sooner or later, we all face the same fate. After a short pause, I asked him, did the departed leave any children? The mourner answered, Ah Rabbi, your question touches on a sore point which pains me greatly. I have two children, a son and a daughter. But really, I don't have them. You see, it was a terrible blow for my wife and me when our son got married in a Catholic church. However, with time we recovered and found consolation in our daughter. She became our source of life and hope. But when she too married a non-Jew, my wife could no longer bear the pain and mourning. She broke completely and couldn't eat or sleep. They made her life into hell. And with heavy sighs and a stream of tears and with great difficulty he continued: "In the Lodz ghetto I lost my parents. Here in Sydney, I lost my wife and children. I remain childless, lonely and solitary." Upon hearing the terrible tragedy that befell this modern day Job, I wanted to get down on the floor and sit Shiva (mourn) with this triple mourner.

The family tragedies that stuck this holocaust survivor were: his parents' murder in the terrifying and besieged Lodz ghetto, surrounded by Jew haters and killers. On the other hand, his children's intermarriage and many like them in Sydney, a city of equality and free will, is the exile's shocking and intimidating curse on us. There was a physical holocaust in the East and a national and spiritual holocaust in the west. Their common factor is Judaic destruction. The Diaspora experience is in essence a destructive decree. As it is written, "Your enemies' land will consume you." (Leviticus 26:38). Don't interpret only your enemy's land, but also your lover's land.

In the Ghettos and Concentration Camps They Longed for Zion and Nothing Else

In those dark days and nights, while they suffered the tortures of the suffocating crowded ghettos, or while they lay on hard cold boards of the concentration camp beds, freezing, hungry and thirsty, they dreamed of restarting life in the holy city of Jerusalem, or on the shores of Tel–Aviv or Haifa. Then they saw Israel as the dreamed of land, as heaven on earth. In their strong yearning, they promised themselves that if they remained alive they would settle in Zion. Their heart's only desire was to go to Israel and help rebuild it to prevent the holocaust's reoccurrence.

However, when the big day arrived and the Russian army opened the camp's gates, the Russians returned to their homeland, the Poles to their country, and of course the Belgians and the Dutch returned to their roots. However, the Jews were different; they did a one hundred and eighty degree turn. They denied their heart's dreams and yearnings. They were drawn to the fertile lands of lava which had cooled off after the holocaust's volcanic eruption. Did the Polish holocaust survivors want to leave Poland? They left Poland only after the Poles violently attacked them, killing even more Jews. The tortured survivors, the exile lovers, wandered to new countries, to again live among strangers, to again be rejected and hated. They moved, closing their eyes to the terrible dangers of assimilation and intermarriage which could destroy their hopes and their children's' future. Meanwhile, their ancient homeland was in the process of a praiseworthy and beautiful reconstruction. It called its children to return, to build and to be rebuilt themselves as members of a free and proud people.

One wonders how they forgot the return to Zion which they had yearned for in the valley of death. In addition, they don't encourage their children to make Aliyah, in spite of this writer preaching Aliyah day and night. Those who became multimillionaires don't even consider Aliyah. It is difficult to take them out from the exile and it is twice as hard to remove the exile from their personalities.

The Generation Follows its Leaders

The leaders and spokesmen of the holocaust survivors took a similar direction. We see this with Elie Wiesel in his story, *Night*. He tells about the dark days in a Nazi work camp: He and his friends would often hum tunes of songs about the Jordan River and Jerusalem's beautiful holiness. He wrote: "We often talked about Palestine. We decided that if we survived, we would not delay even one day in Europe but would take the first boat to Haifa." So stated Mr. Wiesel. However, when the time came, he did just the opposite. Eli Wiesel's biographical sketch, which appears at the end of this book, conveys the following: After the war he traveled to Paris where he obtained French citizenship. He then moved to Israel and then moved to the United States. He resides there permanently and happily obtained American citizenship.

Holocaust survivors and their authors have a home in the "New World," rather than a home in the Promised Land. The Land which Jews dreamed about for two thousand years and sacrificed their lives to reestablish. The survivors' spokesmen chose to live in the America which refused to allow three hundred Jewish refugees to land on its shores. Rather, it returned them to the European inferno. They chose the same America whose president maintained silence, and silenced the world, while European Jews were led to the crematoriums, while the gas chambers polluted European air with the blossoming souls of naive and pure children. They chose the same new homeland whose president refused to meet with the Jewish leadership who were pleading to bomb the railroad tracks to Auschwitz. Ironically, at the same time that the Jewish leaders were pleading, Eli Wiesel's family was transported on those very railroad tracks to the concentration camp. He settled in the same new homeland where the spiritual and national holocaust is proceeding at full speed. "If a flame burned the mighty cedar trees, what will the moss that grows on their trunks do" the worried rabbis asked. It becomes more and more apparent that we have learned nothing form the holocaust!!! Our Fathers inheritance is the nomads' staff and we are still clinging to it!

What is The Solution?
A young partisan who illegally immigrated to Palestine pointed out the real solution. "I ponder what to do with this gift of life that I have received. I want to go to Israel and start a family there. If there is such a thing as revenge, this is it… I shot as many Germans as I could, I killed them, I spit on their despicable faces, excuse me for saying this. However, that was not revenge; it was just anger (*Kisufim Ve Saar*, page 83, by Yitzchak Egoz). Since it's impossible to prevent overwhelming assimilation under present conditions, there is no hope for survival in the exile. The present exile, knowingly or unknowingly, emanates foreign and strange influences which make their imprints on Jewish souls, and fragments them until they disintegrate. The result is that Judaism disappears by itself, with no intention or effort. Tanna Rabbi Shimon says: The Jews who reside in exile worship idols with pure hearts." Rabbi Shimon means that they do so unintentionally and without even noticing it. (Rashi, Avoda Zarah 8a)

They Returned to Live in the Valley of Death
The atrocities in Lithuania were more deadly than in any other county. The Lithuanians took the initiative to kill Jews even before the Germans began

their murder mission. As soon as the Germans commenced invading Lithuania, the Lithuanian underground movement began to transport Jews to murder pits. They murdered the Jews with any means available: guns, axes, and clubs. It seemed like the Lithuanians were too spiteful to allow the Jews a "pleasure trip" to the Treblinka gas chambers. By the time the Germans were ready to implement the "final solution," the 200,000 Lithuanian Jews were already gone. The murderers were not punished and remain free. When Lithuania received independence after the USSR crumbled, the criminals whom the Soviet Union had convicted of war crimes against the Jews were freed. The Lithuanian murderers live freely.

How can approximately eight thousand Jews live in Lithuania today? How could they return to the cities and villages where so many Jews, including their own families and loved ones, were so cruelly and sadistically murdered? Jews returned in mass to Vienna. This city sent its Jews to the next world accompanied by sweet Viennese music. How can Jews bear the bitter memories, while living with the generation whose parents worked hand in hand with the despicable murderers. How can they live with the burning hatred which is still burning strong today? It is crystal clear that these pitiable souls have not learned anything from the holocaust.

The Spanish Expulsion and the Jewish Boycott Against Spain
Look and see how drastically and quickly we have deteriorated and diminished over the years. When the Jews were expelled from Spain, they left with their physical health intact and with some of their wealth. Thereafter, they did not set foot in Spain for hundreds of years. There was no need to make an official prohibition or boycott against living in Spain. Each Jew decreed on himself not to return to the persecuting country. They felt in their hearts and souls the need to excommunicate Spain as a matter of principle upon which their survival and self-respect rested.

Immediately following the Jewish People's most terrible tragedy, in which the Germans cruelly destroyed European Jewry, tens of thousands of Jews, including holocaust survivors, moved to Germany. Jewish history reminds us of: the second Temple's destruction, Titus's victory parade outside Rome, and the construction of Titus's arch to memorialize Jerusalem's destruction. Jews who visited Rome made a point not to pass under Titus's arch which symbolizes our humiliating downfall.

Many Jews Migrate to The Murderers Country
In recent years, German Jewry grew from thirty thousand to two hundred and twenty thousand, due to an influx of Israelis and mainly Jews from the Soviet Union. They have forgotten that divine commandment and human instinct: "Remember what Amalek did to you!" You stand and stare at human beings who have no basic human self-respect. You are drawn to the fertile lands of lava, which have cooled after the volcanic holocaust. It is

known that even animals struggle with all of their might against being pushed into the slaughterhouse when they smell their fellow animals' blood. You stand, shocked and embarrassed at how Jews can shamefully live and educate their children among the nation whose fathers every day reiterated that 'the Jewish People are just fleas and parasites and the only solution is to destroy them.' How can they breathe the same air as these sadistic murderers who poisoned and burned millions of their brothers?

The entire German nation elected Hitler, and supported his Nazi theories. The Germans did not revolt until the allied superpowers had conquered every town and village in Germany. Professor Goldhang researched the allegations that it was only a group of Nazis that took over Germany and instigated organized, thorough, and comprehensive genocide. This allegedly caused the regular German citizens much grief. He proves that everyone in Germany knew, everyone saw, everyone participated, and aided and abetted. He proved that Hitler's hangmen were not limited to the twenty thousand SS men. They comprised half a million to one million ordinary Germans. They were mature reservists who had families. They could have arranged discharges from these slaughter assignments had they desired. Not only did they not want to change their assignments, but they willingly volunteered to kill Jews. In fact, they begged to participate in executing Jews. Hitler's plans answered their secret heartfelt yearnings. They did everything they could in order to increase their victims suffering. Destroying Jews gave meaning of their lives and also served as entertainment.

Egance Bobis was the former head of the Committee of Jewish German Communities. In an interview with the German weekly magazine *Focus*, Bobis told about his relative giving him a picture of his niece who was killed in a concentration camp. He said, "the young child's expression in the picture seemed to ask me why I stay in a country that was responsible for her and her parents' deaths?" Indeed, the souls of one and a half million children who were obliterated by the Germans ask German Jewry: Why do you live in a country which is responsible for their extermination and that of your own fathers and mothers?

Jew Hatred is Not Forgotten

The "other Germany" is not "other" in relation to Jew hatred. "Just as a leopard doesn't change its spots," so Israel's enemies don't change their feelings. A survey conducted by a German weekly newspaper proves that one out of five Germans is anti-Semitic. This is what they admit, however many more are actually anti-Semitic. The younger generation has learned quickly to use anti-Semitic slogans: "Death to the Jews." They even boast, "We will finish what Hitler left undone." Slogans such as *"Yudin Raus"* (i.e., Jews get out) are painted on Synagogues and Jewish communal organizations. In Germany, the number of neo-Nazis attacks on Jews is rising and they are using guns. The German police report that the neo-Nazis have ceased bothering foreigners and now see the Jews as public enemy number one.

Egance Bobis, who suffered from identity problems like most Jews living in Germany, used to say the following. "I am a German citizen Of Moses' religion. Today, Germany is my home". His comments drew fire and hailstone. The anti-Semitic Germans retorted: "They forgot you in Auschwitz." Bobis admitted in an interview with the German weekly, Der Spiegel, in October 1996 that "For the majority here (in Germany) the Jews will always remain foreigners." In his opinion, German Anti-Semitism is a permanent phenomenon. He declared: "I believe that hatred for Jews among the German population is no weaker than it was during the period from 1933 to 1945. The only difference is that then it was more murderous." In other words, Jews flock to Germany to live in the same diabolical and murderous emotional climate as during the holocaust, and it means nothing to them. Apparently they have shed all human feelings and sensitivity.

The Murderers Remember While the Murdered Have Forgotten

The Germans' infected consciences demand that they should hate Jews, because if they don't they would have to hate themselves and their fellow countrymen. Without us there is no one to remind them of their destructive past. The Jewish presence in their cities and suburbs is a silent witness to the cruel murderous campaign which they executed. It constantly reminds them of their terrible crimes. In reaction, their psychology forces them to deny these crimes. This denial expresses itself in hatred towards Jews, through which they deal with emotional conflicts. In the German people's minds, Jews who immigrate to Germany "deserve" scorn and hatred for two reasons. First, the Jewish presence in Germany reminds them of their murderous past. These Germans are therefore forced to live their whole lives with nightmares of gas chambers, with embarrassment, and with feeling like murderers. Second, the Jews are so downtrodden and repulsive, that they choose to live among murderers, among their own parents and children's murderers.

Rabbi Tsvi Azariya, Kelen's Rabbi, writes about these emotional and psychological mechanisms in his book. He writes about the views of two catholic authors who are known as the Jewish People's friends. They asked their Jewish friends, the following seemingly innocent question during casual conversation. How can Jews identify with Germany and be loyal citizens of a nation whose citizens murdered their nation? They could not imagine the possibility of such identification after what happened to European Jewry. One of these authors declared that if his parents, or close relatives had been murdered by the Nazis, it would have been impossible for him to remain in or immigrate to Germany. It is abnormal and inhuman. Both authors emphasized that both the Jews presence in Germany, and their wish to enjoy equal rights with their murderers, arouses the hatred between the murderers and the murdered in the most cruel and sadistic way possible. The Germans "must" hate their victims, because they are convinced that their victims hate them. They don't believe that Jews are capable of fitting into the German nation and being loyal citizens, because it is against human nature, feelings, and instincts.

It is evident from these authors and many like them, that Jewish immigration to and settlement in the country that murdered their people is contemptible and loathsome. The murderers have not forgotten their crimes, yet many of the murdered nation have forgotten them. They have not yet learned the holocaust's lessons.

Jews are Described as Foreign Plants, Sub-Human

Professor Zahar Shavit, in her book, *Avar Llo Tzael* (Past without a Shadow, *Am Oved*, Oxford Library), bases her profound findings on research performed on hundreds of books written for German children and teenagers. The books deal with their country's past and their fathers iniquities. The research showed that these books teach German youth a distorted perception of history. Her analysis of these books reveals that that they have a common historical framework which serves as the foundation for the "story" as follows. "There was a terrible war. Hitler, the Nazi, and a small group of Nazis under his influence, succeeded to take control of Germany. They were responsible for the war, and no Germans really wanted it." Literature written for German children and teenagers reveals that the Nazis did terrible things. However, it emphasizes that the Germans were not Nazis, and the Nazis were not Germans. After the war, all of the Nazis disappeared. It depicts Germany as the war's major victim. The holocaust is squeezed out of the picture and out of their memories. In this German literature, Jews are described as foreign plants in German society, as devious frauds, swindlers, and sub-humans. In addition, the Jews' apparently good character traits are eventually exposed as wickedness towards the German People. Generally, they are represented as threatening bear cubs who are capable of causing serious damage. This is how German youth are indoctrinated. Jews, who still have not learned their lesson, settle in their midst and marry them.

The Jewish–German relationship, which became impossible during the Third Reich, maintained its hostility even after the Reich's collapse. Jews are described as eternal migrants who do not belong in Germany. Professor Shavit notes, the same theme repeats itself over and over between the lines. Wherever there are Jews, there is trouble. Where there are Jews there is dirt and disease. Associating with Jews involves the danger of contracting diseases. This German literature expressed astonishment that Jews don't rush to leave Germany and move to Israel. We can sympathize with this sense of astonishment, since it is natural and correct, even though it stems from a hostile source. How can Jews allow themselves to deteriorate to such shame, lowliness, and contempt? How can they step on that blood drenched land and live among the murderers' children and grandchildren, among Asmodeus's offspring? How can they join their communities? The majority do it looking for upward mobility to the "fleshpot," in its modern reincarnation. These same sentiments are expressed about Jews who have recently settled in Austria and other European countries which cooperated with the Nazis. Take Austria as an example. A survey conducted by the Sociological Institute in Vienna, shows that 31 percent of Austrians are not willing to have a Jewish neighbor. 61 percent of Austrians admitted that they feel uncomfortable around Jews and want to get away from them. Fifty percent of Austrians think that Jews themselves are anti-Semitic and hate each other. It is well known that a profound hatred of Jews exists in those countries and it is impossible to uproot that hatred within one or two generations.

They are eternal nomads who are not accepted anywhere. They are hated and shamed. Their women are tortured, their children dismembered and they are killed in strange, cruel ways. They paint swastikas on their homes and defile their graves. Nevertheless, they shamelessly return to live in countries soaked with Jewish blood. Now Jews have their own country, but still the Diaspora can't get rid of them. "Therefore I have also made you contemptible and base before all the people" warns the Prophet (Malachi 2:9) There is a good reason why the children of Israel are compared to the stars in heaven and the sand on the sea shore. There are times when we ascend to great heights and there are times when we descend to the lowest of the low.

Let's not deceive ourselves that Jews have learned from their troubles, tortures, and deaths. They did not even learn anything from the holocaust, because they continue to wonder from exile to exile, just as they did before. They even returned in the hundreds of thousands to live in that same impure Germany whose sons operated the gas chambers and crematorium.

No, they have not learned the lessons from the holocaust, nor has introspection pierced their souls' depths. "There has been no earthquake in their hearts and no mental revolution in the nation's spinal cord." They are distracted, forgetful, and have no desire for sanctified clarification.

"If the holocaust did not shock them, did not teach them, did not change or mend them" then the outraged poet (Uri Tzvi Greenberg) sees no future for the holocaust survivors, due to their loss of spirituality and faith. They are caught in a world of dead bodies, and with all of their wisdom they have undermined their Judaism and confused themselves.

CHAPTER NINE

THE CHILDREN: THE HOLOCAUST'S MOST TERRIBLE TRAGEDY

THE HOLOCAUST'S most unbearable and cruel chapter of horrors was the way that they killed Jewish children. The Jewish children, the nation's hope and future, could have brought glory and splendor to our nation and to all humanity.

Romkovski, the Jewish *Judenrat* leader of the Lodg Ghetto, made the following speech when his ghetto's children were taken to extermination on September fourth, 1942. This is cited in holocaust sources and research published by the Israeli Department of Education and Culture.

"A hard blow has struck the ghetto. They demand that we hand over our most precious ones, our children and our elderly. I did not merit having my own children and so I dedicated my best years to an adopted child. I lived and breathed together with the boy. It never occurred to me in my wildest dreams that my hands would be forced to deliver the sacrifice to the altar. In my old age, I am forced to stretch out my hands and beg: brothers and sisters give them to me! Fathers and mothers, give me your children… (Shocked and bitter cries are heard from the listeners)…Yesterday they gave me the order to send twenty thousand Jews out of the Ghetto. They said that if we do not cooperate, "we will do it ourselves." The question was asked: 'Should we accept this? Should we do this ourselves or should we leave it to others?' Our orientation should not be 'how many will we loose?' but rather 'how many can we save?' We, meaning myself and those that I work closely with, have reached the conclusion that no matter how difficult, we must perform this decree ourselves. I am obligated to perform this difficult blood-letting operation. I am obligated to amputate limbs in order to save the body! I am obligated to take the children and if not, they will probably take others… (Terrible shrieks)

Today, I am not a consoling person. Rather, I uncover all of your pain and sorrow. I have come like a thief to take what is most precious to you. I tried to modify the decree. Just yesterday I ordered a listing of nine year old children. I wanted to at least save the children ages nine to ten. They did not want to give in to me. I succeeded in one thing: to save the children over age ten. Let this console us in our tremendous troubles."

The day after this bitter announcement, the Germans quickly transported all of the Lodz Ghetto's children to their deaths. To fulfill the murderers' quota, a few thousand elderly marched with them to the death pits.

Grandfathers and grandmothers marched to the abyss. They carried sucking babes and toddlers in their arms, their grandchildren and great grandchildren.

Sadistic Attacks on Children

The way the children were killed instills terrible horror. The sadistic Germans viciously attacked Jewish children in extremely cruel, unusual ways. They did it to destroy the Jewish People so that we would never rise again. Pure, innocent children, who had not tasted sin, were the first to be lined up to murder. They were killed with the cruelest means possible, means which even Satan could not have thought up. One and a half million children and teenagers of the Children of Israel were killed through many strange, cruel methods. Separated by force from their mothers, they were thrown onto the daggers' tip, their sculls were smashed on the sidewalks stones, and they were ripped apart in front of their parents' eyes.

We know that murderers and the worst criminals recoil before the pure and upright gaze of young children. Even criminals feel pity and compassion for lonely children and orphans. The German arch-murderers did not. They cruelly tortured school children and infants in their cribs. Their sadistic feelings lit up like a devouring flame when they saw Jews and especially Jewish children, who represented the Jewish People's future. Here the German beast of prey revealed itself, in all of its abominable evil, as a dedicated champion in the art of murder.

The Most Sadistic Crime in the Annals of Human History

Reports from occupied Poland in 1943, which the Polish government received verified that: "During the ghettos' destruction they shot Jewish children with machine guns, electrocuted them, and suffocated them. There were cases where the German soldiers grabbed infants from their mothers' arms and smashed their skulls on the sidewalk."

Blanka Rosenberg, a holocaust survivor described her memories: "The Germans loved to grab small Jewish children by their legs, swing them around very quickly and then smash their heads very hard against a wall. They just loved it!" One night, General Kotzman from Vienna appeared with his helpers at the Jewish communities children's and orphans' home. In the middle of the night they got five hundred children out of their beds and threw them out the fifth floor windows, straight into the trucks waiting to take them out of the city to their graves.

Yoseph Kleenman told about Dr Mengele, the chaotic world's Asmodeus, and his "teenager selection." The teenagers had to pass through a wooden gate. Each child whose head did not reach the upper board of the gate was directed by Mengele to go to the side with the small children for immediate death. The miserable teenagers, who stood on line waiting for their future to be determined for life or death, instinctively felt what was happening. They put stones in their shoes so they would be tall enough to reach the top of the gate and therefore be saved from the gas chambers. The revelation of the Jewish children's cruel torture arouses awful horror. Holocaust survivors tell how the Nazi storm troopers shot the children and afterwards trampled them with their boots until their bodies were flat. During the destruction of the Lvov Ghetto, small Jewish children were given to the "Hitler Youth" Organization, whose members used the children's heads for target practice.

European Jewry Became Childless and Bereaved

Rabbinic literature relates that when the Edomite tyrant Herod was about to die, a satanic plot occurred to him. He commanded the execution of thousands of Jewish children. He said "I did this so that the Jews will not rejoice over my death. They will not rejoice over their liberation and their redemption. I will slaughter their most precious loved ones when I die. They will cry and wail on the day that I die. Their children's corpses will lie on my dead body." The Nazi despot, in failure and despair, took his own life and died like a despicable dog. However, that same tyrant's will and testament went completely against us. When the world's nations celebrated their victory, we Jews cried and mourned at our babies and children's slaughter. Eastern European Jewry was blessed with children. They had the greatest number of children of any Jewish community, yet after the war they remained childless. Their holocaust survivors remained bereaved of their children. Throughout Europe there remained hundreds of thousands of survivors, yet there remained almost no children. These children were treasuries of life and precious human resources which are gone forever.

One and a Half Million Children

The murder of one and a half million of our children was the most sadistic and barbaric crime in human history. It was purity and innocence versus unfathomable, monstrous evil. Jewish children innocently stood lonely and isolated in the depths of the holocaust. They faced the world of dark death, the horror of suffocating poison gas, and the oven's flame. Even Satan could be moved to tears! How come the earth did not shake and how did we not go insane. "The Satan has not yet created the revenge for these little children's spilt blood!"

How can we find a little consolation for this unforgettable tragedy? What has the Jewish People done to perpetuate the memory of one and a half million victims? At "Yad Vashem" they have established "Yad l' Yeled Yehudi," (i.e., a memorial to the children murdered in the holocaust). It is an impressive memorial and a visit there can be a very moving experience. However, it is just a memorial and nothing more. It is only lifeless stones and cement, which cannot breathe life into the young victims, into our souls, or into our nation.

Those children – that most miserable group of Jews during the holocaust – were the heroes who smuggled food into the ghetto. They were the foundation of the ghetto economy in the fight against starvation. These little smugglers would sneak between the ghetto fences and crawl under the fence to get food for their families. They did this in spite of the danger. When the Nazis and their helpers caught them, they shot them to death instantly. Those small children from the ghetto were willing to sacrifice their lives for their loved ones! What did we reward those brave children with? Forgetting them, ignoring them, and alienating them!

A Life For a Life
Heavy losses like these, such horror and tremendous suffering, demand more from the Jewish People than just words, memorials, ceremonies, museums, and exhibits. They cry for real action – for bringing more life into the world. They demand personal exertion and sacrifice from us. Hevel was the first person murdered in world history. The Torah tells about his parents' feelings and response. Adam and Eve could not be consoled about their son's murder until they bore another child to replace him. "God has appointed me another seed instead of Hevel, whom Qayin slew" (Genesis 4:25). Adam and Eve's pain and mourning for their son's murder did not abate, and Hevel's spilled blood did not stop screaming from the ground until they had another child to replace him. The Jews are like Adam and Eve. We cannot and are forbidden to find consolation and peace of mind for our children's murders. Our infants' and children's blood will not stop screaming to us until we bear another one and a half million children to replace them. A life for a life, we will establish a new, massive, unstoppable, wave of life to replace our slaughtered children.

Adopting One and a Half Million Children's Souls
All Jewish communities, both in Israel and in the Diaspora, should accept the following obligation for the next ten to twenty years. Every family should adopt a Jewish soul of one of the children killed in the holocaust by bearing one more child than they normally would have. This would be a living monument. This can revive the holocaust children souls and replace the tendons and flesh on their burnt bones. This can enable these souls to live on earth and stimulate great success for the Jewish People. This would truly be the "March of the Living."

The Children Were in the Front Lines
"Remember what Amalek did to you." The Holocaust's evil was felt most pointedly when Jewish children were trapped and tortured. The children were the Nazis' first target. Of all of our terrible pain, the pain and mourning for one and a half million children and teenagers is the most constant pain. It never leaves us. Jewish children were symbols of innocence and purity in

their lives and the embodiment of horror in their deaths. How can we not remember that had they lived, they would have blossomed into a burgeoning camp and brought pride to their nation? How many righteous men, scholars, men of spirit, men of great deeds, scientists, scientific inventors, writers, and others would have developed from these children?

It is certainly true that the holocaust valley is filled with dry and burnt bones which can be converted into life and power. We just have to want to do it and to know how to fulfill our obligations to the living and the dead. This is the only way that the holocaust children can continue to live: through our children souls, our spirit, and our deeds. In addition, it is our obligation to improve our nation's demographics. There is zero percent natural increase among the Jewish People, which is much less than needed to maintain our current proportion. According to a Jewish World Congress Institute survey, in all Jewish communities other than Israel, deaths per year outnumber births.

A Positive Survey about Memorializing Holocaust Children

In 1980, a survey was conducted among 300 young Jewish couples in Sydney Australia, to measure the chances of success for this noble project. To our satisfaction, the survey showed that close to 70% of the respondents answered positively to creating a living memorial to the holocaust children. Many of them emphasized that a prerequisite for success is for national institutions to publicize this impressive enterprise through their national publicity channels. In tandem, the holocaust survivor organizations should also publicize this through their communication channels. Some of the respondents also praised this life giving project. According to them this will improve the nation's demographic situation and strengthen Jewish identity.

In response to this survey, we wrote: to over thirty holocaust survivors' associations, to organizations of communities with members of European origin, and to holocaust spokesmen. We acted in the hope that they would join together to awaken upper organization leaders and the masses to support and participate in this project of a living memorial to the holocaust children. After all, they saw the satanic death factories with their own eyes and felt the cruelty and the torture on their own flesh. Many of them also lost their children there. Therefore, it was reasonable to assume that they would be the first to act to memorialize those souls and to raise our nation's low birth rate. Unfortunately, the response was poor.

Ignoring the Nazi Horrors

Forty years have passed then since the Nazi slaughters and we thought that "Its time has past, its sacrifice has been nullified." In addition, the survivors were tired, weary, broken, and fragmented by the suffering and tortures which they endured. The survivors wanted to take their disturbed, nightmare filled minds off the holocaust's most horrible terrors and cruelty, their children's murders.

A Comprehensive Campaign for Property Restoration

During recent years there has been a massive awakening to return Jewish property from European countries. Holocaust survivor organizations have come to life. A world confederation was established comprising organizations representing holocaust victims worldwide. Its main activities revolve around returning Jewish Property to its owners. To be blunt, if after sixty years we can demand reopening dormant accounts and returning properties, then we could also initiate a campaign to adopt holocaust children's souls. On the contrary, today more than ever, we are obligated to carry out this spiritual and nationalist mission because it is a pure and noble ideal. We must also do it because "What will the non-Jewish nations say," and also because "what will we say." What has happened to us? We talk about the holocaust and all we discuss is money? Isn't returning the children's souls to life the same principle as returning possessions? Had we embarked on the human project of replacing the souls of the slaughtered children, then it would be sensible to demand also the return of Jewish possessions.

Journalists Denounce

Journalists in America and other countries, recently accused Jews of taking advantage of the holocaust for money. They accused Jews of looking for dormant bank accounts and monetary claims against insurance companies. They claim that ninety percent of the forced laborers were gentiles and they did not sue for compensation. Only the Jews, about ten percent, sued. In addition, the Israeli government already received "payments" from Germany in 1952. These claims are too painful to bear. We are a plundered and slaughtered nation. The only case that we have is if we prove through our deeds, that we want both our property and our souls returned to us. We can only prove this through adopting holocaust children's souls. There can be no compensation for the millions of murdered souls. No payment can ever compensate the taking of human life. However, we can demand compensation for property damages. On the other hand, without a project of adopting the holocaust children's souls, it will become clear that the Jewish People's reaction to the holocaust is a worldwide property hunt and nothing more. The Jews exert great and might efforts to retrieve their property, while at the same time do not thinking or attempting to restore their lost souls. The poet of "In the City of Slaughter" will admonish us again with his burning rebuke: "Just as in the past you stretched out your hand for charity, so in the future you will stretch out your hand. Just as you begged for charity, so you will beg again."

One Cries for One's Departed Children Yet There is No One to Console

In the Valley of Death the story was told of a bereaved mother who had her four children taken by the Germans. One was a suckling child who was torn from her arms and decapitated it before her very eyes. Her face became white and her eyes became thick and bulged out of her head. Walking determinedly, she turned to the synagogue, entered and went up to the Holy Ark. She opened it and said very simply: Father of orphans and judge of widows..."You say kaddish for my children." She stood there in front of the open ark for hours, pleading her tremendous and shocking claims against heaven. From time to time she would break out in a wailing cry that would shake the synagogue's walls. The mourning mother stood like that from morning to night and did not leave her place until the German murderers set fire to the synagogue. She went up in flames together with the Torah scrolls. The souls of bereaved mothers beg us to sanctify and to memorialize their children's souls. "Thus says the LORD: A voice is heard in Ramah, lamentation, and bitter weeping, Rachel weeping for her children; she refuses to be comforted for her children, because they are not. Thus says the LORD: Refrain your voice from weeping, and your eyes from tears; for your work shall be rewarded, says the LORD; and they shall come back from the land of the enemy. And there is hope for thy future, says the LORD; and thy children shall return to their own border" (Jeremiah 31:14–16).

Educators and Children March Together

Among the chapters on the holocaust of children is the story of the courageous educator Yanush Korchiak. He refused to be saved without the students from his school. He refused to separate from them and marched at the head of the children's death march to Treblinka. He became a symbol and shining example. However, Kortzak was not the only one who did this. The remainder of the school's teachers also went with him at the head of the children's death march: At the front of one class was Korchiak; at the front of the second class was Vilchinska; at the front of the third class was Bronitovska; and at the front of the fourth class was Sternfeld. Aaron Koninski headed an institution in Milna. He also went to his death together with his child students in Treblinka. Tuvya Korn refused to abandon the orphanage when he was informed that aktzia, (i.e., rounding up Jews for transport to concentration camps) would be taking place shortly. He said regarding his students: "I will not abandon my students in order to save my life. Their fate is my fate." He perished together with his students (Sources and research on the Holocaust). This courageous and beautiful phenomenon stemmed from a feeling of Jewish solidarity and brotherhood. It is a generations old tradition of standing steadfastly together in times of oppression. Above all, one doesn't leave children alone, not during the day and not at night, not in the light and not in the darkness, not in life and not in death.

Children's Souls Flying in The Air

Its amazing and shocking how easily we have forgotten our nation's best and brightest. The children, who symbolized innocence and purity, stood alone and abandoned before their cruel murderers. They stood without a caring mother or a merciful father, against a world of wild beasts. Israel was unable to give them their final respect. Their bodies were not ritually purified, covered with traditional shrouds, or buried in the traditional Jewish manner. To our shame, we ignored them and left their souls to disappear into the air, with no address and with no proper burial.

Let us at least do them the kindness of adopting these holocaust children's souls in our children's life-cycle. Let us thus comfort their souls, so that they will no longer be on our consciences.

Shema Yisroel (i.e., Hear O Israel)

Testimony given in the Eichman trial, told about a transport of Jewish children who arrived at Auschwitz. Immediately upon their arrival they were all brought as a group to the furnace. As they stood before the entrance to the crematorium, all at once, like one man with one heart, their pure mouths burst forth their final scream: "Hear o Israel, the Lord our God the Lord is one!" At the most critical and threatening moment of their lives, these tender children had understanding, wisdom, strength, and daring, to unite with their nation and their God. They parted from the world with "Shema Yisroel," "Hear O Israel!" but Israel does not hear and does not answer their cry.

Oy to the Nation that does not do true kindness (chessed shel Emet) to those who have sacrificed for it.

Let us implement this important commandment to become a life-giving project for the Jewish People. Let every family bear one more child. Let them adopt a child's soul who was killed sanctifying God's name! This will revive the children, and bring light to our homes, and consolation to our People.

CHAPTER TEN

DIASPORA JEWRY IS HEADED FOR SPIRITUAL AND NATIONAL EXTINCTION

EASTERN EUROPEAN JEWRY led world Jewry in learning, observing Torah, and in Jewish spirituality. It was a national undertaking which created the nation's spirit. It was the center of large, famous yeshiva's which produced Torah prodigies and men who illuminated the nation's path. It had: Chasidic centers, with their Admors (Rebbes); hostels for world-wide Jewish organizations; and Torah and social welfare institutions. The leadership and culture of these Jewish communities were wonderful examples for all of us.

Judaism's Mother

Eastern European Judaism served as a spiritual and national mother to world Jewry. In spite of the oppression and maliciousness, it maintained a strong, vibrant religious and nationalistic life. Those Jews stringently observed the commandments and they excelled in religious studies and in chasidus [morality and spirituality]. They had their own language, Yiddish, and a highly advanced Jewish culture. Sabbaths and holidays were observed properly. They did not mix with gentiles and were not defiled by them. Rooted in their Judaism and in their father's traditions, they were a special national group in terms of their religion, culture, language, and lifestyle. They carried their special flag proudly and honorably. They were "A nation which dwells alone."

Eastern European Jewry served as a tremendous human reserve for the Jewish People. It was a rich national reservoir, which nurtured and sustained other areas of the Diaspora, together with Jewish communities in the Land of Israel. Eastern European Jewry supported these other communities with its spiritual and moral treasures. These included its tremendous intellectual and psychological assets which were culled from the Torah wisdom and tradition. By Eastern European Jewry's merit, millions of Jews in America lived and the Jewish People's wellsprings continued giving life everywhere in the exile. It strengthened and fortified the Diaspora with Rabbis and religious teachers, with Jews knowledgeable in Torah and in observing God's commandments, and with Jews rooted in Jewish sources and engaging in a healthy Jewish lifestyle. When a group of European Jews immigrated to Jewish communities which were weakening, they brought a breath of life to invigorate the community's Judaism. This happened in the U.S.A., in Latin America, in England, in Australia and in many other places. Eastern European Jews helped these communities to survive.

The Nazis Discovered the Secret of our Existence

The Jewish Peoples enemies also knew about Eastern European Jewry's unique abilities to sustain Diaspora Jewry. During the Israeli police investigation of Eichman, it was revealed that Eichman was positive that if he succeeded to destroy Eastern European Jewry, world Jewry would not survive. Without Eastern European reserves, world Jewry would become meaningless, wither, and assimilate (Eichman investigation, police archives 101).

"Official pronouncements from the Nazi government contain many warnings of Eastern European Jewry's dangers to Germany. It is represented as the largest source of Jewish power, which supplies a tremendous stream of religious Jews who migrate throughout the entire world. It was represented as a huge warehouse which maintains and constantly replenishes world Judaism. Without it, the life force of western hemisphere Jewry would dry up and descend to the netherworld. The Nazis claimed that without additions of Eastern European Jewry's spirituality and creativity, the Jewry of the Western countries would have disappeared long ago. To accomplish this satanic objective, the Nazis used various means and stratagem, taking advantage of every day to destroy as much of European Jewry as possible."

Religion Strengthens the Jewish People

It is well known that until October 1941, the Germans allowed Jews to emigrate from Germany and its conquered territories. Unfortunately, there was no where to go. As Chaim Weitzman said: "The world is divided into two halves. One half expels the Jews and the other half does not allow them to enter." The following was written and signed by the Nazis in that same secret communication on October 25 1940. At that time, Jewish emigration from conquered countries was still legal. "I request that Jewish emigration from conquered Poland not be considered. Jewish emigration from Eastern Europe means a continued rejuvenation of Jewry. This is because the majority of the Rabbis and Talmud teachers come from Eastern Europe due to their traditional religious knowledge. Therefore, every traditional Jew is an important instrument in the hands of American Jewish organizations in their constant sabotage of the world and in order to spiritually revitalize and consolidate the Jewish People."

Eastern European Jewry Acts like Leaven in Dough

The archives of the Jewish Historical Institute in Warsaw, contains another historical Nazi document from November 22, 1940, which describes Eastern European Jewry as leaven in dough. The document is signed by the commanding Nazi officer of the Polish conquered lands, in the name of central Gestapo command in Berlin. This officer was stationed in Krakow. The document was issued to the military commander of the Lublin region,

Dr. Tzainer, and is cited by the author and holocaust researcher, Moshe Prager.

The Nazi document states, "The emigration of Eastern Jews leads to spiritual strengthening of world Jewry, because the mainstay are the Eastern Jews (the orthodox) who provide them with religious stability. They supply a large portion of the Rabbis and Talmud teachers and are in great demand by Jewish organizations in the United States, as they themselves admit. Therefore, every Eastern Europe (orthodox) Jew makes an important contribution to these Jewish organizations in their continuing attempts to strengthen and revitalize American Jewry."

The Nazi beast's sense of smell was well developed enough to sense what the Diaspora Jewry and its leaders tried to ignore. They sensed that without the spiritual resources of Eastern European Jewry, Judaism could not continue to survive in western countries. It is surprising and difficult to understand that our enemies discerned which of our abilities protect and strengthen us. However, our brethren do not sense our effective treasures which could strengthen our defensive system. They discount and ignore them. In truth, the majority of the Jews in the Diaspora march in the same rut which the Nazis planned for them in preparing the "final solution." They do not deviate from it at all. They do not move to Israel and they do not strengthen their Jewish identity according to their fathers' traditions. Rather they sink into the abyss of assimilation and intermarriage which results in extinction. Sixty years after the holocaust we see that through their self-destructive lifestyle Diaspora Jewry is completing the destruction as planned. It is making all of the errors and mistakes necessary to liquidate itself.

The Exile's Destruction

During the Jewish People's entire history we have never been tested by the type of destructive national tragedy which is occurring today. This catastrophe is unique in its destructive powers. Rabbi Dr. Eliezer Berkovitz, z'l, defined our nation's situation correctly. "Many types of destruction have befallen us: two Temples have been destroyed and many Jewish communities throughout the world have been destroyed. However, this destruction is different from all of the rest, not in degree but in type. The holocaust was a unique type of destruction: it was a destruction of the Diaspora itself. This is the first time that the Exile itself has been destroyed. What does this mean? After each destruction, we have never lacked the strength to continue living. This power has enabled us to continue, create, renew and rebuild our lives in every exile. We always returned to this power of redemption and familiarized ourselves with this power that lies dormant in exile. That same power, [the power of redemption] has been demolished in this destruction – in this holocaust."

However, from the Diaspora's destruction sprouted a national medicine – which is unique and no less revolutionary than the destruction itself. Namely the re-establishment of the State of Israel, after two thousand years of its destruction, and the ingathering in it millions of its exiled sons and daughters who came to build the Land of their Fathers and be rebuilt as free and proud Jews.

The Nazi Slaughter's Joyous Completion of Their Mission

It appears as if the Jewish People ignores the bitter truth that Hitler merited and continues to merit fighting the Jews. The Jews that he failed to destroy during his lifetime continue to be destroyed after his death. This is the only front on which his competitors and enemies allow him victory. He destroyed Eastern European Jewry and as a direct result Western Hemisphere Jewry is being destroyed. The holocaust destroyed moral and spiritual sources of sustenance, growth, and development. Eastern European Jewry is no longer there to nurture and strengthen the Diaspora communities. Therefore, they are drying up and dying due to lack of spiritual and nationalistic nourishment. This is the Nazis joyous completion – the victory of destruction. The Satanic forces (*Sitra Achara*) rejoice daily about their victory over the Western Hemisphere Jewry.

National Suicide

Diaspora Jewry's clear national characteristics are: lack of Judaism and Jewish identity, unraveling of the traditional family, marriages at late ages, and a low birthrate. (The birth rate is much lower than is needed to maintain the current status, so much so that the number of deaths exceeds the number of births each year). Above all – there is a plague of intermarriages and Jewish assimilation into the host population.

It clearly demonstrates that the Jewish communities in the Diaspora are presently undergoing a double process of annihilation by which both are causing tremendous losses in souls to Diaspora Jewry. They are losing large numbers of souls to the Gentiles by assimilation and intermarriage, while at the same time fail to maintain their numbers from within, as the number of the newly born is far less than the dying.

The plain statistical facts are, that Jewish life in the Diaspora is in the process of disappearing. The bitter fact is that almost half of the American Jewish Community already consists of non-Jewish spouses and children of mixed marriages. Only 20% of young American Jews declared themselves opposed in principle to mixed marriages. Anglo Jewry estimated at 450,000 Jews in the 1950's, now number less than 300,000.

We have arrived at a critical period, filled with dangers to Diaspora Jewry's existence. Today, due to Eastern European Jewry's destruction, there are no spiritual, life giving, and creative reserves to strengthen and protect western communities. They are in the process of spiritual and national disintegration.

The Ongoing Holocaust

A Muslim legend tells of a Damascus Caliph (Arab leader) who dreamed that the Angel of Death was preparing to kill him. The next day this leader packed his things and fled from Damascus, escaping to Baghdad. He wanted to escape from the Angel of Death and save his life. When he arrived in Baghdad, he was aghast to discover that the Angel of Death was waiting for him. The Angel said, "Caliph, I thought that you had forgotten our appointment here in Baghdad today. How good it is that you yourself came to the place designated to execute your sentence." Then the angel beat him to death. Today the holocaust continues: it has changed its place and form. The Angel of Death has changed his operating area, his strategy and his methods. The Angel of Death has moved from the conquered European countries to the rest of the western world. The Angel of Death has also changed strategy from physical destruction to spiritual and national destruction. However, the principle remains the same: death to the entire nation.

Collaborating with Nazi Plans

Diaspora Jews, including holocaust survivors, unwittingly and unknowingly collaborate in the satanic Nazi plan called the final solution. This plan is currently continuing in today's spiritual-national holocaust. The results of this holocaust will be catastrophic. Eastern European Jewry served as a tremendous Jewish reservoir that invigorated and replenished the spiritual and emotional roots of Diaspora communities. Eastern European Jewry' annihilation caused the remainder of the Diaspora to spiritually dry up. We are awarding the Nazis victory even after their defeat. If the Jewish People in exile disappear, this will be a posthumous victory for the Nazis. Hitler will jump for joy in his grave.

Have we Learned the Holocaust's Lessons?

After the Holocaust, the Jewish People's main problem is what have we learned and what we can do to prevent a future murderer from hurting or destroying us? If the situation didn't hurt, it would be funny. We are fighting a valiant educational and public relations battle to prevent the holocaust from being denied and forgotten throughout the world. In many countries holocaust deniers are prosecuted in law courts. Meanwhile Jews forgot and distanced themselves from the holocaust's significance. It is known that a nation whose memory is weak also has a weak vitality!

Let's say this openly, what difference does it make to us if the gentiles acknowledge or deny the holocaust? It makes no difference! It is known that "Esau hates Jacob," especially when we willingly continue to be holocaust victims. It is unbelievable with what ease we have avoided applying the holocaust's principles and significance to our own lives. We have suppressed the consciousness of Auschwitz, because no nation or group can exist over time without its own territory. We have suppressed the consciousness of the holocaust, because the exile absorbs its Jewish residents, either physically or spiritually. We have not internalized the Jewish significance of the State of Israel as the redeemer which maintains the continued existence of the Jewish chain of generations

From Physical Holocaust to Spiritual Holocaust

To our shame and embarrassment, Diaspora Jewry, among them many holocaust survivors, did not learn from the holocaust. It did not shock the foundations of our experience. It did not change and did not repair. Our world continues as before. We continue in our routine and wander from exile to exile. There is a saying that "a nation which does not learn from history's mistakes is doomed to repeat them." In addition: whoever does not learn from what happened in the past will be helplessly unable to understand what is being done in the present and what will transpire in the future.

In the physical holocaust, Jews went to their deaths like lambs to the slaughter, with no resistance. In today's spiritual and national holocaust, Diaspora Jews are taking giant steps towards self-destruction, with no serious battle to prevent it. In the physical holocaust, the Germans violently and murderously robbed us of our children. In today's spiritual and national holocaust, we abandon our children to assimilation and apostasy, simply by diverting our attention to other matters.

The Jews Accomplish Asmodeus' Goal

Aside from one, all of Hitler's later plans failed. He succeeded in one plan namely to destroy the Jews. The first part was executed during his life by the storm troopers who wiped out European Jewry. The second part is being executed after his death by Diaspora's Jews themselves.

In the present holocaust, the victims do not need S.S. soldiers and trains to take them to extinction camps. Jews themselves are galloping on the tracks leading to the camp of extinction. Above its entrance is the sign: "Assimilation and intermarriage free Jews from the Jewish People." Again, there is no one to bomb these suicide tracks. There is no one to shift the train to the tracks of Jewish life.

The Jews of the Diaspora are granting a belated victory to Nazism, after its failure, death and burial!!!

CHAPTER ELEVEN

TERRITORY FOR THE JEWISH PEOPLE

W{HEN WE READ} the scroll of our People's reoccurring sufferings, oppressions, harsh decrees, blood libels, expulsions, and pogroms, a question jumps out at us. Why didn't the Jews divorce themselves from their enemies and go and live on available deserted islands? It would have been better to live just with bread and water and the problems of poverty, than to live under the constant pressure of fear and enemies violent threats.

This question occurred to me when I visited Mauritius, in the Indian Ocean. This is a large flourishing island which, at the beginning of the fifteenth century, was ruled by Portugal. Since there was no one living there, Portugal abandoned it. Eventually the British took possession of the island and recently Indians immigrated there and developed and multiplied. As a result of their population increase, the island's sovereignty was transferred into their possession. That's how the immigrants became self-governing.

The grave question is: why didn't the Jews choose this path? During the same time period there were islands and huge regions of land that were uninhabited by man. These areas were fit for settling large populations and were just waiting for someone to take possession and settle them. Wouldn't it have been better than being degraded, tortured and murdered, among the nations where they lived? It's impossible to understand the strange and curious fact that the Jewish People, who is so used to wandering from one country and continent to another, to degradation, suffering, and oppression, did not try to settle any territorial area for itself during 2000 years of exile. It is better to live in a barren, dry wilderness and to eat grass in freedom and independence, rather than to live among enemies and murderers as oppressed second-class citizens. What would happen if, in addition to the State of Israel, there were another Jewish State in the world?

Now let us deal with some actual territorial plans for Jewish settlement which started to develop skin and bones with the agreement and help of various governments.

Birobidzhan – Jewish Autonomy

Soviet Russia, a country comprised of many nationalities, announced its policy of encouraging each nation to maintain its own national customs within its autonomous boundaries. The USSR kept its promise and nurtured autonomies for both large and small nationalities living within its borders. In 1928, the USSR undertook a project to settle Jews en mass in their own territory located in a region known as Birovidzan. [This is located in the Far

Eastern Russian, near the Chinese border.] The then president of the Soviet Union, Michael Kleenin, was friendly to the Jews. He decreed that this territory would be a Jewish autonomy within the Soviet Union. It is interesting to quote some of his statements. He said that generally national minorities tend to intermarry into the country to which they have immigrated and they disappear over time. The president emphasized the need to preserve Jewish culture and nationality, which could only be accomplished with an independent Jewish territory. From his words it is revealed that the soviet leader was aware and concerned about the plague of assimilation, more so than Jewish leaders.

The Soviet Union's President's Speech

Here are a few excerpts from the Soviet Union's president, Michael Kleenin's speech, in 1934. He refers to the reasons for establishing a Jewish autonomous territory in Birobidzhan. "The main reason is that Jews are numerous and lack a national governing institution. This is the only nation in the USSR, which numbers three million people and does not have its own national governing institution. I think that creating this territory, on our terms, is the only way to develop proper administration for the People [Jewish People]. I estimate that within twenty years Birobidzhan will be the most developed, if not the only region of Jewish nationalist socialist culture. Moscow, for example, is incapable of maintaining national characteristics in a multinational environment. If one can say so objectively, this multinational environment grinds down each national entity into one collective synthesis as happens in our capital city. A similar thing happens in New York City. For example, what remains of a Jewish worker's nationality after he lives in a city like Moscow for ten years? Practically nothing. If he partakes in cultural life, if he participates in proletarian life, then clearly Jewish interests will fade into the background. He will be forced to forget them… Everyone whose national culture is also dear to them, everyone who wants to develop a Jewish and cultural socialistic national territory must join Birobidzhan and help. I think that the Jews will last much longer in their own area than anywhere else"…

"I look at the question from a political perspective. I think that establishing this territory will put the nation on its feet. Better yet, it will stabilize a soviet base for the Jewish People in the USSR. Establishing a soviet governing unit for a Jewish run territory will generate a large influx of life. Again, I see Birobidzan as a tremendous opportunity, as an opportunity for Jewish proletarians to have a homeland, the USSR, and their own national homeland, they will be a nation!"… (A country for the Jews, Benyamini 129–130) These are true and correct sentiments from his majesty, our dear friend.

The Territory's Quality of Life

An American survey mission who came to Birobidzhan in 1929 and Lord Marley (assistant chairman to the British House of Lords) who visited there in 1933 reached the conclusion that Birobidzhan was well suited for a large settlement with industrial development. This is based on the rich abundance of natural resources, including steel, gold, magnesium, clay, marble, one million tons of graphite, and hundreds of billions of tons of coal. Its rivers have an abundance of fish and provide fertile land for farming various types of crops. This area is twice the area of the complete land of Israel [north to Damascus, all of Jordan and east to Baghdad] and was totally uninhabited before the Jews arrived. The mission found that there were electricity, health services, and schools whose first language was Yiddish and whose second language was Russian. The climate in winter is similar to Switzerland, Canada, and Tokyo. They found much activity there even in the winter, which has many sunny days. Streets, settlements and factories that were established there have Yiddish names.

On his visit, Lord Marley declared that "There is no reason for competition between Birobidzhan and the land of Israel. There is room for both locations and they must both prove themselves through development. In Birobidzhan, there is an advantage that there are no native inhabitants. This land is empty, there are no Arabs and no British government to slow development" (ibid page 130).

The soviet government invested much money in this region. It supplied free housing, transportation, loans, and nine years of tax exemptions. The workers there received up to fifty percent more salary than anywhere else in order to attract Jewish immigration. The United States also sent much aid there. According to Soviet policy, if the Jewish population had reached a quarter million people, Birobidzhan would have become an independent republic with political representation. It could have been the crown of the Russian nations.

Expectation and Disappointment

Approximately two million Jews emigrated from czarist Russia to distant lands much further away than Birobidzhan. However, the immigration to Birobidzhan was miniscule. From 1928 to 1948, only fifty thousand out of the three million Jews in Soviet Russia immigrated there. After a short while, many of them moved on to other areas in the Far East or returned to where they came from. Today, less than ten thousand Jews live there. There is never a vacuum, especially in a praiseworthy project. Since Jews did not go there, Russians and Ukrainians moved there and today total almost one million people. Birobidzhan developed into a large and flourishing territory which is called "the Pearl of the Far East."

The Birobidzhan settlement ended in a humiliating failure. Why did it fail? Some Soviet Jewish writers, together with others who dealt with this subject, blame the Jews. They claimed that, "The Jewish People in the USSR have not yet concluded that they need an independent and normal national life in their own land-based nation." The Soviet leader, Niketa Khrustyav, stated his opinion about the failure of Jewish Birobidzhan: "The USSR is the first nation which decided to help the Jewish People. We gave the Jews Birobidzhan and gave the project special priority. It was a wonderful gift. Birobidzhan has the most fertile land and a southern climate. It has abundant water and sunshine. There are endless forests, fertile land, unlimited natural resources, and rivers filled with fish. But what good came of this? In my opinion, Jews don't like collective work... they are individualists. They always preferred to be dispersed..." (*Midinot L'yehudim* page 165–166)

National Suicide

Dr. Chaim Zitlovitsky emphasized that the blame for the Birobidzhan failure lay on the Jews, because they were led by Jewish assimilationist intelligentsia.

The leaders of the USSR, and especially Lenin, did not believe in a nations' ability to exist without its own territory. Therefore, the Jews had only two options under the communist regime. Assimilating or congregating in one territory and establishing an autonomy with independent educational institutions. The Jews chose the first option. The fact that the Jews were the only People in the USSR that did not have its own autonomous area or educational or cultural institutions acted to its detriment through assimilation. They sent their sons and daughters to the general population's schools. Therefore, they grew up without religious education and Jewish identity leading to over fifty percent intermarriage.

We have treated Jewish settlement in Birobidzhan at length because this is the only historical attempt to create a Jewish territorial autonomy in exile. All of the other many plans never proceeded past the planning stage.

A Jewish Country in New York

Regarding the failure in Birobidzhan, excuses were given that it was located in the Far East. However, what would they say about establishing a Jewish state in the center of the new world, on the island of "Grand Island?" It is a beautiful large island near the city of Buffalo, New York. Mordechai Emanuel Noah was a journalist and a brilliant playwright. He served as the American consul in Tunis and afterwards as a sheriff and judge in New York. Noah toured Europe and witnessed his people's poverty and sufferings among the nations where they lived. He decided to help his nation and take it out of its misery. As a member of the Chovaveh Zion, he believed in the Jewish People's return to its homeland. However, as a politician, he determined that the return to Zion was a vision for the nation's future, but was not practical in his generation. Therefore he decided to establish a national shelter in his country.

Noah planned to start the Jewish state on the island of Grand Island, which is true to its name. It is a wonderful island in New York, 12 kilometers long and nine kilometers wide. Then it was completely uninhabited. He called the island Ararat. There the Jews in exile could find a shelter, just as Noah's ark landed on Mount Ararat after the flood. As a politician, editor of a New York newspaper, idealist and noble and influential political activist, Noah succeeded to attain agreement and support for his plan from the government of New York. As a first step, he purchased more than 10,000 dunams of land on the island, for the initial settlement of settlers emigrating from Europe. It is interesting that he received the money from a Christian friend, who requested to assist this great undertaking.

The Jewish State's Foundation Stone

On September 15th, 1825, a unique festive celebration was held in Buffalo which is located adjacent to Grand Island. The ceremony began with an impressive march. The march was started with a colonel leading an army division accompanied by trumpet calls and drumbeats. They were followed by leaders and members of the freemason's society in their official uniforms. Then Jewish and Christian members of the public followed. After the march, Mordechai Emanuel Noah gave a speech and dedicated the foundation stone for the Jewish State. The following Hebrew inscription was engraved on the stone: "Here O Israel, Hashem is our God, Hashem is One." The following English inscription was also engraved on the stone: "Ararat, a city of refuge for Jews" and the date.

The event was publicized in European newspapers and Noah invited European Jews to move to the new Jewish homeland.

The Chief Rabbis of England and France voiced fierce opposition to Noah's project. In articles in secular newspapers, they proclaimed that Jews are tied by bonds of love to the countries where they live and are loyal and dedicated to their governments. They did not hesitate to slander, saying: that Emanuel Noah's project is a joke, the humorous vision of a false messiah. They proclaimed that according to Judaism's principles, the establishment of the State of Israel will be established through revealed miracles. In addition, it is forbidden for us to take any political or nationalistic steps towards this goal. (Major Noah p. 208–209)

An Additional Failure

The Grand Island Project was a real experiment to bring Jewish immigration to the United States, through a territorial-country solution. The rulers of the State of New York gave their approval. The wonderful island stood ready to accept the Jewish immigrants. However, the immigrants were not interested in a national territory or a Jewish State. During those years hundreds of thousands of Jews streamed into the United States. They dispersed throughout America. Every state and every city found favor as a place to reside. However, they did not go to Grand Island.

All that remains of Mordechai Emanuel Noah's work is the foundation stone. It is located in a museum in Buffalo and testifies to a missed, golden opportunity to establish a Jewish territory.

CHAPTER TWELVE

THE ETERNAL WANDERING JEW

YOU WONDER WHY the Jewish settlements in the East and West did not succeed. Why did both of these Jewish territorial centers fail, both in Soviet Russia and in the United States?

A Solution to the Jewish Problem

From the eighteenth century onwards, there were Jewish organizations and individuals and a majority of righteous gentiles who saw the Jewish peoples' suffering among the nations. They tried to solve Eastern European Jewry's problem. Therefore, they drew up various plans to establish an autonomous area or even a Jewish State so that the Jews could manage their own affairs. Eliahu Binyamini, in his book, *Medina LaYehudim*, recounts in detail 36 territorial plans for Jewish settlement, which were created throughout the world. However, all of the attempts failed even though great fortunes were invested in them. Political possibilities which appeared at certain times were missed due to the Jews' lack of interest.

The incomprehensible mystery repeats itself over and over again. The Jews' degrading and stormy lives among the gentiles were filled with fear of harsh decrees, persecutions, and pogroms. In spite of this they did not attempt to free themselves from the gentiles' yoke by settling in one of the autonomous territories that were allocated for them. We must discover the source of this strange process, which has cost the Jewish People such a heavy price.

The Ivrim's [Jews'] First Exile

From the beginning of our national existence, we have exhibited a major weakness. This weakness results in difficulty in making aliyah and performing the mitzvah of settling the land of Israel. It also results in our developing an unhealthy allegiance to the exile. The Israeli tribes, Jacob's sons, went down to Egypt as strangers. They planned to live there temporarily, until the end of the famine in their homeland. "To live there," teaches that our forefather Jacob did not go to Egypt to settle there permanently, but rather to live there temporarily." However, with time our weakness was discovered. They devoted themselves to Egypt as a permanent home, as the bible recounts: "And Israel lived in Egypt, in Goshen, seized it, and were fruitful and multiplied greatly." This means that they established there permanently (Klee Yakar, Genesis 47:27), that they refused to leave. "And one fifth of the children of Israel went out of Egypt," only one out of five (Mechilta 13:10).

Even though the Egyptians embittered the Jews lives with back breaking work, beatings, tortures, and infanticide, shortly after the exodus the Jews yearned to return to Egypt: "And the whole congregation of the children of Israel murmured against Moses and Aaron in the wilderness; and the children of Israel said unto them: 'Would that we had died by the hand of the LORD in the land of Egypt, when we sat by the flesh-pots, when we did eat bread to the full'" (Exodus 16:2–3). Did the Egyptians really allow the Jews to eat meat, when they would not even give them straw? Indeed it is not written when we ate from the flesh-pots, but rather when we ate bread. The children of Israel would only watch the Egyptians eating from the flesh-pots, while they themselves only ate dry bread (Midrash Rabba, ibid).

The Episode of the Spies

The tragic episode of the spies caused an entire generation to wander in the wilderness for forty years. It also caused bad consequences for the Jewish People for all generations. All of the tragedies, sufferings and sadness that the Jewish People suffered throughout 2000 years of exile are the result of this first unfortunate spy episode. This initiative did not originate from the common people, but rather from the princes. "They are all important men, leaders of the children of Israel." Leaders are given the power to strengthen the nation or to destroy it. "If the nation's leaders behave evilly, the entire nation is drawn after them (Zohar Leviticus page 20). Those spies toured the land of Israel, seeing it through the perspective of their own poor self-image and self-deprecation which was engendered by the exile. "And they spread an evil report of the land which they had spied out unto the children of Israel, saying: 'the land, through which we have passed to spy it out, is a land that eats up its inhabitants… And wherefore doth the LORD bring us unto this land, to fall by the sword? Our wives and our little ones will be a prey; were it not better for us to return into Egypt?" (Numbers 13:32, 14:3).

Lowly and pitiful, without a spark of faith, without any security in the God and redeemer of Israel, without even one spark of hope, they succeeded to strike fear and cowardice in the hearts of the nation. The generation of slaves who left Egypt were startled, they began to sob, "If only we had died in Egypt…and they said to each other, let's appoint a leader and return to Egypt"(ibid 2–4). These people were in no condition to conquer Canaan. They dreamed of the flesh-pots, of squash, watermelon, onions, and garlic, when they should have been hurrying to conquer and settle the Land of Israel. It is clear that that it is more difficult to remove one's soul and personality from a slave mentality, than it is to remove a person's body from slavery. The generation that left Egypt had slavery and inferiority complexes. It was a generation that pictured themselves as dwarfs in comparison to the Canaanites, and the Canaanites as giants. They were incapable of handling the challenges of inheriting the land. Their fate was to wander in the empty wilderness until they passed away. Only their children, who were educated on the Moshe Rabbenu's knees, were capable of inheriting the designated land.

Weeping for all Generations

"And the people wept that night" (Numbers 14:1) Hashem said to them, since you cry over nothing, I will arrange that you cry for generations to come (Ta'anit 29a). Therefore, until today the sin of the spies and its consequences still affects us. This sad event did not end simply with the nation crying. Our forefathers' aversion to the chosen land and the consequent yearning to return to the exile of Egypt has not ended. Throughout all of the Exile's generations, the children are continuing their forefathers' sin of contempt for the Land of Israel. This weeping continues until today.

The spies' generation caused generations of weeping, not only because their deeds served as bad examples to future generations, but also because they bequeathed their character flaws to their descendants. The forefathers' deeds are signs for their descendants. It is known that both heredity and environment are the two most influential determinants in character development and identity.

Inheriting Character Traits

Researchers in the field of genetics found that personality traits do not disappear after death. Physiological, psychological, emotional and mental characteristics are passed from generation to generation through ones' genes. They pass either directly from parents to children or they pass indirectly from previous ancestors to future descendants for all time. Genes are hereditary causes which are located in chromosomes. They are responsible for transferring traits and characteristics from generation to generation in humans, animals, and plants.

Therefore, literally weeping for generations! The generation of the wilderness is dead and buried. However, their genes carrying the characteristics and leanings of self-annihilation are transmitted in their descendants' genes to this very day. These genes manifest themselves: in scorn and revulsion towards the land of their forefathers; in yearning to wander in the international wilderness; and in seizing unto the flesh-pots of exile and ignoring their suffering and their children's assimilation among the gentile nations. They are following in the footsteps of the "generation of the wilderness" who yearned to return to the flesh-pots of exile, even though the Egyptians had exterminated their children. What was not written explicitly in the 5 books of Moses was written in the book of Psalms: "Moreover, they scorned the desirable land, they believed not His word. And they murmured in their tents, they hearkened not unto the voice of the LORD. Therefore He swore concerning them, that He would overthrow them in the wilderness. And that He would cast out their seed among the nations, and scatter them in the lands" (Psalms 106:24–27). In other words, the descendents of the generation of the wilderness carry their forefathers' harmful traits in their very bodies. They disperse throughout the Gentile countries where they continue their own downfall and the cessation of future generations.

The Only Exilic Nation in the World
It is well known that Jews are literally a nation of wanderers. In almost every era of Jewish history, we find the Jewish nation continuously wandering from city to city, from country to country, and from continent to continent. It is one nation which is different from all of the other nations in that they live in their own lands in an established and orderly manner. The Jewish People is the only exilic nation in the world. It is the only an extraordinary specimen and an unnatural spectacle. There is no other nation that clings to exile so persistently. This very behavior agitates anti-Semitism. It is well known that the Jews are the most hated nation. The Jews have special characteristics which single them out as eternal nomads who are dispersed and scattered among the nations.

Analysis Required
Repentance is the process of rehabilitation and purification after a sin. It first and foremost requires acknowledgment of the sin. Similarly, healing a nation and returning it to proper functioning, requires the first step of analyzing its disease and its spiritual weaknesses.

It would be proper for us to claim that foreign forces forced us to remain in exile and do not permit us to leave. However, the truth is that no nation forced the exile on us. Rather, we ourselves choose it with our own free will. Nebuchadnezzar, the king of Babylon, did exile us to Babylon. However, from then on we ourselves wanted the exile. We loved it so much that we refused to leave. This bacterium which is called exile is spread throughout our blood and our national experience. The fact is that the Jewish People are very attached to exile both in body and spirit and cannot extricate itself. Indeed, the traits which our forefathers in the generation of the wilderness perverted appear in their descendants to this very day.

Self-Centered Leadership
The spies also passed on corrupt and destructive traits to their descendants. Israel's princes and leaders in the wilderness placed their own interests above the nation's. They were concerned with maintaining their power and status. They knew that after entering the Land of Israel, their situation would deteriorate and they would loose their positions as tribal princes. It was clear that other leaders would be appointed in their stead (Zohar, Shelach 30). In order to prevent this, the spies who were princes of Israel, prevented

implementing the policies that would have best served the People. They did so in order to maintain their leadership positions. They preferred their personal advancement over the national good. The main motive of the spy's opposition to entering and possessing the land was lust for political power, rather than concern for the nation's good.

The Babylonian Exiles

After the first Temple's destruction, the Jewish exiles had the opportunity to return to their forefather's land. Good King Koresh, a friend of the Jews, announced: "King Koresh of Persia proclaims: Hashem, the Lord of Heaven, has given me reign over all the countries of the world. He ordered me to build a house for him in Jerusalem, in Judah's tribal territory. Whosoever there is among His people – may his God be with him – let him go up to Jerusalem, which is in Judah, and build the house of the LORD, the God of Israel, He is the God who is in Jerusalem. And whosoever is left, wherever he lives, let the men of his place help him with silver, gold, goods, and with beasts, beside the freewill-offering for the house of God which is in Jerusalem." (Ezra 1:2–4). This great king sent soldiers to guard the new immigrants during their journey. He also gave them a generous immigrant's monetary allowance to get started. He commanded to give them royal treasury money to build a new temple and to return the Temple's holy vessels which Nebuchadnezzar had plundered. Nevertheless, most of the nation did not make aliyah (move to Israel). Even the priest, who should have set an example of cherishing the holy land, did not make Aliyah.

"By the Babylonian rivers, we sat down and wept, when we remembered Zion" (Psalms 137:1). They cried for Zion, but they continued living near the Babylonian rivers. They could not tear themselves away from the fleshpots of exile to rebuild their plundered land. In the course of a short while thereafter the situation reversed for them: The bitter life of exile became sweet and the sweet life of the Land of Israel became bitter. Among the millions of Diaspora Jews, only "82,360" made Aliyah (Ezra 2:64). These immigrants were comprised of "Ten different lineages who came up with Ezra from Babylon: ... Chalal (child of a Cohen who is married to a Jewish woman that is forbidden to him), convert, freed slave, Mamzer, Nasin (Givonim who converted in Joshua's time), Shtuki (one who knows his mother but not his father), and Asufi (one deserted as a baby, who does not know either of his parents)" (Kiddushin 69: a). The people with status or from respected families remained with their communities in Babylon.

Ezra sent letters to Jewish centers in Babylon, urging people to move to Zion to help rebuild it. However, the deep sleep of exile enveloped them and the Redeemer's calls did not succeed to awaken them. The genes that they had inherited from their forefathers in the generation of the spies, transmitted scorn for their homeland and the stubbornness to wander among the Gentile nations.

The Blame was Laid on the Babylonian Jewry

In reaction to their refusal to settle the land of Israel, Resh Lakish blamed them for the Jewish state's weakness and destruction. The Gemora tells us that when Resh Lakish was swimming in the Jordan River, Rabba Bar Chana of Babylon came to shake his hand. Resh Lakish told him, "The Holy one hates you because you did not move to Israel in Ezra's time. "If she be a wall, we will build upon her a turret of silver; and if she be a door, we will enclose her with boards of cedar" (Song of Songs 8:9). This means that "if you had behaved like a wall, all of you going to Israel in Ezra's time, you would have been similar to silver which never rots. However, since you have gone to Israel like doors, only a small minority went, you are similar to a cedar tree which can rot" (Yoma 9: b)

It's in our Nature to be a "Nation of Exile"

Our exile began hundreds of years before the Second Temple's destruction. There were already large Jewish population centers in Rome, Greece, Germany, and Spain. There was an enormous Jewish Community in Yeb, Egypt which had a temple whose beauty rivaled the Temple in Jerusalem's beauty. This community was destroyed by its neighbors. Twenty thousand Jews were killed and the remainder was sold into back-breaking slavery. During the entire period of the Second Temple, more Jews lived outside of Israel than inside.

A normal nation is bound to its land with bonds of love. It remains loyal to its land even when the nation collapses. A noble People remain loyal and firmly committed to their homeland in the face of military defeat. However, the Jews choose to leave their land. They wandered, seeking shelter in foreign lands. The Romans vanquished them, but did not exile them from their land. Since then the Jewish People continue in a state of constant wandering. Anti-Semitic pressure and economic factors pushed the Jews to emigrate. However, many times the Jew's natural tendency to take up the nomads stick was more motivating than anti-Semitism or economic factors. For the Jewish People, exile is an ongoing phenomenon. This is not true for any other nation. Other Nations from time to time wandered in distant lands; however the Jewish nation made wandering in exile an ongoing activity.

The Spanish Expulsion

Don Yitzchak Abarbannel was a *Talmid Chacham* (Jewish religious scholar), an exalted politician, and a finance minister of Portugal and Spain. In the introduction of his commentary to the book of Kings, he describes the expulsion from Spain as the worst national tragedy since the Jewish exile from the land of Yehuda (Judea). "And three hundred thousand People without strength, traveled by foot. My nation, all ages including youths to elderly people, babies, children and women, departed on the same day from all of the king's territories. Whoever has enough spirit to leave should leave (Spain)…and there's tragedy, darkness, and despair. Pushed out and rejected, they faced many bad and evil troubles, such as robbery, heartbreak, hunger, and disease. Some sailed to sea through very stormy waters. I will also choose their direction; I will travel by ship through the middle of the ocean." He and his family reached Naples, Italy.

The Golden age became the Death and Torture age. This is the mechanics of exile. Many of the refugees accidentally drowned or were intentionally drowned. Many were captured by pirates and were sold as slaves. Approximately 20,000 died from the difficult travel conditions and diseases. Who can count how many parents saw their children kidnapped before their very eyes and were helpless to save their children? How many parents saw their children dying from hunger and disease, but could not save them? The Spanish exiles dispersed in every direction. About fifty thousand were convinced by torture and sufferings to become heathen. Some of these only acted as Christians in public, while maintaining Jewish belief in private. However, the vast majority sacrificed their lives with courage and pride. They remained loyal to their God and their People. Ninety thousand settled in Turkey. Twenty five thousand settled in Holland and another twenty five thousand in Morocco. Twelve thousand went to France and another twelve thousand went to Italy. Ten thousand went to Algeria and two thousand to Egypt. A hundred and twenty thousand exiles ransomed their way into Portugal. However, only four years later they were expelled from Portugal. It was decreed that they had to leave all of their children age fourteen and under in Portugal to be brought up as Christians. They wandered to every country except for their homeland. They exiled the Jews from one exile and the Jews streamed to the next exile. They oppressed and persecuted them in one Diaspora country so they moved to another Diaspora country. They did not leave the exile, even when the gentiles burned them at the inquisition's stake and kidnapped their children. As a wandering People they remained in exile in terms of "a dead body which does not feel the scalpel." Their main priority is to remain in exile, even if this entails partial suicide! Therefore, this is "Weeping for generations."

A Missed Opportunity to Return to Zion

Abarbannel could have been a second Zerubavel or Ezra. He could have changed the course of Jewish history for the better. He could have set an example and guide his People to settle in the land of Israel, especially since the Turkish Empire was very open-minded about Jewish nationalism and religious observance. Turkey had conquered the Middle Eastern countries, including Israel, just twenty five years after the Spanish expulsion, and they improved the conditions for Jewish immigration and settlement. The Turkish sultan welcomed the Jews warmly. He ridiculed the Spanish king for expelling such quality people, many of whom were professionally qualified to contribute to society. Very unfortunately, only a few hundred families of the Spanish exiles moved to Israel. They moved to Jerusalem, Safed, Tiberius, and Gaza and lived in peace and tranquility.

On the other hand, the Spanish exiles continued to wonder from bad to worse. The one hundred and twenty thousand exiles who had found respite in Portugal for four years were then exiled again were just one example of this phenomenon. In Italy and other countries the exiles were persecuted and oppressed with evil decrees and pogroms until they were again forced to flee to new countries. Abarbanel personally suffered this curse. He was forced to leave Naples and moved to Sicily and then to Corfu. His riches were stolen from him and he lived a life of poverty and suffering. In the end, he wondered to Venice, where he remained until he passed away.

The Hope for the Advent of the Messiah

If the majority of the Spanish exiles had settled in the Land of Israel, their number would have reached over a million by the beginning of the past century. Through natural birthrate we could have possessed both sides of the Jordan River. Instead, a messianic movement arose among the generation of the exiles. That generation believed that the redemption would come only through revealed miracles and that the messiah was just around the corner. In medieval times, the rabbis generally encouraged hope in messianic redemption.

How can an ancient, intelligent nation, enlightened by religion and a moral culture, when endangered see miracles as its only hope for salvation? This is especially true in light of the Rabbis' teaching that "We do not rely on miracles" (Pessachim 64b, and Kiddushin 39b). In times of danger, one is obligated to make every effort to help himself. He is forbidden to rely on miracles. It is commanded, "Never put a person in a dangerous situation saying that they will perform a miracle for him, in case they don't." (Shabbat 32)

This messianic sentiment brought false messiahs. They deceived Jews into believing that they were God's messiahs who had come to redeem the Jews from exile. Some of these false messiahs knew that they were not the messiah and deliberately deceived people for financial gain or for respect. Some of them were visionaries who misunderstood the situation and mistakenly believed themselves to be the true messiah. The common outcome of these false messiahs was to cause the Jewish People much sorrow, evil, depression and loss of faith.

The Cure for the Illness

Once there was a very sad Chassid who cried loudly during prayer. People asked him why he was so upset. The Chassid answered, I want to speed up the coming of the messiah and the Jewish People's redemption. A wise old man approached the Chassid and said your honor, please forgive me, but do not pray in vain. First, we must pray that the Jewish People merit to be freed from the diseases of the Diaspora. Only then can we hope and pray for the complete redemption. Rav Shmuel Moliver, the leader of the Hovaveh Zion movement, emphasized this principle. Indeed, why does Israel's future redemption require two messiahs, first Mashiach Ben Yoseph and afterwards the Mashiach Ben David? Rav Moliver answered that according to the truth (Kabala) we need two messiahs. The first will take the Jews out of the exile and the second will take the exile out of the Jews.

The Messiah Among the Jews and Among the Nations

Judaism gave the world the Messianic concept and even supplied one if its sons to serve in this position. However, they took this idea to extremes. They took "the same man" not only as the messianic king of this world, but also as a part of God. They made him into a messiah who saves and redeems in both this world and in the next world, who redeems from hell and atones for man's sins. In spite of their complete belief in their messiah, they did not accept him as a national and political savior and redeemer. They refused to place their national fate and well-being in their Messiah's control and to rely on miracles. They reserved this national function for themselves. They free their country from foreign conquerors and defend their country with their blood and their lives. If needed, they will fight bloody wars for their homeland, instead of waiting for their messiah to save them.

On the other hand, the Jewish People don't believe in a messiah who is the son of God. They know that he can't atone for his nation's sins, yet they have exempted themselves from their national obligations. The Jewish people threw their national responsibilities on the shoulders of the Mashiach. He alone is to gather the exiles and to transport them on eagles' wings to their homeland. He will argue for them, fight their enemies, and bring the complete redemption. Everything should be miraculous. Therefore, Jews neglected the most important areas of their lives. Jews forgot, or due to their compulsive addiction to exile, removed their focus from the main point that belief without action is insufficient and ineffective. One must fulfill the belief in the coming of the messiah with practical deeds applicable to the current reality.

The Jews' and the Gentiles' Emancipation

The emancipation took place in the nineteenth century. It granted full equal rights to all citizens and led to a sharp rise in nationalism. That generation's intellectuals became aware that every nation and language has the right to cultivate its own nationality and culture. The emancipation led to the Haskala movement, the enlightenment. Those on the sidelines of the emancipation believed that it would damage Torah nationalism. They feared that it would destroy the barriers between nations. The members of the enlightenment deluded themselves into believing that the other nations would be like them and would disregard nationalism. However, the opposite occurred. The emancipation caused a rise in the nationalistic struggle among those nations and tribes oppressed by large, racial empires. Emancipation also increased the small nations' zealousness for their own national culture and language. For the Jewish nation the Emancipation had exactly the opposite effect. The Jews relinquished their homeland, denied the national significance of the Jewish religion, and opposed gathering the exiles and redemption.

The Haskala and Reform movements viewed that the emancipation was their hope for "redemption" and their messianic ideal. Their goal was to integrate into Christian society. Their strategy was to adopt Christian culture. They edited their prayer books, removing all prayers for return to Zion and redemption. They became alienated from Hebrew and used foreign languages as a norm. This unfortunate delusion caused us to loose a large portion of our countrymen to intermarriage. The emancipation brought the Jewish People spiritual and national impoverishment. The number of Jews declined and entire European Jewish communities were lost. The increasingly poisonous anti-Semitism proved that the emancipation was no more than empty trickery.

How Socialism Impacted on the Jews and Other Nations

From socialism's very inception, Jews adopted it in varying degrees. The first Jewish socialists' desire was to bring redemption to all mankind, but not to the Jewish People. The Jewish socialists fully believed that the universal socialist revolution would eventually solve the Jewish problem as a side benefit. These were the bitter illusions which stole our best sons. Socialist doctrine vehemently opposed manipulation and oppression. Yet when it came to the Jewish question, the socialist movement sided with the most extreme anti-Semites to persecute the "Zionist chauvinism" and to announce that the Jews have no right or hope to continued national life.

The Jew's disproportionately large, mass participation in revolutionary national messianic movements led to increased anti-Semitism. The long bitter exile taught our nation to cling to brilliant slogans and worthless promises of false messiahs. Time and time again cosmopolitan ideas have taken control over us. They have uprooted us spiritually and nationally, undercutting our Jewish identity and our original holy values of being a holy people on our holy land. Many of our young people sanctified their lives to build the world under the kingdom of socialism. They sacrificed their every effort on the altars of the proletariat and on every other kind of "ism" and strange, non-Jewish ideal. Exiled and nomads, they gave everything to all of the various countries and peoples of the world. They participated in all of the national and tribal freedom movements instead of dedicating themselves to our redemption in our People's land. "They guarded the vineyards of others, but neglected our own vineyard." (Song of songs 1:6). Our sons neglected and abandoned the essence, the absolute truth, the basis upon which our hopes and strength are built. They forgot, "If I will not be for myself, then who will be for me?" and that there is no one to depend on except our Father in Heaven.

How Communism Impacted on the Jews and Other Nations

Communism developed every nation's aspirations for national and cultural autonomy and independence. Only the Jewish communists negated the concept of nationality. They incited against Zionism and undermined it. They sided with Israel's' enemies and murderers. The Soviet Union's policy was to establish autonomous areas for every nation, whether small or large, and to cultivate each nation's culture and language. As we wrote previously, the former Soviet Union established the area of Birobidzhan in 1928 as an autonomous area for the Jews. It was nicknamed "the Pearl of the Far East." The USSR also gave much help to the Jewish settlers. Then president of the USSR, Klenin, summed-up the situation. He viewed Birobidzhan as a great opportunity for a national Jewish state. This state would ensure the Jewish People's continuation and preserve it from intermarrying into the other nations. Lenin also did not believe in continued national existence without a national territory. Therefore, the Jews of the USSR had two options: either to assimilate and disappear, or to live together in an autonomous Jewish territory. The Jews chose the first option. They did not want to understand what the other nations knew from experience and instinct.

Opposition to Jewish Autonomy

The Jewish communists in the USSR were displeased and passive when they were promised government aid, together with aid from Diaspora Jewry, for a Jewish autonomous area. This led to three million Soviet Jews without an autonomous area of their own.

The Jewish communists emphasized again and again that communism had already solved Russian Jewry's national problems. According to them, Russian Jewry had already achieved a full national life. They waved the ideological banner which obligated the continuation of Jewish Bundist life in exile. [The Bund was "The General Jewish Labor Union"] and most Jewish workers were members. The Bund also opposed the founding of a Jewish country.

The problem of Russian Jewry was solved in the most tragic way. During the communist regime, Russian Jewry degenerated as a nation. The Jewish religion and culture completely disappeared. Its institutions and organizations were closed down and disappeared completely and intermarriage and assimilation raged. Even though the Soviet government continually tried to uproot anti-Semitism, Jew hatred was not uprooted. Just the opposite occurred; anti-Semitism increased more than it was in Tsarist Russia. The Soviets collaborated with the Germans in murdering Jews. All of the myths of the communist "golden age" were shattered to smithereens. Marxist doctrine became a mockery. Communism, supposedly the greatest of the salvations, remained nothing more than a slogan.

The Nation of Exile

We have seen that throughout time and in all of the varying situations Jews grabbed onto the exile. Regarding the messianic concept and the eras of emancipation, socialism, and communism, all the other nations experienced a national and lingual blossoming. However, the Jewish People experienced the exact opposite.

They disassociated themselves from their nationality and denied their homeland. This perpetuated "weeping for generations!" The Jews did not want to live together in a Jewish territory. They gave up on freedom and honor, preferring to be nomads among the nations. All of the hatred, scorn, oppression, pogroms, expulsions, inquisitions and destructions they faced did not lead to the universal and natural understanding of the need for an independent and normal national life in their own territory.

Therefore, we have become weak, very weak!

CHAPTER THIRTEEN

THE YEARS OF MISSED OPPORTUNITY

IF WE REVIEW the one hundred years prior to the founding of the State of Israel, we see the reoccurring theme of missed opportunities. Time after time we failed to seize opportunities. We knew how to wander from land to land but not to the land of our forefathers. We were expelled from one exile after another, yet we delayed returning to Zion. We always blamed our national failures and setbacks on foreigners. We blamed others for our mistakes and helplessness. However, we, and not others, always paid the high price for our mistakes. We paid with our children's lives. Our children paid with their lives for our mistakes and sins.

Gentiles Started the 'Love of Zion' Movement

It is very strange that among the first to feel the desire for Zion were the righteous gentiles among the Christians, both missionaries and statesmen. The dispersed Jews' suffering touched their hearts and they decided to dedicate themselves to help the Jews. They believed that the time had arrived to fulfill the prophesy of the "chosen People" returning to the holy land.

During the 1840's, there arose a competition between the English and French for the return of the Jews to the Land of Israel. At the same time, Napoleon publicized a pamphlet requesting that Jews dedicate themselves to rebuilding the Land of Israel under the protection of the liberation of France. In England, in 1840, an organization was established by fervent Christians who believed that the time had come to fulfill the Jewish prophecies of returning "the chosen People" to its land. They also believed that God willed that the British should be God's agent to fulfill His will to redeem Israel. There is a long list of English statesmen and authors who defended and demanded the return of the Jews to the Land of Israel, during the period of 1840-1880.

A British Minister Demands the Jews' Welfare

Henry Palmerston, a Prime Minister of England, was a friend of the Jewish People. On August 11, 1840, while still serving as the Minister of Foreign Affairs, he sent a telegram to the British Ambassador in Costa. He wrote, "It is well known that the European Jews are very wealthy. It is clear that in whatever country a significant number of Jews immigrates it will benefit greatly from that wealth." Palmerston continued that, if the Jewish People return to the Land of Israel under the government's protection, it would bring a great blessing to the Ottoman Empire, which ruled over the Middle East. Palmerston diligently continued to take care of the Jewish problem. In a telegram in 1841, he emphasized again and again, that it would be very beneficial for Turkey if the European and African Jews could be influenced to settle in the land of Israel. Palmerston, at the beginning of his above letter, wrote that it is known to him that among the dispersed European Jewry there is a strong feeling that the day is near when their People will return to their land. In truth, that feeling was spreading among certain Christian groups. However, among Jews there was no awakening to return to Zion, and no Jewish leaders arose to implement Palmerston's initiative (Foundation of the State of Israel, Leonard Stein, 81). According to research studies and to Menachem Ursishkin's notes, at that time one could have purchased all of the Land of Israel, including the other side of the Jordan, at a very little cost. However, the Jews did not supply the merchandise!

Treasured Individuals
Among those who propagated reviving the Jewish people on its land, Rav Tsvi Hirsh Kalicsher and Rav Yehuda Alkali deserve special mention. They were active in the middle of the nineteenth century. Rav Kalicsher was famed as an outstanding Jewish scholar, and author of books on Jewish law, Judaism, and the redemption of Israel in its land. His books, articles and pronouncements were spread far and wide. In those works he promulgated a "mass return to the Land which we inherited from our forefathers." He believed in the coming of the messiah at the designated time. However, he proved from the Bible and Talmud that the redemption will begin naturally with the Jews becoming interested. This will lead to gathering the dispersed Jews to the holy land with the help of the major governments. He wrote, "We are waiting for Israel's Redemption. Don't think that the almighty will suddenly come down from heaven to earth and say to his People: Go! Don't think that he will send his messiah to blow the great shofar for the dispersed Jews, gather them to Jerusalem, make a wall of fire, and bring down a Temple of fire…certainly not; I call upon you to use your intelligence! All of the prophecies will come true at the right time, at the end of days. However, first the beginning of Israel's redemption will come slowly and through natural means."

For decades Rabbis Kalicsher and Alkali preached the idea of returning to Israel. They argued with both Haredi Rabbis and those of the reform movement. They preached to the needy and the ordinary people. In numerous pamphlets and articles they explained the need for a "mass return to the Land which we inherited from our forefathers." The generation is obligated to fulfill the mitzvah of settling the land of Israel. Just as other nations sacrifice their soldiers and lives for their country and their liberty, the Jews are also obligated to fight for their lives and to sanctify their inherited lands. They should buy many destroyed cities in the land of Israel, fields, and vineyards, to live there and to work the land. Day and night these Rabbis proclaimed their message to the heart of the nation. Rav Kalischer succeeded to win multitudes, including many influential people, to his ideas. Rav Kalicsher laid the foundation for the "Hovaveh Zion" movement. He inspired the national religious movement of German Jewry, which over the years spread to other countries.

An Obligatory War for the Jewish People's Complete Emunah

Rav Kalicsher and Rav Alkali, together with their friends and few followers, made enormous efforts to ennoble the Hasidim and the Haredim. These groups viewed the nationalist movement as the complete contradiction to the Jewish religion. These two rabbis were well entrenched within the camp of the Jewish believers. They were Torah Giants, and used their knowledge in Torah, in Jewish law and in the deeper meaning of the Torah (Aggada) to gain acceptance for the concept of returning to Zion among God fearing Jews. However, their idea did not gain acceptance in that group. Most of the Hasidim and Haredim viewed the idea of redemption as a slight reform of Jewish faith. They saw human effort to bring redemption as 'forcing the end of days.' They expected a miraculous redemption, complete with wonders like the miracles performed during the exodus from Egypt.

They did not Deliver the Promised Results

For over sixty years nothing was done regarding British Prime Minister Henry Palmerston's plans and his suggestions to obtain a permit from the Sultan for mass settlement in the Land of Israel. It was Theodore Herzl who believed that the dire financial situation in Turkey could motivate the Sultan to grant permission for mass Jewish settlement in the Land of Israel. Herzl believed that he would do this in exchange for large loans from wealthy European Jews.

In May, 1901 Herzl traveled to Constantinople, accompanied by two members of the Zionist Action Committee. They were received by the Sultan for a long conversation. Herzl succeeded to gain the Sultan's trust in the Zionists' loyalty to Turkey and its government. He also succeeded to arouse the Sultan's heart through promising large financial aid which the Zionist Federation was prepared to give to obtain a charter for Jewish Settlement in the Land of Israel. Herzl made a very strong impression on the Sultan of being a "prophet," and Herzl promised to write out a plan for settling the Land of Israel. The Sultan's statements raised Herzl's hopes that in exchange for obtaining large loans for the Turkish government, he would obtain Jewish national goals. The Zionist Federation allocated 2 million pounds sterling for this purpose. Herzl traveled to the capital cities of Europe to influence wealthy Jews to donate the required funds to purchase the land-charter for the land of Israel. However, the wealthy Jews did not join Herzl's plan. Only a quarter of a million pounds were collected, and that was what broke Herzl's heart.

It only requested a loan, not a donation. If Herzl had come to the Sultan with two million pounds sterling as a non-returnable gift, the Sultan would have given him all of the Land of Israel to do with as he pleased. This episode led to multiple opportunities being missed to resettle the nation in Zion. However, the biggest and most decisive missed opportunity in the nation's life will be clarified in the next chapter.

Jewish Opposition to Zionism

It is interesting to note that the Munich Jewish community opposed having the Zionist congress meet in its city. In response, Herzl was forced to change the meetings location to Basel, Switzerland. Even more so the Chief Rabbi of Vienna and the Rabbis of large German congregations published their opinions in the major newspapers. They wrote, "The ambition of those who call themselves Zionists is to establish a Jewish State in the land of Israel. This opposes Judaism's messianic objectives, as taught in the holy Bible and in later works. Judaism obligates its adherents to faithfully serve the country where they live and to improve that country's welfare with all of their hearts and all of their might." Herzl defined their position well: "Flattering proclamations to curry favor with those who hate them" (Dubnow 21, 200–206). What an awfully bitter lesson was in store for them!

The majority of English Jewry was more frightened than enchanted with Theodore Herzl's ideas. In Germany, no less than in England and France, almost all of the influential Jews, strongly opposed the Zionist movement. They shrieked the words of the pierced Jewish slave, "I love my master, and I will not go free."

CHAPTER FOURTEEN

THE HEIGHT OF MISSED OPPORTUNITY

BRITAIN, THE MIGHTIEST empire in the world, ruled over the Land of Israel and also the land East of the Jordan River. For the first time of 2000 years of our cruel exile, the superpowers, Britain, the United States, France, and Italy, recognized the Jews as having the right to self-determination. As a result of this announcement, the League of Nations [the forerunner of the United Nations] unanimously decided to establish a national home for the Jewish People in the Land of Israel. To accomplish this, all of the nations of the world allocated an area of 118,000 square kilometers, which included both sides of the Jordan. In other words, all of the nations of the world recognized and authorized the establishment of a Jewish homeland in the Land of Israel. According to historians' testimony, these mighty empires believed that both banks of the Jordan are the natural and logical living space for a Jewish homeland. For the first time since the destruction of the Second Temple, the right was granted to every Jew, because he was a Jew, to live in the Land of Israel. Unbelievable! A miracle!

The English announcement about the national revival in the Jewish People's historic homeland sounded like messianic announcement. The occupying forces permitted immigration to Israel. The Arabs responded immediately and claimed, "We are the majority and you have deprived us of our rights!" According to Professor Friedman, the British reply was "The Jewish situation is a special case. The land belongs to the Jews. They are only temporarily the minority – and you are only temporarily the majority." This answer was based on the belief that there would be mass Jewish immigration to the Land of Israel, which would form a Jewish majority in Israel."

Zionist Righteous Gentiles

Historic facts prove that the British themselves adopted the Zionist idea of the Jews return to their land. This was before Herzl, as we have previously written. Lord George, who served as the British Prime Minister at the time of the Balfour Declaration, was in the religious group that believed that world salvation depended on the Jewish People returning to the Land of Israel. Balfour served as the British Foreign Minister and the declaration to establish a Jewish homeland was named after him. He was a righteous Gentile and a friend of Israel and was moved to tears when he heard Weitzman lecture about Zionism in 1914. He admired the Jews as the most talented nation, even though it was dispersed and oppressed among the nations. He felt it proper to arrange a secure shelter for them in their historic homeland.

Balfour explained his approach to the Jewish Question, and what caused the declaration. "The Jews are the most talented nation that the world has seen since the Greeks of the fifth century. They were exiled, dispersed and oppressed… If we can find them a shelter, a secure home in their homeland, they will flourish and achieve greatness… The oppressed Jews of the Eastern European Ghettos will find new life in Israel and will develop a new identity and great strength. The educated Jews of the world will transform the university in Jerusalem to a center of spiritual life and an incubator radiating science and art. "Both the Prime Minister and myself were influenced by the desire to give the Jews the place that is rightfully theirs. A great nation without a home is unjust." (The State of Israel Institute 131–133 and onwards) The enlightened statesmen of the righteous gentiles understood and took care of the Jews' national needs, much more than the majority of Jews and their leaders.

These and similar incidents demonstrated that British leaders responded sincerely and truthfully to the Balfour declaration. The British Prime Minister, the Foreign Minister, many English statesmen and writers saw Zionism not only as a righteous national movement, but also as a channel to compensate the Jews for the slander and attacks which they suffered. Similarly, it could express the nations' gratitude for the religious and cultural treasures with which the Jews had enriched the world. Balfour said this amazing statement to Weitzman, "Christian culture owes the Jews a debt that it cannot repay. In spite of your dispersion, you contributed to our religion, our science, and our philosophy. And what great contributions they were!"

A Jewish High Commissioner

Another clear proof of the British government's orientation to completely carry out the Balfour declaration was the appointment of Lord Herbert Samuel as the High Commissioner of the land of Israel and East of the Jordan River. According to Chaim Weitzman, he was an enthusiastic Zionist who observed Jewish religious tradition. He also served as a member of the British cabinet and the president of the local government office.

The London Zionist Federation organized a thanksgiving ceremony celebrating the Balfour declaration in the London opera house on November 2, 1917. At the ceremony, Lord Herbert Samuel said the blessing "next year in Jerusalem," and he fulfilled the blessing by moving to Jerusalem in the post of High Commissioner. However, the Jews did not follow him. They did not move from the countries they were exiled to. Every year, after the Pessach Seder, and at the end of the Neilah service on

Yom Kippur, Jews repeat "Next year in Jerusalem." However, they never fulfill, 'this year in Jerusalem'.

My father, may he rest in peace, told me that when Herbert Samuel came to Israel as the High Commissioner, He found the Jew's very exited as if the Messiah had come. The ruler of the land of Israel is one of our brothers. All of Jerusalem Jewry turned out in Shabbat finery to greet the "Commissioner of Judea," the Zerubavel of the 'end of days'. On Shabbat the High Commissioner came to pray at the great synagogue of Yehuda Hachasid in the old City of Jerusalem. The distinguished guest was honored with the blessings for the haphtarah. When the high commissioner said, "A stranger will not sit on his seat and others will not inherit his honor" a shuddering passed through the giant congregation at the mention of the soon to arrive messiah. Tears of Joy and thanksgiving to Hashem (God) dripped from their eyes, "that (HaShem) kept us alive, and maintained us and brought us to this time."

Unbelievable

The reform movement, just like the bundists, opposed Zionism and the Balfour Declaration. They claimed that Zionist activities are ineffective and do immeasurable damage to their Jewish brothers. Zionism verifies the enemies' claims that Jews are really strangers in the countries where they live. German and French Jewry poured the cup of flattery to the Nazis fathers by protesting against Jewish nationalism. They pronounced that Germany was their only homeland and Berlin had replaced Jerusalem. "Any discussion of the in-gathering of the exiles opposes our love for our homeland. We do not mourn over the nullification of our independent nation status that we maintained in former times. The opposite is true. We are happy and how good is our portion that we merited to live among the enlightened nations. For this we praise HaShem and give him thanks." What lesson can be learned from this! To our sorrow, shortly thereafter these "enlightened nations" reverted to being beasts of prey. Then they yearned to find safety in the same Land of Israel which they had rejected.

Paying Lip Service

The Jews in exile, especially those in Eastern European countries, received the Balfour declaration with great rejoicing and feeling of salvation. For them, it was like a note from heaven informing them of the Jewish People's redemption and the salvation. They saw in it the messianic period, whose footsteps they visionalized. In the Eastern European communities, the declaration touched the hearts of the oppressed Jews who were hated by their neighbors. Mass thanksgiving ceremonies were held. Afterwards the Jews marched to the British Consulate, with demonstrations of joy, praise and thanksgiving to England. However, this was the end of the matter. Joy yes, but no action. Dancing and excitement yes, but no immigration to the

Land of Israel. "And the people saw it, they removed and stood afar off" (Exodus 20:18).

The days of the messiah arrived, screamed the headlines in a Jewish newspaper.

However, they left the messiah alone in the Land of Israel. They moved to America and the other countries of the exile. The Jewish People mainly just paid lip service to the Balfour Declaration. British documents reveal many expressions of astonishment and embarrassment that Jews did not come to the Land of Israel.

Mass Arab Immigration to Israel

In contrast to Jewish aloofness to Aliyah, many Arabs from all of the surrounding countries streamed to the land of Israel. The Job market attracted them to Israel. There were abundant employment opportunities In Jewish settlements. Afterwards, the mandate government implemented projects to establish railways and a road system. As a result, Zionism gave birth to the exact opposite of its desire – the expansion of the Arab population in the Land of Israel.

The British Are Disappointed

The British believed that within five years a Jewish autonomy with a Jewish majority would be formed. Professor Verter is an expert in the history of the Balfour Declaration episode. He notes that Weitzman led the British to believe that within one generation there would be two million Jews in Israel. Winston Churchill described the appearance of a Jewish State, under the auspices of the British crown, which would contain three to four million Jews. Many statesmen also foresaw this. Indeed, everyone with any intelligence could have foreseen mass Jewish Immigration for two reasons. First, the pressure of ongoing persecution would push the Jews towards the Land of Israel. Second, the holiness of the holy land – the historic homeland of the Jewish People – would attract Jews to the Land of Israel. The British were disappointed by the meager Jewish aliyah. The above historian cites that in addition, the British believed that in 1917 there was already a large Jewish presence in the Land of Israel. At the end of the First World War the British conducted a population survey and when they discovered that there were no more than 56,700 Jews in the Land of Israel, the British were dumbfounded. In addition, the non-Jews numbered approximately 600,000, ten times the Jewish population.

How is it possible to build an autonomous homeland with only 56,700 Jews? How can they live together with a vicious Arab majority of 600,000 Arabs, screaming for violence? The British were astounded at the Jews' wasting an opportunity for a national Jewish homeland. Dr. Weitzman lamented, 'Jewish nation, where are you?'

Wandering From Exile to Exile

Even though there were continual huge waves of Jewish emigration from European countries, they went to foreign countries. They wandered from exile to exile, but not to the Land of Israel. From 1882 to 1922, 2,600,000 Jews left Europe, intending to settle overseas. During those years only 75,000 Jews immigrated to the Land of Israel. Statistically, only three percent of migrating Jews migrated to the Land of Israel. In addition, many of those Jews later left Israel. During that period, the Zionist Congress put the vision of the Jewish people's redemption and return to our father's land on the world stage. They envisioned return in response to an overwhelming yearning to end Jewry's suffering and embarrassment at its enslavement. By the same token, the redemption would free the wandering Jews from the stigma of persecution and of being despised, a mockery among the nations.

Based on the many facts that have come to light, there is no doubt that the international community and especially Brittan, gave the Jews their homeland on a platter. They had only to come and take it, yet they turned their backs on the offer. The Balfour declaration was backed by the British and the international community. It was an incentive for the Jews to leave the cursed, destructive exile and to immigrate to Zion, the living homeland. However, we fell in love with the exile so much that we refused to leave it… We bitterly missed a golden opportunity!

Missing the Ripe Years

The nation did not answer Zion's call. At the time when political Zionism was crowned with the success of the Balfour declaration, the vast majority of the Jews and Jewish leaders were revealed as not large enough to take advantage of the huge national opportunity. If they had taken advantage of this window of opportunity which suddenly arose, the Jewish people could have established the Jewish state on both sides of the Jordan River. For four years the gates of the Land of Israel and the East bank of the Jordan River were wide open for Jewish immigration. However, they missed the grace period between 1917 and 1922. The tragedy of the Balfour declaration was the Jewish People's absolute aloofness in establishing a Jewish State. The sin was that we failed to accomplish an essential national goal that was within our reach. Because of our sins we have lost our common sense and have been exiled from our land.

As early as 1919, Max Nordau warned that if the Zionist movement failed to bring five hundred to six hundred thousand Jews to the Land of Israel within a short time, the international political dynamics were likely to change to our detriment. Indeed, a change for the worse did occur. After the Jews failed to supply the goods in such a pitiful way, Arab pressure forced the British to change their policy towards Zionism. The British felt that they were loosing out from both sides. British interests changed as soon as they realized that the Arab population outnumbered the Jews ten to one. The admiration and support for us changed in favor of the Arabs. Nations conduct their policy according to their interests. Jewish aloofness to aliyah caused the British interests to favoring the Arabs.

The Loss of the Other Side of the Jordan River

In 1922, Brittan decided to divide the Land of Israel. Brittan tore the East bank, the other side of the Jordan, from Israel. This comprised 77 percent of the land of Israel as defined by the mandate. 90,000 out of the 117,000 square kilometers which were destined for the national homeland were removed from the mandate's order. A Saudi prince named Abdullah took control of the situation. He speedily moved Bedouin from Saudi Arabia and neighboring countries to the other side of the Jordan and they gave him the emirate [leadership] over it.

It is written in the Torah that the East bank of the Jordan was conquered before the land of Canaan. which is the Land of Israel on the west bank of the Jordan. "Over the Jordan" became the inheritance of the Tribe of Reuven, Gad and half of the tribe of Menasha immediately after Moshe Rabbenu conquered it. During the entire period of the Judges and for most of the First Temple period, the Eastern side of the Jordan was a part of the kingdom of Judea and Israel. During the second temple period, Jewish wise men also viewed the lands east of the Jordan as wholly integrated into the Jewish state. Jewish cities and villages existed there for hundreds of years. We can see in an ancient Mishnah which speaks very practically about 3 regions to remove produce in the shmita year. They are Judea, the other side of the Jordan, and the Galilee (shve'et 9:2).

In addition, the three regions of the land of Israel mentioned above are divided regarding the subject of marriage (Ketuboth 13:10). The three regions also apply regarding possessions (Baba Batra 3:2). The most interesting is the Mishnah in Menachot (8:3), Tekoa (produces the finest) oil. Abba Shaul says the next best oil is from Regev which is on the other side of the Jordan. All of Israel provides kosher oil, however, they would bring oil for the Temple service from Tekoa and Regev, on the east side of the Jordan.

From the times of Moshe Rabbenu until the destruction of the second temple, the side east of the Jordan was an integral part of the State of Israel. After the destruction, Jews continued to live there, farm the land and eat its produce. Three quarters of the land of Israel slipped through our hands because the Jews missed the opportunity for mass immigration to their land. Is it not an unforgivable sin? Declarations are not enough to lay claim to land acquisition. Rather acquisition requires that one takes physical possession. Without immigration and without a nation of people, there can be no state.

The Determining Factors are the Specifics of the Situation

The world has not ceased to marvel about the non-violent revolution in South Africa and about the white man's giving away his rich land to the colored population. The Bores, the white Africans, were in South Africa for about 350 years. They developed a flourishing economy with farms, factories, and gold and diamond mines. They ran a modern vibrant regime with an excellent army. However, they made one mistake which cost them loss of governmental control. Unlike Australia and new Zeeland, South Africa limited immigration and the white population remained a minority of five million as opposed to twenty million blacks. In spite of all of their advantages and their claims that the blacks immigrated after the whites had already settled the land and begun developing it, the whites were forced to transfer control of the government to the blacks. This is because the land belongs to the people who belong to the land, who are there in body and flesh. One cannot gain possession of a country through declarations and official decisions, even by major empires and the League of Nations. The Torah emphasizes this, "and ye shall possess it, and dwell therein" (Deuteronomy 11:31). "Rabbi Ishmael taught: and ye shall possess it, and dwell therein. How does one possess it, by dwelling in it!" (Kiddushin 26a). A nation possesses a land when it lives in the land!

A Strange Phenomenon

You ponder that throughout the entire period of exile, Jews remembered Zion, turned to it in prayer, and asked about the welfare of its prisoners. They prayed, "May you redeem us soon and gather our exiles from the four corners of the earth." They vowed, "If I forget Jerusalem, may my right hand forget its cunning." However, when the redemption and the salvation arrived, they forgot and ignored it. They continue to live in a threatening, dark Diaspora, to wander from one country of exile to another, but not to their own rightful possession. This is a reflection that we still posses our forefathers' genes from the generation of the wilderness. This is an inheritance that we have not yet abandoned. The exile's mental slavery is so rooted in our being that even when the opportunity arises we cannot stand up straight like free people and proclaim loudly, enough slavery! The time has come to be a free people in our homeland. We are going to Zion!

The Mystery of Our Passiveness to Redemption

The beginnings of the redemption provide us with a strange and incomprehensible mystery. For generations, Torah observant Jews have tried enthusiastically to bring the redemption through holy means. How is it that the vast majority of the people who put flesh and blood in the national skeleton of Israel during the period of Hovave Zion, were Jews who threw off the yoke of Torah and mitzvoth? It is very hard to understand. Historically, religious Jews were always the first to immigrate to Israel, both in medieval times and after the Spanish expulsion. Rabbi Yehuda HaChasid led a group of 1,300 Jews who immigrated to Israel in 5480. A large group of the Vilna Gaon's students immigrated in 5537. They reached the conclusion that yearning alone does not accomplish anything, "Thought without deeds is like a soul without a body." Instead, one must hasten the redemption with action – physically settling the land of Israel. Those and others like them laid the foundations for the centers of the old settlement in the land of Israel so much so that their number reached thirty five thousand by the year 5640.

We are not surprised that the reform Jews and the Bundists vehemently opposed the Hovave Zion movement, the Balfour Declaration and immigration to the Land of Israel, because they were already on their way out of traditional Judaism. They had already erased Zion and Jerusalem from their prayer books and from their hearts. The religious Jews' reactions are astonishing. They especially had the holy obligation to obey the Torah's command and to seize the historic opportunity to be zealous in the holy work of gathering the exiles and of the mitzvah of settling and building the land of Israel. This was especially true during the Hovave Zion Period and during the years of the Balfour Declaration. Famous Rabbis, who were great Torah Scholars, served as harbingers of Zionism. They saw the settlement of the land of Israel as one of the greatest, most important commandments of the Torah. Nevertheless, a small number of eastern and central European rabbis joined together to rally immigration to Zion, yet the nation as a whole ignored them.

The Jewish State on the Horizon
All of the nations of the world recognized the need to establish a national homeland in the Land of Israel for the Jews. They voted for it unanimously in the League of Nations. Thanks to righteous gentiles who admired the Jewish People and who were leading Britain at the time, Britain, the largest empire in the world, made proclamations similar to those of King Cyrus (Koresh) of Persia. 'Whichever members of your nation desire, may their Elokim (God) be with them, and let them go up to Jerusalem and build a national homeland for the Jewish People.' The Jewish State was seen on the horizon! However, our tragedy was that there was no Jewish interest to support this historic proclamation. In contrast to what these world leaders and righteous people thought and expected, the Jewish People did not wake up from its own free will to move to Zion. We did not learn the lesson from the terrible mistake which our forefathers made by not taking advantage of Cyrus's proclamation for mass Jews emigration from Babylon to Judea. According to the Rabbis, this caused the destruction of the second Temple. The wise men of the generations testify that in general a developed person or a developed nation does not make the same mistake twice. Rather they learn from experience which is the best teacher. Apparently this does not

apply to us. Even bitter experience is ineffective and worthless. Therefore, this nation of ours is an expert of national suicide.

Our strange and inexplicable phenomenon is that of a dreamer. He prays and yearns for thousands of years to gather the exiles and for redemption. Yet when the time is ripe he refuses to be redeemed. Rather he screams like a crane, "I love the exile and will not go free!"

Opposition to The Return to Zion Movement

The opponents of Zionism and returning to Zion claimed that the majority of the Zionists were not religious, and that among them were heretics who had rejected Torah and Mitzvoth. These were the people who constituted the second Aliyah which took place during the years 1904 to 1914. The majority were people who had studied in yeshivas and students who had turned their backs on Jewish tradition to embrace social ideologies and socialism. The Haredi leaders' opposition was based on the suspicion that their students might leave the Torah's lifestyle if they lived in the Zionist framework.

These non-religious Jews only numbered few myriads. When we take into account that in 1882 the old Yishuve numbered only 35,000 people and in 1919 there were only 56,700 Jews in the Land of Israel. The vast majority of the Polish, Hungarian, Lithuanian and others were pure Torah observant Jews who believed in their Admorim and rabbis. The rabbinic opinions served to light their paths and they followed them faithfully. If they had called their flocks to go up to the Land of Israel, hundreds of thousands would have gone. They could have been the vast majority in the Land of Israel and the decisive voice in all of the matters of the community and its leadership. Unfortunately, a huge camp of loyal Jews was frightened off by a small group of non-religious people. They withdrew and left the battlefront in the hands of the non-religious minority.

Eastern European Jewry in Distress

The Jewish masses in Eastern Europe lived in a climate of hatred, pogroms, unemployment and poverty. Poland had over three million Jews and was a poor country lacking in resources. The living situation there was very difficult. Jews were choked by economic banishment which was directed against them, and also by the barrier of anti-Semitism which increased from year to year and increased their distress. Previous Prime Minister Yitzchak Shamir once said that the Pollocks imbibed anti-Semitism with their mother's milk. During those years Mr. Yitzchak Greenbaum proclaimed that that there were one million too many Jews in Poland. The Jews wanted to tear him apart, saying that his proclamation would only help the anti-Semites, who were destructive enough without his help. Entire exiles lived like people sick with malaria, yet they dug into position in Exile and continued living their personal and communal lives as they always had. They cut themselves off from the voice which called from Zion.

They Refused to See the Situation

There was no need for genius or prophetic ability to see that a poisonous and destructive anti-Semitism was spreading over all of Europe. This was because the Jews were sitting on a volcano whose lava was building up. This volcano was likely to blow up one day and destroy everything in its path. It was not hard to see that the only real, long-term solution was to return to Zion. The holocaust did not just spring up in a sudden unexpected outburst. It was a continuation and a culmination of a prolonged process, which included visceral hatred towards Jews, oppression, destruction, evil decrees, expulsions, crusades, inquisitions, the decrees of 5408 and 5409, the holocaust of Yemenite Jewry, and many other incidents between tragedies. These all caused the loss of a high percentage of the Jewish People. The Europeans' rampant hatred showed itself fully when the German army invaded other European countries in 1939. In most European countries, the local population had already conducted pogroms, cruelly killing Jews and plundering their property, even before the Nazis could evict the Jews from their homes.

Our adherence to exile and our chronic wandering within exile is what prevented European Jewry from seeing the situation clearly and anticipating the direction of anti-Semitism. Meanwhile, righteous gentiles recognized the processes which would probably occur, which would bring a tragedy to the Jewish People. Let's mention just a few of them. At the time Lord Balfour and the President of the Soviet Union, Michael Klinin: "If Jews want to save themselves from oppression, pogroms, and destruction, then they must confine themselves to a Jewish autonomous territory or intermarry and disappear into the people that they live among." From the beginning of the spread of Nazism, Jabotinsky traveled from country to county and from city to city. He cried with great pathos for the Jews to end the exile, and warned that if they don't the exile will end them. He sensed the terrible danger that awaited the Jews. He, like Trotsky, foresaw the tremendously threatening fire which was about to breakout and destroy the Jews. However, his cries did not touch the hearts of millions of Jews who were killed in spite of their intellectual rationalizations and philosophical justifications for remaining in exile.

Also, during the period of the mandate and in the days of the certificates, the British decreed a selection for aliyah. Yet, there were tens of thousands of Eastern European Jews who had the one hundred thousand British pounds which would have enabled them to immigrate to the Land of Israel without special permission. These Jews did not need special certificates and could have immigrated to Israel as wealthy people. However, they did not take advantage of this option. They remained with their money in the valley of death.

More Severe than the Sin of the Spies

It could be that the sin of abhorring the land of Israel during the time of the Balfour Declaration was more severe a sin than in the generation of the spies. In those days the Land of Israel was inhabited by the seven nations. Their inhabitants were tall and strong and lived in fortified cities. The children of Israel had to conduct long hard wars which lasted many years and they lost many lives. The Balfour Declaration changed all of that. It was wonderful to see that Divine providence repeated what it had done with Persian King Cyrus' declaration for the Jews to return to the Land of Israel. These were miracles and wonders! A new light began to shine on Zion! The redemption of Israel would materialize, without the Jews having to rebel against the nations or going to war to conquer land. With the Balfour Declaration, the British, together with the other nations of the world, gave the Jews their traditional homeland on a silver platter. They said to the Jews, it is prepared for you, come and take it without having to fight and sacrifice for it. Just immigrate and settle there and it will be yours…How marvelous! Isn't it? However, the Jews did not immigrate to their homeland, as if they abhorred it. During those years, they streamed to foreign countries in the millions. However, all they could do for their homeland was to heave a sigh. During those same fateful years for the Jewish People and the land of Israel, millions of other Jews remained in Eastern Europe. They suffered from tremendous hatred, discrimination, oppression, persecution, and apprehension about an uncertain and dangerous future. Does world history record any stranger of more difficult story of national suicide than ours?

Contempt for the Commandment of Settling the Land of Israel

Israel is not ruled by astrology. The Jewish People's existence and prosperity depends upon the commandment to settle the Land of Israel. This was the only commandment that even Godoleh Yisroel (Torah Luminaries) and Hassideh Yisroel (saints) failed to fulfill several times during the course of history. This kind of disrespect and negligence was not found for any other Torah mitzvah. Gathering the exiles and performing the commandment to settle the Land of Israel is equal in value to all of the other commandments combined, states the Talmud. There were those who nullified these important obligations based on an Aggada (A type of rabbinic legend) about three vows. Regarding these three vows the Talmud teaches us that, 'this teaching has the status of an Aggada, a legend: An Aggada does not legally forbid anything or permit anything. It does not render anything impure nor does it purify anything (Jerusalem Talmud, Horayot 5:5). Also, we do not learn [Jewish Law] from an Aggada. (Jerusalem Talmud, Peah 8:1). We do not teach from an Aggada (Jerusalem Talmud, Chagigah 80:1). Others conditioned the fulfillment of settling the Land of Israel on a revealed miracle of the coming of the messiah. Until then, "Sit and don't act." However, Jewish law opposes this passivity and forbids it. One is forbidden to rely on miracles (Pessachim 24b & Zohar 1:111). One should never put himself in danger and say, it will happen a miracle for me (Ta'anit 20:a). How correct the Rabbis were when they said about the above matter, "When the Shepard makes a mistake, his flock follows after him in his mistake."

Let us Acknowledge and Confess our Bitter Mistakes

Let us examine our weaknesses and admit our foolishness and transgressions. We have ignored the realistic opportunities for redemption which Divine Providence has placed before us. We have tarried in exile, and have missed ripe moments one after the other. We have disappointed our friends who wanted only good for us. We remained with our enemies who sought our lives. All of our sins in delaying our return to Zion, have brought unimaginably cruel revenge. Six million of our bothers, men, women, and children suffered all types of hell before being crowded into gas chambers, sent to crematorium and turned into ashes. They are forever before our eyes. Their hands were outstretched for help that never came. They could not defend themselves and salvation was not forthcoming.

History remembers and records what we would rather forget and ignore. We did not fail because the nations of the world were aloof. They preferred us over the other nations. They offered us our homeland and expected us to come and take it. We failed terribly because of Jewish indifference to our own fate. For years the gates of the Land of Israel remained wide open, expecting its children to return to their source. However, the Jewish People did not want to come to the Land of Israel and their leaders did not encourage them. They waited for Hitler to push the people, but by then it was too late…

We Paid an Astronomic Price

What a cruel and catastrophic price our nation has paid for our mistakes. Million of our people remained in European countries known for their violence, until they fell into the hands of the Nazi storm troopers. Had there been a Jewish country in Israel before world war two, it could have saved a large portion of those Jews who perished in the holocaust. Don't ask, where was Hashem [God]? In truth, it is better to ask, where were the Jews?

Free Will [Free Choice]

Judaism makes man free to do what he wants. He is free to choose his direction in life and to decide each individual action. Judaism holds man responsible for his actions and rejects the idea that Hashem brings good to man without his efforts. According to the Mishnah, "In the process of the world being judged for good, everything is determined according to the majority of the deeds" (Avot 3:15). Everything depends on free will. According to one's choice is the outcome: good or bad. "Man's deeds are in his control. God does not force a person or decree what he will do" (Rambam, The Laws of Repentance, chapter 5). "See, Today I have put before you life and goodness and death and evil...The blessing and the curse, choose life so that it will be good for you and your progeny" (Deuteronomy 30:15 & 19). What did we choose from the above? We chose evil, the curse of exile which leads to annihilation. We preferred to remain in exile even when we had the viable alternative to live in the Land of Israel. The eventual fate of the exile, sooner or later, is eradication. "And ye shall perish among the nations, and the land of your enemies shall eat you up" (Leviticus 26:38). This is both Torah law and nature's law. All this we have taken upon ourselves.

Diaspora Jewry is again in the midst of a spiritual and national holocaust. Today's holocaust, just like its predecessor, has annihilated millions of victims over the years. Will you ask where is God or will you acknowledge the unfortunate fact that the current holocaust's victims choose with their whole being to participate in exile. They don't leave the Diaspora even though they loose their most precious possession – their children. Personal or national suicide has no safety net, not from heaven and not from earth.

Nature Does Not Tolerate Deviants

As we said above, man, animals, and birds have natural instincts to live in a certain territory. This territorial instinct leads them to fight until the death for their territory. The creator designed the world so that each nation would have a land which is especially fitting for them. The Jewish People were given the land of Israel. We, who have chosen the deviant, abnormal, nomadic lifestyle, have adopted this abnormality for normal life. This mistake has led to poor choices. We have assimilated this deviation into our very feelings, thoughts and lifestyles. No one was capable of saving us from the exile's [mental and emotional] slavery. We stubbornly persisted in our nomadic lifestyle, defying the laws of nature. Whoever ignores and refuses to live by the rules of nature which the Creator established, will eventually be victimized by nature. The deviant can exist for a certain time. After that time, nature will overcome him and will drive him out of the world, either through a physical holocaust or a spiritual holocaust.

Until When?

We have discussed this at length because many people have not learned the holocaust lessons with all of their nuances. They refuse to negate the exile, with all of its terrible violence. They continue living as if the situation in exile has not worsened and the situation in Israel had not improved. Some of the Diaspora Torah leaders are under the influence of this illusion and expound it. If there is another yeshiva or Kollel, they think that Judaism is getting stronger and they voice this very loudly. Unfortunately, they ignore the process of Diaspora Jewry's disintegration. Everything is focused on small groups while the masses are getting lost. For every Jew who comes closer to God, one thousand are lost.

The Exile Incites Assimilation

Whoever tempts himself into believing that Diaspora communities have a chance of long-term existence is making a big mistake which will cost him his descendant's lives and the lives of those who believe his opinions. In the Diaspora there is the constant danger of foreign concepts invading one's spirit, simply because it's a foreign land and incites to assimilation. The result is that many religious parents loose their children to assimilation and even intermarriage. Some of them join the conservative and reform movements and from there it is easy to leave completely. The plague spreads and infects healthy people as well. Diaspora Jewry is emptying out spiritually and loosing its forefathers' spiritual and cultural treasures. This process is creating a vacuum which is being filled by western culture. This in turn tears the Jewish soul away from the its source and so destroys it. Today there is no question whether or not there will be another holocaust. The bitter truth is that it is transpiring before our very eyes. It is a silent holocaust, a spiritual and national holocaust. Rather, we are trying to close our eyes to the present catastrophic situation.

They were Mistaken About the Land of Israel

The admore of Belz, Rav Aaron, arrived in Israel as a refugee from the holocaust. When he arrived, he told Rav Shalom Raman-Kook, Rav Avraham Yitzchak HaCohen Kook's son-in-law, "We made a mistake in our approach to the land of Israel." Rabbi Yisachar Shlomo Teitel, z'l, a leading rabbi of Hungarian Jewry, was extremely anti-Zionist. In his book, *Eim Habonim Smecha*, he admits that he was mistaken. On almost every page he screams about the tragic mistake of not getting the Jews to go to the Land of Israel while there was still time. In spite of all this, whole Jewish populations refuse to do a spiritual accounting. They continue to strengthen their roots in exile, just as the European Jews did before the holocaust. They claim that the main thing is to rehabilitate Judaism and to learn Torah and to fulfill the commandments. Aliyah to Israel is not mentioned favorably. They correctly recognize the danger of foreign influences, yet they ignore the natural law that it is precisely living in a foreign land which causes this danger. This happens at the same time that we have merited to establish the state of Israel which proselytizes its inhabitants towards Judaism. Israel has also developed into the greatest center of Torah luminaries and Torah study and observance in the Jewish world. Even during the first and second Temples there were never as many yeshiva and kollel students as there are today in the state of Israel.

Scorning the Precious Land

HaRav Hillel Mishkolov, the main student of the Vilna Goan, said the following fiery words, "[Let us explain,] "In our many sins." Many are the sins including the great sin of "and they scorned the precious land." In addition, many of Torah scholars did not know that they were caught in the sin of the spies. They were caught in the klipot (husks) of the sin of the spies with many false logical arguments and empty, repulsive claims. They also hid their logic with scattered reasoning that the commandment to settle the Land of Israel does not apply today. This opinion has already been disproved by both Rishonim and Acharonim. Today's 'spies' want to be bigger than the Tanaim and Amoraim, who determined that settling Israel is equal in proportion to all of the commandments of the Torah. The Ramban set the commandment of settling the Land of Israel as a positive commandment of the Torah. 'And you will inherit it and settle it'... Who in the last generations was greater than the Vilna Gaon? He urged his students on with fiery speeches to go to the Land of Israel and to work on gathering the exiles. He put many efforts into encouraging his students to bring the end of days through settling the land of Israel. "Almost every day our Rav talked to us with trembling and excitement because "in Zion and Jerusalem there will be refuge," and not to be late for the time. Who can describe our rabbi's great concern as he spoke to us in holiness and with tears in his eyes."

Rav Hillel Mishkolov continued, "How painful was the fact that many of our Jewish brothers, among them the richest Jews in Russia, who enthusiastically intended to travel to the Land of Israel at the order of the Gaon of Vilna. Unfortunately, they were cooled off by Torah leaders who did not know or understand Torah. This is what the Goan wrote: "In the gathering of the exile, the Sitra Achara [The Satan (the forces of evil)], may be so strong as to put false ideas and foolish conceptions about Torah even among Torah scholars in order to delay the redemption. For example, the spies at the time of Moses were Torah scholars, yet the Satan sidetracked them" (Kol Hatur chapter 5).

Leaders Who Err Due to Misconceptions

Dr. Dov Yosefi's note is fitting to our subject. "When an individual errs due to his misconceptions and doesn't want to think about the facts because of his personal philosophy or economic interest, he has a personal problem. However, when a leader errs due to misconceptions, this is a tragedy because he spreads the misconceptions to the nation which leads to national catastrophe. This unfortunate phenomenon, which has plagued our people for generations, is also typical of our epoch, the time of returning to Zion, and it is protruding in our time."

The Sitra Achara of the Diaspora

You stand beaten, amazed and embarrassed. Does it make sense that Torah observant Jews who live in the Diaspora, who every week read the weekly portion twice with its translation, don't sense that the Torah and the land of Israel are one and the same, as Hashem commanded. Why are they careful to keep the first and not the second. They degrade the commandment to settle the Land of Israel? All of the Torah from beginning to end is the land of Israel. There is practically no weekly Torah portion that does not deal with: the land of Israel; the events that occurred there; its laws; its unique qualities; its holiness as Israel's inheritance; inheriting it; settling it; as a covenant between Elokim [God] and his People. Even more so, the Rabbis testified that everyone who lives in the Land of Israel is without sin, because the land atones for its Jewish inhabitants' sins (Ketuboth 111a, Yerushalmi Kilayim 9:3). Even more than this, whoever lives in the Land of Israel permanently is promised that he will inherit the world to come (Pessachim 113a and Yerushalmi Shabbat 1:3). In light of the greatness and holy Godliness of the Land of Israel, the following innocent question arises. How can God fearing, observant Jews, adhere to the exile and become estranged from God's inheritance and covenant with the Jewish People? Everyone will testify that Chazal said in both Talmuds and in the study halls that the Torah's commandments are directed towards an independent life in the Land of Israel. This is so because the only actualization of Torah study and observance is in the land of Israel. It is the "land that Elokim [God] watches over at all times. God's eyes are upon it from the beginning of the year until the end" (Deuteronomy 11:12)

Even more, the whole Diaspora lifestyle opposes Torah. The Torah relates to exile as the most terrible curse on the Jewish People and its existence. "The exile is difficult. It is equal to all of the curses in the Torah put together" (Sifre, Akev 43). The Torah emphasized this principle, "Everyone who lives in the land of Israel is similar to a person who has a God. Everyone who lives outside of Israel is similar to a person who does not have a God... and it is as if he worships idols" (Ketuboth 110b). These are difficult and painful issues, yet this is the truth.

Generally, even our Diaspora brothers who eagerly imbibe rabbinic teachings and live by them. However, they ignore the commandment to settle the Land of Israel. They ignore the stark truth and the foundation of everything, which is that the Holy One hates lies and deceit. They continue to pray evening, morning and afternoon: "Blow the great *shofar* [rams horn] of our freedom, raise the flag to gather our exiles, and gather us together from the four corners of the earth." All of this is at an era when the gates of our forefather's land are wide open and the land yearns for her sons to return to their borders. The Vilna Gaon's statement that, during the ingathering of the exiles, the Sitra Achara [power of evil] will get stronger was very true. Indeed, Satan's power rules even when we have merited The Jewish People's redemption in our land.

CHAPTER FIFTEEN

THE HOPE OF TWO THOUSAND YEARS

SINCE THE DESTRUCTION of the Second Temple and our exile generations have yearned for our People's redemption to our land. This yearning was accompanied by prayer, pleading, mortification, and fasting. The Rabbis compared the ingathering of the exiles to the creation of a new world for the Jewish People. "The ingathering of the exiles is greater than the creation of heaven and earth" (Pessachim 88a). Jews aspired to regaining Zion; they mourned, lamented and fasted because of the Temple's destruction, and they prayed for its rebuilding. Many generations were nurtured with the hope of returning to Zion. This hope helped our forefathers to keep going during all of the uncertain years of the long, cursed exile. Throughout the generations we confessed, "Because of our sins we were exiled from our country." Our hearts were pained because, "we are unable to immigrate" to Israel. We waited impatiently for the opportunity to return to our land. We said that when the opportunity to make aliyah comes, we will give a writ of divorce to the exile and stream, in mass, to our forefathers' land.

Our generation was the happiest generation, because we witnessed the fulfillment of the generations old dream. What we prayed for, hoped for and yearned for came to us as redemption and blessing. However, we did not pack our suitcases and move to Israel, but remained stuck in exile. Faith and yearning for Zion on one hand and solidifying our position in exile on the other. The mitzvah of returning to Zion and settling there was generally not observed. The majority of Jews preferred to remain in the lands of their dispersion. The prophet announced: "The remnant of Israel shall not do iniquity, nor speak lies, neither shall a deceitful tongue be found in their mouth" (Zephaniah 3:13). We make the prophet a liar when we do iniquity, speak lies and have deceitful tongues.

Immigrants Who Did Not Immigrate

Jews continue with their anomaly in spite of the holocaust and the establishment of the State of Israel. The immigration today continues in the same vein as it generally has been. Chaim Weitzman termed this aliyah as "Judaism of catastrophes." They immigrated to Israel from countries that were hostile to the Jews, or were in dire economic straights, and only when other countries would not allow them in. Those who had the opportunity to go to another country forgot everything and ignored their homeland completely. The fall of Iran's shah was truly a tragedy for Iranian Jews. Those Jews who managed to flee did not go to Israel. Some of them used

Israel as a "way station." Today they are in New York or Vienna. Today, there are 60,000 Iranian Jews in America. Algerian Jewry followed a similar pattern with, 85% relocating to France. There they are loosing over fifty percent of their children to the plague of intermarriage. Moroccan Jewry built Jewish communities in France, Montreal, and Latin America. Cuban Jewry did likewise: 10,000 went to America; 500 went to Israel; and some returned to Cuba. What happened to those Jews who left the USSR? Eighty percent went to America and to other countries, but not to Israel. They did this while they could have taken advantage of the way stations in Vienna and Italy en route to Israel. More than ninety percent of those Jews who chose to go to western countries rather than Israel, are well on their way to assimilation.

Who Believed that the South African Zionists Could do this?

We had hoped that the South African Jews, the dedicated and enthusiastic Zionists, would stand in line to immigrate to Israel. Only a few made aliyah, while the vast majority dispersed to Australia, New Zealand, the United States, and Canada. Only 20% of Jews who left South Africa moved to Israel. The Chairman of the Jewish student union in South Africa was not ashamed to state: "Ninety percent of the Jewish, South African Students intend to leave South Africa, however, many of us don't even consider making Aliyah to Israel." On one hand, South African Jewry flees due to the Black overthrow of the government and the resulting personal danger. On the other hand, many Israelis stream into South Africa looking for a new home. Reliable sources report that close to twenty thousand Israelis have settled there! It is strange that while Jews are fleeing South Africa other Jews are immigrating there. These are all our Jewish brothers, what a contradiction? They are chronic wanderers who have no rules or principles. They allow themselves to wander wherever the wind blows them, even if it is an evil spirit.

I remember that when South African Jews, who were known as enthusiastic Zionists, began to stream to Australia, a few journalists proclaimed that it was a Zionist crisis. I published then an article in the newspaper explaining that the idea of Zionism and the exalted value of ingathering of the exiles are not threatened by this crisis. However, this was a crisis for South African Jewry, who was unable to separate from the unnatural and negative phenomenon of living in exile, according to foreign lifestyles. They are always ready to move on and to wander from one exile to the next. The true and straight path which is the glory and the beauty of a nation living in its own land is no less true because many of its son's are mistaken. The commandment to live in Israel, with all of its treasures and blessings, is not damaged by poor souls who are unenlightened by normal Jewish nationalism.

Above everything, where did the South Africans choose to settle? They have chosen cities and countries where the contagious plague of assimilation and intermarriage rages. Where it consumes fifty percent of the Jewish population and will certainly strike South African Jewry's children as well.

The Large Emigration
In our naiveté, we believed that our dispersed nation's wandering would end with the establishment of the State of Israel. We said, Jews are once again being connected to their roots, in their forefathers' land, and will rest under their grapevines and fig trees. Men, like the produce growing in the fields, are dependent on their territory for their existence. Mankind adds the historical inheritance of the land. Jews add to this the religious belief that the holy land as an estate defined by the covenant between God and Israel. Unfortunately, we are infected with a bacterium called exile, which has invaded our blood and our collective experience. It pushes our people to move all over the world, even though the Jewish state has finally been established. Seven hundred and fifty thousand Israelis emigrated to the Diaspora since the State had been founded. These statistics are shocking!

Many Israeli youth are confused and pitiful. They are like beggars collecting door to door. They stand at the American, Canadian, Australian, South African and other embassies, their hands outstretched, begging for entry visas. The experienced consulate clerks can recognize them as chronic drifters. In their hearts they mock them: "The Jews are gypsies, with no land and no home. They will continue to drift forever…"

Exile to Your Hearts Content
Who could believe that after two thousand years of bitter exile, with anti-Semitism in full force, Israeli's would prefer to seek their future in foreign countries where they have to struggle for a living. It is doubtful whether they will make an adequate income, but it is clear that they will not make a secure Jewish life. Exile is an unnatural, negative phenomenon. However, the lowest and most miserable are the people who willingly exile themselves. They exile themselves for greed, they surrender to emotional helplessness. The wise men teach us that "Countrymen who willingly left their national homeland and their natural life, and moved to live in other countries, are considered parasites, who changed their colors and developed a strange nature."

The Educational System's Failure
The failure of the Israeli educational system is the root of emigration from Israel. The educational system ignores the historical fact that only education based on Jewish tradition can immunize, strengthen, and equip our youth to face the crises and challenges of the future. As Jewish identity weakens so does connection to the Land of Israel, driving the emigration rate up. A tree

with no roots will be uprooted by any normal breeze. Without deep roots in our forefathers' tradition and in our national history, our children will not be able to withstand the winds of evil which try to destroy us. Our entire national existence is based on spirituality, belief, and religion. These are the symbols of our life and the secret of our existence. Everything has its price, including distancing oneself from Judaism and rejecting values and idealistic vision. One pays by losing one's spirituality and one's emotions. Abandoning our forefathers' tradition destroys the basis of Jewish identity for the next generation. Our children are left with empty souls and perplexed hearts. Zionism without Judaism cannot last. Without values based on ideals there can be no love for the Jewish People and its land. Without love for the country nothing will be accomplished. Therefore, our youth goes searching for the fleshpots of the United States, mistakenly imagining that they will find an easier livelihood there.

Among them are 1,800 Israeli professors and lectures, 902 doctors who studied medicine in Israel, 324 scientists, and 171 high ranking military officers, 25,000 high tech workers, and 15,500 kibbutz members living in the United States today. 600 shlichim (teachers, government representatives, etc.) went to America and did not return. 10,400 Israel students are pursuing higher education in the Diaspora. These facts demonstrate that even the new generation raised in Israel is not immune to the genetic disease of wandering. Life without vision, values, beliefs and our forefather's tradition can cause our youth to flee to drugs, alcoholism, and even to exile.

Most of those mentioned above, who left Israel for the Diaspora, held safe jobs and good salaries in the Jewish State. Some of them even enjoyed high salaries there. But their lust for more money and being addicted to the wandering stuff, made them desert their homeland for a foreign and anti-Semitic environment. There to lose their most precious possession – their children, of whom seventy percent end up in intermarriage and assimilation.

Source of Power
Emigration from Israel does not exist among Torah observant Jews. They will not leave the good land for a better physical life in a foreign country. They know the land of Israel's great value to the Torah and the Jewish People. Religious education has succeeded in cultivating roots strong enough to resist the storm of wanderlust. The strength of the connection between Judaism and retuning to Zion can be seen from the fact that religious Jews form the vast majority of immigrants from developed countries. A community which has deep Jewish roots displays a strong bond to its land.

Kibbutz members who left Israel state that they were not taught any special love for Israel. They claim that "if a movement wants to emotionally bond its members to the land, it must follow the example of the national religious Jewry. The religious kibbutz movement is the ideal solution. Take all of the kibbutz children and educate them like the religious kibbutz movement does and there will not be emigration" (Kibbutz L.A. 29). We heard the same ideas from emigrants to Australia.

The Ideal Education

The national religious education is outstandingly successful, especially in the Yeshiva high schools and Hesder Yeshivas. This success is reached by inculcating a deep system of values. These values nurture strong behavior, deep roots in the Jewish religion and culture, and love for the Jewish People and the land of Israel. The national religious education raises youth who are free of complexes about making decisions based on fragmented souls. They don't leave their country and don't avoid the draft. The opposite is true. They volunteer for the best units in the army. National religious education raises a magnificent generation, which is an example in every field: morally, nationally, and personally. It participates fully in Torah, in pioneering, and in every field of human endeavor. This generation is fully motivated to serve its people and its country and to defend them with their body and soul. Indeed, religious education is capable of strengthening Israeli youth against the plague of exile, and awakening their sleeping love for the Land of Israel. This forges a connection that is not broken. Our national uniqueness and our religious mission are intrinsically integrated together. A tree needs its roots to maintain itself. The secret of our past existence has been educating our children in Jewish tradition and history. This will continue to be the foundation of our future.

Integrating Israeli Emigrants

Sociologists' findings ((Kivunim 117 [43] 6) clearly show that the vast majority of immigrants in America – and in our experience in the other countries of exile –feel very distant from Jewish communities in their new country. They are unwilling to integrate into communal life of the synagogue, Jewish day schools, and Jewish social clubs. Above all they prefer to send their children to secular public schools. Apparently, the Yordim's (emigrants) first priority is to ensure their children adjust quickly to the lifestyle, language and culture of the Christian environment. On the other hand, the local Jewish communities are not open to accept these immigrants.

Sociological findings reveal that the parents, the first generation, try to maintain their cultural roots and Israeli identity. However, their children, the second generation, do not try to maintain anything. They prefer to integrate into the general gentile society, rather than into Jewish society. This second generation adopts the habits, customs, and national culture of their new country. Their bond to Israel weakens. A new generation arises that does not know Israel. Sociological findings reveal that the second generation does not integrate into the local Jewish community. Sociology presents us with the painful conclusion that second generation of Yordim will assimilate and intermarry into gentile society at faster than normal rate.

Israeli Children on Foreign Soil

There is a very sad, touching picture of nice Israeli children, speaking Hebrew, who have been exiled from their land, where they studied and associated with each other with love and brotherhood, under the blue sky of freedom and independence. Their parents condemned them to crisis and upheaval in a strange and hostile environment, and to anti-Semitic attacks from their classmates. We met them on various occasions and saw the tears in their eyes and felt their pain. They were pure and naïve children who were unluckily born to parents who treated them cruelly. We explained this in the previous section: "Parental Cruelty to Children" (Chapter 6). These young victims suffer emotional torture. It causes them internal stress which may cause them permanent emotional scars. This is really an abnormal lack of parental compassion. Even birds and animals feel compassion for their chicks and puppies. They protect them from every attacker.

It is well known that there is a significant rise in anti-Semitism in all of the countries where Jews live, including the United States. Energetic youth can be cruel towards the Jewish youth that they hate: They can tease them and mock them with insults and humiliations. These young victims naturally feel inferior and humiliated among these non-Jews. There is no worse emotional distress than to have a religious and national identity which the surrounding environment embarrasses them for. This cruelty causes them to feel sick of their outsider identity and to eventually reject it. As a result, these young Jews develop very painful conflicts which afflict them throughout their lives. It is no wonder that these youth dropout, en masse, from the Jewish People. To our great sorrow sociological studies confirm this. One reaps what he sows!

Unsettled and Embittered

Professor Aaron Harrell Fish's comments confirm the Israeli emigrants' children's suffering: "I can testify that it is not good for Jews to live in exile. Externally, their lives appear alright, however, what happens to them inside is not good. I know Israeli families who live in Canada. They feel cold [inside their hearts], even though they have a car and other amenities. Their children suffer and cry a lot and don't know why. During my vacation, I visited an Israeli family in Providence. They had a fourteen year old son. He was unable to articulate his uneasiness, but something was very wrong with this boy. This was expressed when he refused to eat any foods other than watermelon, hummus, falafel, and olives (all are Israeli foods). He refused to eat anything else. Could a boy who is unable to explain himself, explain any more clearly what he is missing?"... (Yahadut, Zionut veMedinah 49)

The Yordim's (Those who have moved away from Israel) Children's Distress

Professor Naama Tzabar Ben Yehosha, from Tel Aviv University, traveled to the United States. There she conducted research on Kibbutz members who had exiled themselves, en masse, to the United States. In her meetings and interviews with them, she could feel the children's emotional distress. 'The teenagers generally rebelled against being uprooted from the kibbutz' social network... They were in an emotional crisis. Had they remained in the Israeli kibbutz, they would have received emotional and social support from their friends. Now they must face both their emigration crisis and their teenage crisis in a foreign country, culture and mentality. They have to deal with two crises at once. I met with fifth and sixth graders who were "angry" with their parents for months about the injustice that their parents had done to them...The problems caused by emigration damaged the entire family core. The emigrants' children felt physically and socially isolated from their peers, teachers, and the unfamiliar environment. The parents don't feel any better and therefore they are unable to help. The children feel the emotional storm, just like their parents. In addition, they also have stormy feelings towards their parents...The children also have strange, difficult, and ambivalent feelings towards their Israeli identity. They feel an identity conflict. They feel the heavy burden of living in two different cultures simultaneously. They are Americans in school and Israelis at home. Therefore, they often seek revenge against their parents by rejecting Israeli culture. Not only do they refuse to speak Hebrew, but they also boycott anything Israeli. They are fed up with their Israeli identity, and abandon it. They put their efforts into becoming "Americans." (Kibbutz L.A. 97–9)

One's Most Precious Possessions

An ancient Roman story tells about a very fashionable lady who visited the noble princess Cornelia. During the entire visit, all that this lady talked about was her beautiful clothing and precious jewelry. Eventually, she turned to the princess and said, I am sure that you also have precious jewelry, could you please show them to me? The princess left the room. After a short while she returned, hugging her two children under her arms. She proclaimed, these are my most precious jewels! Indeed, our children are our most precious jewels. For Jews they are even more. They are the continuation of our life and faith. As it says in Nedarim 64: whoever does not have children is considered as dead. Our matriarch Rachel said to Yaakov: Bring me children, without children I am dead (Genesis 30:1). Our children are the horizon. They are the channels through which will bring future generations. The Torah portion which tells of Yaakov's death is called VaYehee [meaning "and he shall live"] because our forefather Yaakov lives on in his descendants.

Jews remain in exile because their prime motivation is to pursue the material comforts of life. This motivates them more than their children's happiness and wellbeing. They are chasing after the imaginary fleshpots which are "over the sea." However, they are forfeiting living by Jewish values and love of country which would enrich both them and their children. They are neglecting their children and their children's sense of well being. The Greek philosopher, Socrates once protested, if I could climb to the height of heights in Athens, I would raise my voice and warn people. I would say, "Citizens of Greece, you work by the sweat of your brow to accumulate fortunes. At the same time you neglect your children's welfare and their internal richness. However, one day you will have to give all of your possessions to them." Likewise, if I could march in the street of the Diaspora, I would raise my voice calling: Dear Brethren, you are toiling day and night to acquire money, while you are neglecting your greatest treasure: your children's Jewish future, who are trapped by the Diaspora Moloch, who swallows them up.

Leaving the Land of Israel Leads to Losing your Children

The findings show that the second generation of emigrants from Israel, the children of the emigrants, assimilate and intermarry at much higher rates than Jews whose families were born in exile. The children of the emigrants intermarry at the astronomical rate of 70%. Its unbelievable! According to the opinions of sociologists, one can assume that the existence of assimilation among the Israeli emigrants' camp will carry in its wake the third generation, the children of the remaining 30%. In other words, Israeli emigration will result in the emigrants' descendents' complete assimilation. The majority will assimilate in the second generation and the remainder in the third generation. We are witnessing the destruction of 750,000 Israeli emigrants, who should have reached now one million people. Eternal wanderers until they disappear in intermarriage. A silent holocaust! This is definitely a severe crisis for the Jewish People and for our state. This is a threat to the state's existence at a time when the demographic axe is waving over our heads.

Jeremiah (22:10) says: "Weep ye not for the dead, neither bemoan him; but weep sore for him that goes away, for he shall return no more, nor see his native country." Regarding this verse, The Gemora in Moed Katan (27:) explains, "Do not cry for the deceased and don't pace up and back for him. In other words, don't cry too much for the deceased. Don't pace up and back more than the normal mourning period. However, for the Jews who have gone to a foreign country, cry your head off and don't stop crying. Cry because they will never return to see their homeland and its intrinsic worth." This kind of loss deserves weeping for generations. Not only physical destruction is called ruin and annihilation. But also spiritual destruction including assimilation is true ruin and annihilation.

A National Catastrophe

We are facing the terrible catastrophe of the disappearance of the vast majority of our people of the Diaspora. Many times more Jews are disappearing than the number of Jews who were in the Land of Israel when the State was established. It is not the result of external attacks. Rather, it is the result of a rapid internal breakdown within the Jewish People. These Jews are disappearing into gentile society. This is a process of loosing the Israeli emigrants' children from Judaism and from the Land of Israel. It is surprising that the Israeli press defends emigrating from Israel. The press relates to it as if someone was moving from Jerusalem to Tel-Aviv, or from Tel Aviv to the Golan. The press acts as if the struggle for the Land of Israel and the loss of the vast majority of our people is of no interest to it. Perhaps this behavior stems from their emotional leaning towards national suicide.

The Fervor for the Golden Calf

In nature, if a person is missing one sense, such as sight, he will be blessed with more developed senses such as feeling or hearing to compensate for his blindness. The emigrants from Israel are missing love for their homeland and their natural connection to their land. Therefore, they try to compensate for through acquisition, through love for money and a passion for profits. They go into exile in search of the golden calf. The undeniable truth is that if someone is willing to work, he can get along very well in Israel. However, the grass is always greener on the other side of the fence. They abandon their principles and don't despise any method of making money. They aspire to wealth. They are willing to sacrifice their children, their peace of mind and their true happiness on the imaginary alter of wealth. They are prepared to leave their familiar homeland, where they lived with their family, connected by a shared set of values and ideals. They lived with the feeling of freedom rejoicing their hearts in the exalted mission of the Israeli independence. They part from their close relatives and good friends, to whom they were bound with ties of love and friendship. They move to a foreign country, where anti-Semitism lurks in everywhere. In this foreign country they lack human and social relations and live in permanent conflict and depression. Money blinds them. They don't understand that not all that glitters is gold. Many disappointments and tragedies are anticipated for them in the new foreign country.

Performing Hard, Low Status Work

There were six Jewish catering companies under Sydney Rabbinic supervision, which I was honored to have authority over. Some of these companies' kitchens were small and stuffy due to improper ventilation. One kitchen was located in someone's garage which did not even have a window. It was hard to breathe because of the suffocating heat and steam from the cooking. To our surprise, all of the cooks were women and daughters of emigrant Israeli families. In Israel they would not have been willing to work in the Hilton Hotel or King David Hotel kitchens. Some women worked as cleaning ladies in schools or hospitals. Building contractors employed Israelis to do all kinds of physically hard manual labor. They are willing to work hard under difficult conditions. Some worked as traveling salesmen, selling kitchenware and other small items door to door. If those same emigrants were willing to work that hard in Israel, they would be able to succeed even better here in Israel.

Both in Australia and Los Angeles, we found many Israelis in dire poverty, some actually hungry for bread. One must remember that even in these countries there is a high rate of unemployment. Australia has an unemployment rate of 6%–7%, which is approximately 600,000 unemployed people. In America there are approximately five million unemployed. That rich country has the highest discrepancy in the world between classes. There is a tremendous variation in the economic level and lifestyle between the various economic strata of society. There are thirty six million people under the poverty line and three million homeless in the United States.

In the beginning of 5762 (2002 CE), a businessman named Lev Levayav, revealed the sad and difficult reality. Approximately sixty thousand Buchara Jews living in America were in dire financial straits. Mr. Levayav was serving as the president of the Buchara Jewry. Their financial situation was so terrible that Mr. Levayav turned to the Buchara community, numbering approximately 200,000 Jews in Israel, to help their American Jewish brothers deal with their economic poverty. This is the present situation of Israelis who immigrated to the "land of gold"…

It is interesting to see Professor Na'ama Tzabar's research on former Kibbutz members' lifestyle in Los Angeles. "These immigrants are willing to do any work, including hard and stressful work. They do low-level work and their earnings are less than they were in their native country. They get by with very little and are willing to delay satisfaction. Some sell candies, movies, and seafood out of private cars on street corners. They do every kind of work! Kibbutz girls do all types of jobs including working in kindergartens and babysitting in Jewish homes. They also do cleaning and work as waitresses. Some of them admitted to being materialistic. They abandon their values for money and enter into the spiral of doing anything to earn more money. About twenty two percent of all of the new Israeli immigrants to America live under the poverty line. This is twice the number of the new immigrants from Europe."

Family Tragedies

In spite of all their difficulties, their sufferings and disappointments, these poor miserable emigrants write to their friends and families describing how good their new lives are. They feel that they must justify their decision to emigrate. They are therefore forced to hide the truth from their friends and family. Unfortunately, we have seen many family tragedies resulting from this emigration. I remember an Israeli taxi driver in Sydney, whom we had ridden with several times. One day, when he came to pick me up, he was feeling so sad and depressed that he almost caused an accident. Then he confided in me that he was worried and embarrassed because his son was marrying a gentile that very day. That day I gave him a tried and true recommendation how to save his other children from the same fate. A few days later, he returned to me. He said 'Rabbi, I have decided to take your advice. I am selling my taxi. I, my wife, and my two daughters are returning to Israel. He had the wisdom and courage to draw conclusions from his experience of exile, and to return to his own country. However, almost none of the Israeli emigrants leave the exile, even when it threatens to steal all of their children through intermarriage. They are unable to admit their failure. On the other hand, they are aware that that their children's intermarriages cause friction and arguments between the parents. They accuse each other that the other was to blame for emigrating from Israel. Indeed, how can parents remain complacent when their children have gone to graze in foreign fields? Sometimes, the tear between the couple is so great that they can no longer remain together. They emigrated to find prosperity and satisfaction, but it disintegrated into broken and bereaved families. We knew bereaved parents who were drowning their troubles in alcohol. They could no longer face themselves, their loneliness, nor their emptiness. They fled from their homeland to exile and now they flee from themselves to the drunken stupor of alcohol…

The Lesson

There is a story about a man that always went about with his head bowed and back bent. His eyes were dimmed, showing no joy or life. His childhood friend, who had not seen him for many years, was embarrassed to see him so miserable and depressed. He remembered his friend as an emotionally stable and courageous man, happy, and full of life. After much investigation, he learned the reason for his friend's drastic personality change. This poor man once found a gold coin in the street and was very happy. In his desire to find more coins, he always walked bently, looking down for more finds. Over time, he did find more coins. However, he destroyed his posture and ruined his eyesight. What a terrible price he paid for the glitter of coins. For them, people are willing to go from light to darkness, from freedom to slavery, from redemption to mourning and grief…

Wandering from Exile to Exile

Although the return to Zion has gone from being a prophecy to being a reality, only a small minority of our people have willingly and lovingly moved to Israel. For example, Although the Former Soviet Union has recently endured economic hardships, all of the peoples have continued living in their homelands. Jews acted differently. They emigrated from their homeland, en masse and went to whatever countries would permit them entry. They even went to Germany. Regarding those who moved to Israel they acted in the most natural and noble manner. They returned to their homeland, to the land of their fathers. This is in contrast to 700,000 Jews from the Former Soviet Union who gave up on moving to Israel. They went to America, and tens of thousands of Jews who went to Australia, New Zealand, and other countries. About two hundred thousand Jews who left the Soviet Union settled in Germany, the country which methodologically spilled Jewish blood like water. They have lost their values together with their Divine image, their self-respect, and their humanity. Similarly, almost all of the Cuban Jews left due to economic difficulties stemming from the communist regime. Meanwhile the general Cuban People continues living there as they always have. Today, Argentina is in economic distress. Naturally, the Argentineans don't even consider immigrating to another country to seek their livelihood. However, her Jews, who have lived there for over one hundred years, are looking for ways to leave the country. They yearn to make their fortune in the United States or in Spain, where wandering Jews have not set foot for generations. But not to the Jewish homeland. They are eternal wanderers. They float around the world for a while until they disappear.

Lack of Appreciation

This same process reoccurs in other countries. For example, South Africa was a wealthy country. Every house had male servants and maids. The white Christian population has a 5% emigration rate due to the Black takeover of the government. The Jewish population has an emigration rate of over 50%. Almost all of the young Jews have left South Africa. The vast majority emigrated after having benefited for a few generations from the best South Africa had to offer.

Among those who severely criticized South African Jewry's departure was the Chief Rabbi of South Africa. In the Jewish world congress journal "B'Tfuzot, The chief Rabbi claimed that the emigrants were ungrateful compared to those who decided to remain in South Africa."

In addition, he claimed that that the Jews who left and intend to leave, also sin against the country. "With all that the country has invested in their education and their professional training for promising professions, this is how they repay the country"...However, it is doubtful that his statements will be listened to and can stem the tide of these Jews dispersing all over the world. As we have seen earlier, the chairman of the South African Jewish Student Union declared that 90 percent of the Jewish students intend to leave South Africa and don't consider going to Israel. And so, they wander eternally until they disappear entirely. They confirm our enemies' opinion that Jews are not at home anywhere and are a nomadic people whose only ideal is materialism.

The Exiled Jews' Spirit

Pierre Goldman was a leftist revolutionary and a brilliant author. A whole series of literature sprang up around him. In his book, *Dark Memories of a Polish Jew who was Born in France*, he reveals the true status and attitudes of the Jews in exile. Goldman was born in France in 1944, the son of Jews from Poland. He explains why it never occurred to him to go to Israel. "I was a stranger in Israel, like in every other country. I was too Jewish to be or feel Israeli. I was too Jewish to settle in one country. In my perspective, in my being, Israel was just another place in the Jewish Diaspora, another exile." He wrote about his being born in France, "In my most inner being I was never a Frenchman. I was just a Jewish exile with no promised land. Eternal exile, with no end, ever. I was not a member of the proletariat, but neither did I have a homeland. No homeland except for the exile. The same absolute exile, the same Jewish exile, the Diaspora" (Memories page 56). He felt the hatred of those who supported the philosophy of "France to the French". Goldman is typical of "the interior exile," the never-ending exile, which is the lot of the wandering Jew.

Everyone is rooted in his land and emotionally bound to his country. Every animal remains in a certain territory, a bird's nest, a fox's tunnel, and a leopard's lair. For wandering Jews there is only exile, never ending exile.

It is Good for Him to Die for the Exile

A homeless creature, exiled and wandering from exile to exile, he is chased and tortured. Though they make pogroms against him and murder his wife and children, he refuses to leave exile. He is unwanted. They embarrass him and slander him. They paint swastikas on his synagogues and communal institutions and even torch them. They desecrate his graves and destroy his tombstones. Yet he does not move out. The exile cannot get rid of him. He didn't even learn from the poison gas and the crematorium. Even after all this he continues wandering, just like before. They tried to uproot the exile from his heart through providing a safe shelter for him and his descendants in the land of his forefathers. But even this did not help. It is impossible to take him out of the exile. There are also Jews who speak in God's name. They use the messiah as an excuse to remain in exile until his arrival. Through this they change the messiah's mission from rescuing and redeeming to devastating and destroying his people. Wandering Jews also stream from their homeland to the purgatory of exile. They are willing to sacrifice their most precious possession – their children upon the exile's alter. There they are mercilessly annihilated because, "it is good for them to die for the exile." These children are love sacrifices to the Moloch of exile...

Spiritual AIDS Disease

The bacterium called exile lives in our blood and in our national experience. This bacterium has infected wandering Jews with a spiritual AIDS which eats away their souls and spirits. This disease acts by breaking down the spiritual and national immune system, by destroying the threads of Jewish life. It exposes its victims to infections caused by the negative, destructive influences of the non-Jewish environment. Powerless to resist, the exile forces push them to assimilate. The result is a self-inflicted plague of assimilation and intermarriage of holocaust proportions.

I Believe

I am fully convinced and I believe with complete faith that our divine sages were completely right when they declared: that the commandment to settle in the Land of Israel is equal in importance to all the Torah commandments all together (Sifri Deut. 12:29). This is completely and literally true, for it is the base for the survival of the Jewish People in body and soul, its growth, success and bliss.

I believe with full faith the Rabbi's interpretation of the Torah verse, "In order that your days and the days of your children multiply in the land" (Deut. 11:21). Your children will live long lives and multiply in the land of Israel, but not in foreign lands. This too is the truth and will remain so forever.

CHAPTER SIXTEEN

ISRAELI ALOOFNESS TO "THE SILENT HOLOCAUST"

A BITTER, TRAGIC spectacle is occurring before our very eyes. Large parts of our nation are being torn off our national body. The plague of spiritual assimilation and biological intermarriage attacks us mercilessly. It makes major inroads in the Jewish communities of the Diaspora. The tie to Judaism loosens and disappears and hundreds of thousands of Jews disappear through the kiss of death. This same angel of death constantly travels to every Jewish community in every country of the Diaspora. The foreign environment oppresses the national personality and blurs its Jewish identity. Exile fragments the nation's soul, because life in exile is drawn into a process of assimilation. This process occurs whether people are aware or unaware of it.

The Second National Holocaust
In this generation, we are loosing just as many young people as during the holocaust. These terrible statistics are publicized periodically by experts and by the most prestigious national institutions in Israel and the Diaspora. These statistics should shock every Jew who fears for the fate of his people. Jews should scream out to the masses in the Diaspora about the dangers they face, the dangers resulting from self-destructive assimilation into their surrounding cultures. Jews should spur them on to move to Israel as the only way to save themselves from extinction. Although once in a while one hears a comment, but no serious or significant steps have been taken to stop the plague of assimilation. We have not deviated from the standard Jewish activities used during normal times.

Jewish Nation, Where are you?
The Israeli Government does not seem to deal seriously with the tragic fate of Diaspora Jewry. It simply ignores the dangerous situation which worsens every year. We are dealing with a silent holocaust, and a silent extermination. It is an accelerated process of mass assimilation into the surrounding population and no one says a word or lifts a finger. It's as if the Jewish People has decided to commit suicide.

You are dumbfounded, outraged, and appalled as to how long we can remain passive and silent, facing the national kiss of death of such a large part of our nation? We are a nation losing more than 60,000 youngsters each year to mixed marriages. As years pass, millions of Jews drop out and disappear quietly. Diaspora Jewry is currently going through a critical and awful breakdown, a breakdown that endangers its very existence. Where is the shock over what is happening to a large part of our people? Where is the trembling soul? In fact, there is no worry and no concern – as though they are not our brethren and not a part of our nation. We should be alerted heaven and earth with our roars to awaken the nation to its critical situation!

No initiative to stop this disaster is being taken coming either by the State of Israel or by any of the centers of Diaspora Jewry. We are not doing anything to enlist the power of the nation against this dangerous struggle. The national institutions are not doing anything out of the ordinary. They are acting as though we are in normal times, protected from both external and internal dangers. However, they are not arousing the masses to defend themselves against the malignancy. As a result, the Diaspora Jews, as always, have their heads buried in the sand. What will we be able to respond, when future generations blame us, rightfully so, for standing by the abyss of the loss of our nation, for doing nothing to save it from descending to those depths, from a national Jewish perspective? What memorial will they establish to the millions lost to assimilation and inter-marriage?

The Meager Aliyah from Western Countries

We are perplexed by the meager Jewish Aliyah from Western countries. We complain about their sitting on their fleshpot and refusing to settle in the land of our fathers. Truth be told, this painful question should be directed at us! Have we clearly and sincerely stated the reality – that the Diaspora is an unnatural phenomenon, a temporary delusion whose physical and spiritual extinction is anticipated? Have we warned them that if the Diaspora is not liquidated, the Diaspora will liquidate them, and that they are headed for disintegration and termination? Have we informed them that Aliyah is in their best interest – saving their children from assimilation; that settling in the Land of Israel is not only a mitzvah from the Torah, but Jewish defense as well? We absolutely have not informed them!

Money is the Answer to Everything …

The State of Israel has demanded monetary assistance from the more prosperous countries to assist in Jewish Aliyah from distressed countries and assistance to the State during times of financial distress. However, Aliyah was not advocated as a value for survival, as a means of saving souls, or as a historic demand of the nation to its wandering brethren.

Over tens of years, from the establishment of the State of Israel, they promised Diaspora Jewry, that Jews living in Western countries were fulfilling their Jewish obligation and loyalty to Israel by providing financial support. They repeated this mantrap almost to the point of brain washing. The leaders of fundraising campaigns for Israel repeatedly thanked supporters; "You, our fortunate brethren, who sit comfortably in prosperity, please give generously to assist your poor and unfortunate brethren, who have immigrated to Israel from distressed countries! Give charitably as you do not need saving or redemption." As a result, it became absorbed into the consciousness of Western Jews that Israel was a refuge for poor, depressed Jews from distressed countries. However, Aliyah was not meant for the prosperous Jews. What a wonder that today they are not coming on Aliyah! Simply put, we did not present the whole truth about the shortcomings of the Diaspora and we did not educate them toward personal fulfillment! This process removed the insight and path from Zionism. It enabled one to be a loyal Zionist, even a Zionist leader and activist, and still deny the Diaspora's shortcomings. Zionism's most critical error is: it did not create an atmosphere that the place for every Jew is in Israel, and that the Diaspora is not his natural home.

A Forlorn Picture of Life in Israel
Even more so, the United Jewish Appeal, unintentionally became a factor in the prevention of Aliyah from Western countries, and fatally sabotaged it. The fundraising lecturers painted a black picture of the economic and security conditions in Israel, in order to encourage our brethren to donate considerably. I remember a major-general from the IDF, who was invited as a main speaker for the UJA campaign in Sydney. This man, with all of his military knowledge, dedicated his speech to the threatening danger to the State of Israel from missile launchings on three fronts, from the Syrian, Iraqi, and Iranian…. These things obviously opened the pockets of the listeners. On the other hand, this raised worry and fright for the State of Israel's existence and its security, and as such struck a blow against Aliyah.

My Personal Scenario
I myself experienced this several times. When I spoke at UJA campaign parties for Israel, I described life in Israel optimistically, by emphasizing the good in Israel and its citizens. The campaign fundraisers commented to me that it would be more effective to emphasize the poverty, suffering, and sacrifices of the Israelis, in order to encourage greater donations.

The Whole World is One
This trend is general and knows no boundaries. In the years that I lived in the United States, I very often heard the UJA campaign fundraisers and spokespersons emphasize sad and terrifying things regarding the economic situation and Israel's security. The UJA pamphlets described life in Israel as difficult and dangerous. Some of the descriptions included; "The Israelis pay the highest taxes in the world, workers' strikes disturb the daily life, the number of young criminals is on the increase, men are away from their homes 30 to 40 days a year for army reserves – making family life and

running a business difficult, government debt has reached nine billion dollars," and more.

Gloomy and terrifying stories arouse depression and deathly fear. The Jews of the prosperous countries unintentionally received a distorted, shocking picture of the condition of the State of Israel and the life of its settlers. For tens of years they told these frightening and awful stories in overkill to the masses, and relieved them of any desire to make Aliyah. It's no wonder that Jews from the Western, more prosperous countries, avoided Aliyah. Who would endanger himself and his family, to establish his home and life in such a poor and dangerous life-threatening place, full of obstacles?

Entrenched in a Stance

These stories once again force me to reiterate the illustrative incident: one day during WWII, when Winston Churchill visited the front, he asked one of the soldiers what his task was — the soldier, instead of responding that he was protecting his homeland, answered that he was protecting his position...Indeed, they made the subordinate the essence and the essence subordinate. They make an effort to protect the public position, instead of protecting the homeland.

The Result: Parents' Opposition to Aliyah

As a result of the depressing picture of the economic situation and the security in Israel that was painted by the UJA spokespeople, it is no wonder that parents vehemently opposed their children's Aliyah to Israel.

It was very late one night when I received a call from the President of a Sydney synagogue, who requested that I come to his home to calm his wife who was having a breakdown due to bad news that had come her way. When I arrived, I found her sitting and crying over the bitter news. In between her sobs she told me that her only son was about to drop a bitter tragedy upon them. When I heard this, I naively imagined that her son fell in love with a non-Jewess. However, she continued to expound of her "tragedy" between her sobbing. Her son had decided to settle in Israel, this poor land full of life-threatening dangers! She pleaded with me to convince him to change his mind. I was shocked at her words! I jumped out of my seat and raised my arms towards the heavens and called out: "L-rd Almighty, I wish that this tragedy should befall me, my relatives, my friends and every Jew. So that they would merit to raise families in Israel, descendants who are faithful to their religion and their nation; instead of being lost to assimilation and inter-marriage in the Diaspora!"

The matter ended positively. In the end, the parents sold their large, prospering business in Sydney and followed their son on Aliyah as permanent residents, building a faithful, devoted home in Israel.

Aliyah vs. Honoring One's Parents

As a result of several similar incidents that repeated themselves among Australian Jewry, I publicized a religious teaching. According to Torah law, children should not listen to their parents when they are preventing them from performing the mitzvah of settling in the Land of Israel. They should make Aliyah and settle in the Holy Land. According to Jewish law the laws of settling the Land of Israel supersedes the laws of honoring one's parents. Settling of the Land of Israel is honoring HaShem and the existence of Israel, and the parents are also obligated to settle in the Holy Land (see my book: הנשירה לאור ההלכה, paragraph: Aliyah vs. Honoring Parents, page 192).

Chapter Seventeen

Establishing a Rescue Council

OUR NATION'S CURRENT situation is very similar to that of heroes of a well known Chassidic story. Once a Jew got lost in a thick forest. He was there for a few days and could not find his way out. Eventually, in the distance, he saw a man walking towards him. He was very happy because he hoped that his deliverer had come and would show him how to get out of the forest. The stranger said to him, "I have also been lost in this great forest for many days. I don't know how to help you, although I can tell you one thing. Don't continue in the direction that I came from. There is no salvation there. So let's keep going together to search for our way out of the forest to freedom."

Rescue for Those who Have Lost their Way

Also, we cannot continue to be lost and without guidance. We must help our brothers who are lost in the Diaspora. They are caught in a whirlwind of assimilation and intermarriage and have no idea how to get free of it. The direction that we have chosen is "sit and don't do anything." The result of this is national loss and destruction. Every year that passes without action causes the Jewish communities in Diaspora to wither. We must find another way to fight this plague of assimilation. The severity of the situation obligates us to change direction immediately to take care of the spiritual and national holocaust, which is destroying Diaspora Jewry.

We have not lost the battle since we have not even started to fight. We must draft all of the nation's resources to fight with all of our strength to solve the current problem.

This Epoch's Special Demands – a Rescue Council is Needed

A rescue council should be established. It should be composed of idealists who are organizers and doers, dedicated to the objective of stopping the spiritual and national disintegration. First and foremost the council's function should be to activate all of the varying Jewish organizations wherever there are Jews. In rabbinic organizations, in synagogues, in temples, in Jewish clubs, in youth organizations, and every place where there are any Jewish activities, one must reach every Jewish home throughout the world. Jewish values must be taught to a generation which is disconnecting from its glorious past and forsakes its historical and religious connection to the Jewish People and to the Land of Israel. We must summon our best resources including many lecturers to conduct this campaign to save the Jewish People. The rescue council should be responsible to organize and send influential, well spoken Rabbis; Israeli authors; lecturers; educators; and youth leaders. These professionals will be able to analyze potential painful questions about our national existence and raise the State of Israel's goals. They should make short visits to Jewish centers, university campuses, to ignite enthusiasm and to awaken the Jews to properly defend their spirituality and nationality. The rehabilitation must be done in every country, in every city, in every community, and in every neighborhood in the Diaspora.

Knowing Oneself and Discarding Illusions

We must accept that we are not a normal nation, as we have explained in previous chapters. Psychology has determined that the main condition for emotional stability is knowing oneself and discarding illusions. Know thyself! If you have a weakness, don't ignore it and don't fool yourself. Acknowledge your weakness and try to solve the problem through normal and natural channels. If we drop our illusions that we Jews are like the other Peoples in every way, we will have greater ability and strength to overcome that troublesome arena in which we differ from the norm and nature, and for which we pay such a tragic price.

The only way to end this national crisis is by taking drastic measures. A moderate remedy will not be effective. Aspirin can lower fever and help pain but it does not cure a disease. A strong antibiotic is needed to destroy the bacteria carrying the disease. To reveal a hand-breadth and to conceal two hand-breadths will accomplish nothing. We must present Diaspora Jews with a complete analysis of the components of their weaknesses and their failures. It must be completely true, without making the situation look better than it is. This may deeply shock our brothers. But it may also change their values and way of life.

Losing their Most Precious Possession

First and foremost, we should constantly bear in mind that Jews who live in the Diaspora are at risk of losing their most precious possession – their children – through assimilation and intermarriage. This will bring 4,000 years of Jewish heritage to an abrupt end for these families.

Sociological research has found that "the worst crisis is among Jewish students on college campuses around the world. The vast majority of them are fleeing from their Jewish identity, yet they cannot fully integrate into any other entity. Despite the illusion that they may choose to abandon the heritage of their ancestors, there exists a barrier which cannot be denied. The typical Jewish student is trying to run away from himself but is not really being fully accepted into whichever group he is trying to join. He feels that the world of his fantasies is closed to him. He is unsure of himself and peace of mind eludes him."

It should be noted that these words are describing normal times. But what can be said of the shattered mental state of Diaspora Jewish youth in these crazy times. Today, hatred of our people is raging like an inferno among the nations of the world, and a new era of crudeness and immorality is emerging at universities in the US and around the world.

The Rise of Anti-Semitism

We wanted to believe that after the horrors of the Holocaust and the establishment of the State of Israel, anti-Semitism would disappear from the face of the earth. Yet the wave of enmity towards Jews and Israel which is sweeping the entire world, and Europe in particular, is the worst since the Holocaust. It is perhaps worse than the era of incitement that preceded the Holocaust, which paved the way for the genocide of the Jews.

Today's anti-Semitic outbursts are indicative of a deep-seated hatred. These incidents should sound warning bells particularly for European Jews, as well as other Diaspora Jews around the world. How can one raise children in such a poisonous atmosphere?

The new wave of anti-Semitism is spearheaded by three distinct groups which have banded together in an unholy alliance: the fascist-anti-Semitic Right, the far Left, and the new Islamic hate mongers whose message is flooding the world. In the UK and USA there has been a significant rise in anti-Semitic activity. The US alone is home base for some 3,000 anti-Semitic websites, with a total of thirty five million anti-semites. Meanwhile, the notoriously anti-Semitic fabrication, *The Protocols of the Elders of Zion*, is still being published and distributed around the world.

Anti-Semitism is a disease of humanity for which there is no cure. Sometimes it is dormant for a period, but it always returns and re-erupts with ever greater intensity. "Hatred towards the Jews has become inflamed among the gentiles. It focuses on all the usual negative factors. He is an outsider, his religion is different, he is an economic competitor and, of course, he was the enemy of their god."

The Problems of Diaspora Jewish Youth

Representatives of the Rescue council (Va'ad Hahatzala) should explain to our fellow Jews in the Diaspora the severe mental anguish which their sons and daughters experience in an anti-Semitic environment, surrounded by a toxic hatred and acts of violence towards Jews and their institutions.

The young Jew living in the Diaspora is sensitive to all the shifts and developments in the rancid anti-Semitic atmosphere. He senses the deep and irrational loathing towards his people. He sees the defamatory graffiti sprayed on the walls of Jewish institutions, cursing and abusing his people. He sees the desecration of synagogues and cemeteries and vandalism of graves. He feels that the very fact that he is a Jew is a blemish and an obstacle which stands in the way of all he desires. The young Jew tries desperately to flee from his true identity, seeking refuge in other cultures and playing hide and seek with himself. But in beating his retreat he loses his sense of self-worth and he suffers from a constant inner conflict of wills. He suffers ongoing mental anguish which will give him no peace throughout his life.

We bear a moral obligation to tell our fellow Jews in the Diaspora that which is clearly apparent. Jewish parents, who raise their children as outsiders among anti-Semitic gentiles, hurt their children to a degree that may rate as psychological abuse. (The concept of abuse includes the causing of psychological damage, as we explained in chapter 6.)

Parents cannot blindly ignore the mental anguish of their children. They should realize that young people cannot grow up with self-respect and a sense of human dignity when they are surrounded by a society that degrades and despises them. This is a recipe for individual and national collapse. It is known that people do not perceive themselves as free if they do not live as equals among equals and as an integrated part of the surrounding society.

The Best Cure for Anti-Semitism

The cure for anti-Semitism will not come from adapting to an abnormal existence. It will come through the normalization of the Jewish existence in our homeland. Only in the Land of Israel is a Jew a real human being in the true sense of the term. There he is fully able to exercise his rights and obligations and his Jewish identity as a right and a privilege. Only in the State of Israel can each Jew live with self-respect and dignity, with a sense of belonging and comradeship. In an atmosphere of freedom and independence unmarred by a sense of anomaly.

Shock Therapy

Moreover, representatives of the Rescue council, to fulfill their national duty, may need to shock and scare the Diaspora Jews by stating the bitter and terrifying truth: through the process of assimilation in which they are mired, they are unwittingly executing the next stage of the Nazis' Final Solution (as described in chapter 10).

In the pre-Holocaust era, the migration of eastern European Jewry always strengthened and invigorated world Jewry. This population produced countless rabbis, teachers, and regular Jews who were learned in Torah and faithful to the path of their ancestors. Eastern European Jews who immigrated to the West infused their new communities with spiritual-religious vitality. Nazi documents reveal that they were aware of this secret of our people's vigor. They were convinced that if they could succeed in destroying Eastern European Jewry, Jews worldwide could not longer survive. Without them, the energy sustaining western Jewry would dry up.

It is a catastrophe and a disgrace that through assimilation, the vast majority of Diaspora Jews are blithely following the plan prepared by the Nazis in their Final Solution. These Jews are personally carrying out the second phase of Hitler's demonic plan. They hand Hitler a posthumous victory.

This silent Holocaust obligates us to embark on a national offensive and raise the alarm loud and clear. Our people must know that they are sinking into the mire of self annihilation, in accordance with Hitler's accursed design. We need to sound the red alert about the spiritual Holocaust transpiring among our people, until all Jews around the world have woken up and a sense of national unrest has been generated. This will lead to revolution in the thinking of Jews everywhere and is the only way to halt this calamitous and self-destructive trend.

The Aliyah Movement

The primary role of the rescue council and its representatives will be to expose the non-viability of the Diaspora, based on the idea that "among those nations you will not be tranquil." It will lay the groundwork for the ingathering of the exiles of Israel. Through intensive activity they must create a positive attitude towards aliyah as the ultimate national and religious obligation of every Jew. This will ensure the future existence of the Jewish people.

Never before was the Jewish people in such grave danger of disappearing completely, and in such immediate need of a safe-haven in their homeland. They need a place to call their own to ensure the existence of their children and grandchildren, and prevent them from being lost to the irresistible forces of assimilation and intermarriage.

Liquidation of the Diaspora

We need to lay out the complete picture before our fellow Jews in the Diaspora. We need to shake their hearts and awaken them to their only chance for self-preservation. We must reveal to them in plain language the awful truth that we have reached an epoch where the Diaspora Jews are faced with a choice: to either make aliyah to the State of Israel or disappear into the abyss.

Eliezer Livne predicted this when he said: "Our era will see the end of the Diaspora. The destruction will come in part through integration and assimilation and in part through the establishment of the State of Israel (i.e., through *aliya*). Throughout Jewish history there has never before been an era such as this one. We stand on the brink of the end of the Diaspora. Jewish life in the Diaspora cannot persist… There is almost no hope that they can preserve their uniqueness as Jews in the long term. Even today many of them don't know why they are Jews."

This single most decisive factor that has kept the Jewish people distinct throughout their long and bitter exile has been their faithfulness to Torah and mitzvot. In the past, the Diaspora was nurtured by culturally rich roots that drew their sustenance from Torah and the heritage of our forefathers.

The Jews of the ghetto were confident of their spiritual and ethical superiority over the society that surrounded them, and every day were proud to pronounce the blessing thanking God that He "did not make me a gentile." They viewed their oppressors with derision and disdain. Today's Diaspora Jew has the exact opposite perception of his situation.

In the past Diaspora Jews constructed tall and impenetrable walls around their communities: through particular styles of dress, through a national language, and an independent way of life. Torah study was their main delight, and they pursued it day and night while following the mitzvoth to the letter. The Divine Covenant was always at the heart of every Jewish community. "Whichever place Israel was exiled to, the Divine Presence was exiled along with them and they sheltered in It's Wings" (*Talmud Yerushalmi Ta'anit*). Wherever the Jews went they established their own mini-Torah state on foreign soil. Their pure faith, the practice of mitzvoth and the lofty sense of being the "Chosen People" was the key to Jewish ability to persist in exile, and avoid assimilating among the other nations with whom they lived side by side.

The Process of Diaspora Disintegration

On the other hand, today's Jews have lost all of these safeguards. They see the gentiles as superior to themselves and want to be like them. They have changed their language, their dress and their way of life. There is no doubt that the Jews of the Diaspora will be unable to maintain a distinct identity without maintaining the traditions and lifestyle that set them apart from other people. Yet the lifestyle of the majority of Jews in New York, London, Sydney and Paris is not particularly different from the gentiles that surround them. They don't learn Torah and they don't observe mitzvoth. As a result Judaism has ceased to be a bond that unites them. There is almost no hope that they will be able to preserve their unique identity in the long-term.

Nowadays, only about half of the Diaspora Jews still identify themselves as Jewish, and they have only minimal knowledge of their Jewish heritage. Fifty-six percent of Jewish parents in the USA have said in surveys that it would not bother them if their children married non-Jews. Add to this the depressing fact that some 70% of young American Jews are not receiving any Jewish education. They are growing up with no knowledge whatsoever of the Jewish nation and Jewish values and without any spiritual or cultural connection to their people.

There is clear evidence that the Jews of the Diaspora are rapidly approaching oblivion. It is a simple fact that the Jews of the Diaspora cannot persist as a nation in exile. They have neither the desire nor the capacity to resist the influence of their surrounding societies. On the contrary, they are rushing wholehearted to be absorbed into it.

Aliyah (moving to Israel) is the True Rescue

It is our duty to go out with a vigorous distress call about the plague of assimilation and intermarriage raging in the Diaspora. There is no future for the existence of Jews and Judaism in the Diaspora. Our existence can be assured only in Israel. This realization must be inculcated into the People, until the communal leaders and the Rabbis will believe it and preach it to their congregations as a prescription for Jewish life. This includes the Jewish movement that for years has preached, "Not to go up as a wall" and "Not to rebel against the nations of the world." They must know that the time has come to rebel against exile and to go up to Israel as a wall. Also Torah observant Jews must understand that while they themselves may succeed to remain true to their People, Diaspora dangers threaten their grandchildren. Their grandchildren may well leave their nation and Judaism for the surrounding culture. Unfortunately, these events are no longer rare. Human nature is for minority groups to assimilate into the majority population. The reality is that in the Diaspora the bonds to Judaism loosen and become undone. The surrounding environment directly and indirectly influences our youth and Judaism weakens and disappears with or without prior intention. Let all of the Jews know that in the State of Israel the Jewish People will continue to grow and to flourish, even without the Diaspora Jews' children. However, their children cannot continue to survive as Jews without being in the State of Israel. In our time, only moving to Israel has the power to save from assimilation and to promise that their future generations will remain Jews. There is no doubt that moving to Israel is truly saving Jewish souls.

The chain of Jewish continuity in the Diaspora is breaking down. In the countries of the Diaspora one Jew in every two is marrying out. In some of them, two out of three are lost in intermarriage. Israel is the only place for Jewish survival. Either you go to Israel, live there as a Jew and raise Jewish descendants, or you stay in the Diaspora and lose your children and definitely your grandchildren in intermarriage.

Will People Listen to our Call?

The main question is will Diaspora Jewry be willing to listen to our message and follow our advice and suggestions? Will all of our toil be in vain? Mr. Ori Gordon, may he rest in peace, addressed this question. According to his vast experience in this matter, "I was a youth and now have grown old. I have learned one thing about Diaspora Jewry. If one makes claims against them, as hard as these claims may be, if the claims are made honestly, openly, with true and demonstrated love, they listen with real attention. They patiently and fairly judge the claims. They pay respect to the person who made the claims even if they disagree. Even if there is a difference of opinion, there are no bitter feelings. There are no arguments or hostility. This is not only because Diaspora Jewry's way of arguing is praiseworthy, but because in their hearts they sense that we are one People" (Kivunim 31:69).

Our experience confirms these sincere words. The first chapter of this book, entitled "The Deafening Silence of Jewish Leadership" – obligates ending the exile and moving to Israel. This chapter was printed a few years ago in the Jewish newspaper, *The Sentinel*, in Chicago. In spite of this chapter's anti-exile slant, it received tremendous attention and publicity. It appeared in the editorial section and received positive appraisal by the newspaper's editor. A summary of the main points of the chapter were widely quoted in the general Chicago newspaper, the Sun Times and also on regional television. According to the above editors, this article raised much interest and heated debate in the Chicago Jewish community which numbers 260,000 souls.

These facts emphasize the practical value of the Rabbis instruction. "If someone tells you I worked and was not rewarded, don't believe him. If he tells you he did not work and was rewarded, don't believe him. If he says I worked and was rewarded, believe him! (Megilla 6:) Indeed, "Shall the horn be blown in a city, and the people not tremble?" (Amos 3:6). If we call out the alarm and instructions will they not listen?

Recovering from the Slumber of Exile
Once a fire broke out in an apartment. In the apartment a very drunk, very overweight man was in a deep sleep. A few people tried unsuccessfully to save him from the fire. They tried to push the sleeping man through the door and did not succeed. Then they tried to push the sleeping man through the window but they failed again. Then an old and experienced man passed by and advised them. Why are you trying to save the man while he is sleeping? Instead, wake him up and he will leave himself.

The holy and educational goal placed upon us is to awaken our brethren from the slumber of the destructive exile. We must make them aware that the exile is a danger to their existence and that returning to Zion is a vital necessity for the continuation for them as of all of the house of Israel.

Adopting the Souls of the Holocaust Children and Increasing the Jewish People
Don't spend your time on projects which are unproductive, like marching with flags in Poland, the largest Jewish graveyard in the world. They call this "the march of the living." What life does this march engender? Does our nation increase by even one extra person through this march?

The great horror of the holocaust can be manifested in two real ways. One way is for the nations involved in it to return Jewish property. The second way is for the Jewish People to restore the Jewish souls to life. The nations: Germany, Austria, Switzerland, Belgium and others have done their part by returning property and compensation payments. However, the

Jewish People have not restored the lives of the lost Jewish children's souls. This can be accomplished by each family bearing an additional child to compensate for the number of children lost in the holocaust. This has been explained in chapter nine. We have been satisfied with empty words without action. It's infuriating…

The spokesmen of the rescue council should explain to all of our brethren that increasing the Jewish People is today's major challenge due to our demographic problem. Our birth rate is among the lowest of all of the nations. It is much below than needed to maintain our present level. The annual death rate outnumbers the annual birthrate. We are also reaching new highs in intermarriage.

Our nation's drastic situation requires a change of strategy to deal with the silent holocaust. We must cease being defensive and make an offensive spiritual and nationalistic campaign to save our People. We must take decisive action with the same ingenuity and drive appropriate to the grave danger.

A national project of this scope is capable, with God's help, to breathe a new life into our nation. It can strengthen the nation's demographic situation and deepen Jewish identity everywhere in the world.

CHAPTER EIGHTEEN

ALIYAH TO ISRAEL IN HALACHA (JEWISH LAW)

THE BOND BETWEEN the Jewish People and the Holy Land was maintained throughout the centuries and in all the lands of the exile through and by the Torah.

The Holy Bible is in every sense the Book of the Holy Land. That land is the background of its story and the focal object of promise and fulfillment.

The Sages of the Talmud and of the Midrash constantly emphasized the attachment of the People of Israel to the Land of Israel. They made extensive use of the Haggadah as an agent through which to imbue the people with a love for their ancient land.

The longing for the return to Zion and the belief in its ultimate fulfillment, was an integral part of Jewish life in exile and grounded into the very being of the Jew. He could not help having it brought home to him through the observance of his customs and ceremonies, festivals and fasts, many of which were associated with Zion, that this was the land of his people and that there was Divine assurance of its being restored to its original owners. Three times a day the Jew turns towards Jerusalem, in the course of his religious devotion and stressed the bond between himself and the Holy Land, praying for the return of his exiled people.

The Legal Aspect

The problem of "Yishuvei Eretz Israel," the advancement of the Settlement of the Land of Israel, occupies in the Talmud a real pragmatic legal principle. This problem was responsible for bringing about Rabbinic legislation with regard to the elimination of waste, the prevention of sales of land, the promotion of agricultural activities, the development of towns, and the encouragement of settling and of acquiring houses and fields in Zion.

This chapter is devoted wholly to only one of those items, namely, the settling in the Holy Land. With this thought in mind, we shall examine the various legal problems, scattered throughout the Talmud, in which the policy to promote the settling in the Land was a decisive factor in their determination. Upon further examination of the methods adopted by the Talmudic sages in their efforts to achieve their goal, we may divide the cases into the following four groups:

Statements and rulings to foster settling in the Holy land.

Laws and ordinances adopted by the sages in their process of coping with this problem.

Cases where the sages were prepared to overlook a certain precept or a prohibition in order to promote the settling in the Land.

Cases where penalties were inflicted upon those who ignored their obligation with regard to dwelling in the Land of Israel.

Each of the four groups consists of cases of two types. Those, where measures were adopted to encourage immigration into the Land, and others where measures were taken to discourage emigration from the Land.

Statements and Rulings

"The Land of Israel is holier than all the other lands" (Kalim 1:6).

He who dwells in the Land of Israel and recites the "Shema" morning and evening and speaks the Hebrew language, is certain to have a portion in the world to come" (Yerushalmi Shkalim, 3).

The commandment to settle in the Land of Israel is equal in importance to all other commandments of the Torah taken together" (Sifri, Deuteronomy 12:29).

One should always live in the Land of Israel, even in a town whose inhabitants are mostly Gentiles; one should not live in the Diaspora, even in a town whose inhabitants are mostly Jews" (Ketuboth 110b).

The Talmud gives here a ruling as to how far one should suffer privation in order to continue dwelling in the Land of Israel. "One must not emigrate from the land of Israel unless the price of two Saahs is one Selah, meaning that one may leave only when the country has been stricken by such a severe famine that the price of food has jumped twice as much. Rabbi Simeon expresses his opinion there, that permission for leaving the land may be taken only when one does not find food to buy at all, but should he be able to find food to buy, and, of course, also to find employment, then, even if the price has jumped up to four times as much, he must not emigrate from the Land (B. Bathra, 19a).

The first three references quoted under this group are mere statements about the importance of the Land of Israel and about the significance of residing there, while the last two rulings, laying down definite conditions when one must retain his residence in his Land and under which circumstances one may emigrate.

Laws and Ordinances

This group consists of cases in which specific laws and ordinances were introduced in order to curb "Yeridah," the migration of Jews from the Land of Israel and to encourage "Aliyah," the immigration of the people to their land.

The Mishna in Shvieit (6:6), states regarding Terumah, i.e., heave-offering, that one must not bring it into the Land of Israel from abroad. Yet with regard to Bikkurim, i.e., the first fruits, we find in the Mishna of Bikkurim (1:10), that these may be brought from abroad. Why has the same rule not been applied to both? Wherefore is Terumah different form Bikkurim with regard to the Diaspora?

The Tosfot and other commentators on the Mishna in Shvieit, explain that the purpose of prohibiting heave-offerings from abroad into the Land was because, since the priests were in the habit of visiting farmers in order to get their regular heave-offerings, they might have extended their visits to those farmers outside the Land of Israel and be tempted to settle there. Not so was the case with regard to Bikkurim, since the bringing of the first fruits was a personal obligation incumbent upon the field owner, according to the Yerushalmi (Shvieit 6:6). The priests were not visiting the farms for Bikkurim and there could, therefore, be no ground for temptation of leaving the Land.

Here we find that a special prohibition was introduced by the Mishna, with regard to heave-offering from abroad in order to prevent emigration from Eretz Yisrael.

A similar case, but of a much broader field, do we find with regard to the Rabbinic decree of "Tumat Eretz Ha'Amim," i.e., the impurity of the lands of the Diaspora. Jose Ben Joezer and Jose Ben Johanan, the first of the Zugot, introduced this decree (Shabbat 14b). From the discussion in the Talmud Bavli (ibid) and Yerushalmi (Shabbat 1:4), we learn that this decree was reaffirmed by the sages of the successive generations, and that while at first it was applied only to the ground of those lands, later, eighty years before the destruction of the Temple, this decree was extended to include also the air of those lands. The reason for adopting the principle of "the impurity of the lands abroad," seems to be, as referred to in the above mentioned Talmudic sources, the fear for Jewish corpses that might be buried anywhere in those lands. A Jew who stepped upon a grave became unclean for seven days.

An interesting, and in this connection a very suggestive explanation is found in Tosfot (Nazir 54b). The reason given there for declaring the lands abroad impure, was in order to curb the migration of Jews from the Land of Israel.

Jose Ben Joezer and Jose Ben Johanan lived during the early Hasmonean period and served as the heads of the Sanhedrin. In their days, mighty battles were being waged in the Land of Israel between the Hasmonean and Syrian-Greeks. If the theory of the scatted corpses and limbs of Jewish victims was responsible for declaring the lands impure, then there is all the more reason for this principle to have been applied to the Land of Israel, where the wars between the Jews and the Greeks were raging.

On the other hand, the theory of curbing migration fits in precisely with the historical facts. In the early Hasmonean age, owing to the wars that were going on, in the Land of Israel,between the Jews and the Greeks, many Jews left the land for peaceful neighboring countries. A necessity arose to check mass migration of Jews. That is why the heads of the Sanhedrin, Jose Ben

Joezer and Jose Ben Johanan, decreed the "impurity of the lands of the Diaspora…"

A similar threat of mass migration existed also during the last decade of the reign of Herod the Great, who was hated by the people and when it was overcast with gloom and warfare, and during the first decade after his death, when civil wars broke out, Jewish masses once again started to leave their homeland for more peaceful and prosperous countries. It was then, as the Talmud states, that the decree of "the impurity of the lands of the Diaspora" was reaffirmed by the Sages, even more severely, including also their air.

We could go a little further, in saying that this decree was intended to serve a double purpose. In addition to discouraging emigration from the Land of Israel, it was meant also to encourage immigration from abroad. For in those days millions of Jews were living outside of the Land of Israel.

Overlooking Prohibitions

To maintain and strengthen the marriage-bond is one of the main commandments of the Torah. The sages of the Talmud speak in strong terms against the dissolution of a marriage. They say: "The Alter sheds tears over him who divorces his first wife" (Gittin 90b). Yet a marriage may be dissolved, should one of the couple insist on leaving the Land of Israel or refuse to settle there against the will of the other. "If the husband insists on going on Aliyah to the Land of Israel and she refuses, she should be compelled to go there. Should she persist in her refusal, he may divorce her without payment of the Ketubah, i.e., marriage settlement. On the other hand, if the wife insists on settling in the Land of Israel and he refuses, he should be coerced to go there. Otherwise, she may divorce him and get her marriage settlement…" (Gittin 110b). The Talmud then goes on to say, that if the dispute between husband and wife is about leaving the Land of Israel, the above rulings are applied. Another case, which although it is not specifically associated with aliyah, but with the general principle of Yishuve Eretz Israel is worthy of mentioning. For it indicates so well the idea we are dealing with in this group. A Jew who buys a house or land from a non-Jew in Eretz Israel is permitted by the Talmud on a Sabbath to tell a Gentile to write and execute the deed of sale, although in ordinary cases the telling of the Gentile to do some work is prohibited on the Sabbath, because of "Shevut." Fearing that the seller might back out a day later, the Talmud granted this permission for the promotion of the settlement of the Land of Israel (B. Kama 80b: Gittin 8b).

We see here that the Sages were prepared to overlook the desecration of the Sabbath and a well-known prohibition of breaking up the marriage-bond and denying the payment of the ketubah, which is due to her, by the law of the Torah, in order to promote settling in the Holy Land. This they did, because they regarded settling in the Land as a commandment of the Torah (Tosefta, Avodah Zarah 5:2): Sifri, Deut., 12:29).

Penalties Inflicted

In this group, we can go back to very ancient times, to find a case where Jews are penalized for not going on Aliyah. At the beginning of the Second Jewish Commonwealth, a large number of Babylonian Jews under the leadership of Ezra went on Aliyah to Zion. Very few Levites joined him in that venture. Ezra decreed, therefore, as a mater of penalty, that tithes which used to belong to the Levites should be given to the Kohanim (Chulin 131b; Ketuboth 26a).

An interesting case is found in the Mishna and in the discussion of the Talmud which follows it: If a Jew of the Land of Israel sells his slave to someone abroad, then the slave immediately wins his freedom as a result and the buyer loses the money that he paid for him, as a matter of penalty for causing him to leave the Land of Israel. The same principle of law is true with regard to Aliyah, as recorded in the Talmud. A slave who had escaped his master abroad and reached the Land of Israel, thereby won his freedom (Gittin 43b).

Aliyah is a Mitzvah

The sages of the Talmud, as we have seen, adopted various methods in order to encourage Aliyah, discourage Yeridah and promote the settlement of the Land of Israel. The practical question for us is, whether Aliyah to Israel is a legal Biblical duty and whether it could be regarded as one of the 613 percepts of the Torah? Nachmanides included the Mitzvah of settling in Zion in the Taryag Mitzvoth and set an example by settling himself in the Holy Land. Maimonides, on the other hand, did not include it in the 613 Mitzvoth. He, however, quoted the Talmud with regard to the prohibition of leaving Israel: "It is forbidden to leave Eretz Israel even temporarily. Although one may leave the Land in order to study the Torah, or to marry, or for business purposes, one must return as soon as possible" (Maimonides Codes, Kings, 5:9).

He also lay down as a Halacha, the Talmudic ruling that one should always live in the Land of Israel, even in a town whose inhabitants are mostly Gentiles, and one should not live in the Diaspora, even in a town whose inhabitants are mostly Jews. Maimonides, as we see, conformed fully with the Talmudic attitude regarding settling in the Land of Israel. But he did not include it in the Taryag Mitzvoth in his Sefer Ha'Mitzvot, for another reason, which we may be justified in suggesting.

The Mitzvah of settling in the Land is based on the Biblical page: "For ye shall pass over the Jordan, to go in to possess the land which the Lord your God giveth you and you shall possess it and abide therein" (Deuteronomy 11:31). Maimonides might have maintained that this passage has to be regarded as an indivisible whole, namely, that the second part of the passage "and abide therein," is not binding unless the first part "and ye shall possess it" has been realized. Under the conditions of his time, when the Land of Israel was in foreign hands and Aliyah was a dangerous process, Maimonides had not, for this reason, included it among the 613 Mitzvoth. Today when the first part of that Biblical passage has been realized with the independence of Israel, Maimonides, too, would have regarded the second part as a legal Biblical duty and would have included it in the Taryag Mitzvoth.

Most of the Rishonim and Poskim maintain, however, that Aliyah to Israel is a Torah Mitzvah, even during the time of dispersion, when the land is not possessed by the Jews.